**The Rights of Youth
American Colleges and
Student Revolt, 1798–1815**

Steven J. Novak

The first major student revolt in American colleges came at the turn of the nineteenth century
in unprecedented riots and rebellions. Though
on a small scale in contrast to the campus turmoil of the 1960s and 1970s, in many ways it
was equally significant. Yet its history has never
been written.

In this book, Novak asks why upper class,
Federalist, and socially conservative students
became rioters. He portrays them as a postrevolutionary generation—the Sons of the Founders—who wanted to outdo their elders in na-
tionalistic deeds. He argues that they were
politicized by their Federalist fathers. When
their generational and political goals were frustrated, they were rechanneled into surrogate
political activity—student revolt. To restore
order, colleges adopted a new disciplinary tool
—the blacklist—that effectively suppressed the
resistance. Rebellions continued, but more as
an adolescent rite than as a practical means of
achieving student power.

In addition to important findings on the causes
of rioting, Novak offers acute observations
about the part rebellion played in defining the
antebellum college. In the 1780s and 1790s
American educators were devising a republican

THE RIGHTS OF YOUTH

education adapted to the principles and needs of the new nation. Student revolt was the undoing of experimental and Jeffersonian programs. Professors attributed resistance to Jacobinism and freethinking and reemphasized the classics to counter radicalism and unrest. Novak describes how the downfall of republican education coincided with the rise of the evangelical movement in the colleges, leading to a struggle for control of the colleges of national import.

Although it had antecedents in the colonial era, Novak shows that the classical, evangelical, paternalistic old-time college as an American institution was a peculiar product of the backlash against modern philosophy and student revolt at the turn of the nineteenth century.

Steven J. Novak teaches History at the University of California, Riverside.

THE RIGHTS OF YOUTH

American Colleges and Student Revolt, 1798-1815

STEVEN J. NOVAK

HARVARD UNIVERSITY PRESS
Cambridge, Massachusetts, and London, England   1977

*Publication of this book has been aided by a grant
from the Andrew W. Mellon Foundation*

Library of Congress Cataloging in Publication Data

Novak, Steven J   1947-
    The rights of youth.

    Bibliography: p.
    Includes index.
    1. Student movements — United States. 2. College
students — Legal status, laws, etc. — United States —
History. I. Title.
LA229.N68   371.8'1   76-43109
ISBN 0-674-77016-1

PREFACE

"THE RIGHTS of man have been discussed, till we are somewhat wearied with the discussion," wrote the English moralist Hannah More in *Strictures on the Modern System of Female Education* (1799). "To these have been opposed, as the next stage in the process of illumination, . . . the *rights of women*. It follows, according to the natural progression of human things, that the next influx of that irradiation which our enlighteners are pouring in upon us, will illuminate the world with grave descants on the *rights of youth,* the *rights of children,* and *the rights of babies.*" Her reductio ad absurdum was closer to the truth than she realized, for at this very time a struggle for the "rights of youth" was going on in American colleges. The history of this adolescent uprising has never been written. It took place on a miniature scale in contrast to the campus turmoil of the 1960s, but in many ways was equally significant.

As Mrs. More's remark implied, the rights of youth emerged amid the ferment of the French Revolution and the Enlightenment, giving youthful protest ideological content, whether merited or not. American student revolt also occurred in a postrevolutionary republic passing through great social change. It coincided with the bitter conflict surrounding the election of Thomas Jefferson, when the administration of the federal government passed for the first time to the opposition. This was a formative period in the history of American higher education, as the relatively open, liberal institutions of the late eighteenth century were transformed into the narrower, evangelistic colleges of the early nineteenth century. Student riots and rebellions were both a symptom of this reaction and an inadvertent catalyst of further conservative change. Finally, student revolt took place during the emancipation of childhood described by historians of the American family and adds to our knowledge of the history of adolescence and youth, one of the newest historical fields. In this sense, perhaps the title should be called "the *rites* of youth."

The college records for these years give only a skeletal account of campus disorders, as they were more often concerned with the apparatus of their institutions than with the life within them. Another shortcoming of such records is that they present only the "official" side of events. Campus revolts produced a literature of their own — student petitions and manifestoes and faculty reports. While these are of great interest, neither professors nor students were entirely candid in their public utterances. For academic opinion, the best source is the correspondence among members of the academic community. Here, in an unguarded manner, professors revealed their attitudes toward political and intellectual movements as well as toward student unrest.

For students, letters are the best documents portraying their side of events. In order not to neglect students, I took pains to find their letters, though these are poorly indexed and scattered in libraries throughout the country. There were no student newspapers or periodicals in this period, though a few abortive attempts were made, the most successful being *The Harvard Miscellany* (1811) which lasted just one year. Student literary societies kept minutes of meetings and debates but had little to say about rebellions. The local newspaper was typically a four-page weekly in which two pages were devoted to advertising and the remainder almost solely to national and international affairs, taking it for granted that everyone in the community knew all the local news. When college disorders broke into newspaper columns, as they sometimes did, it was evidence of public concern. Not every question can be answered by this historical record, of course, but the available material is fascinating and sufficient.

I am indebted to Professor Henry F. May for the idea of studying these riots and rebellions and for encouragement, gentle criticism, and subtle discernment which served as a model of scholarship.

A grant from the Graduate Division of the University of California, Berkeley, made it possible to examine unpublished materials in colleges, archives, and historical societies on the East Coast.

I am grateful to the following institutions for assistance and permission to quote from their manuscripts: Harvard University, Princeton University, Yale University, Brown University, Duke University, Transylvania University, the University of Virginia, the University of North Carolina, Dartmouth College, Dickinson College, Williams College, Union College, the College of William and Mary, the Historical Society of Pennsylvania, the Massachusetts Historical Society, the New-York Historical Society, the Boston Public Library, the North Carolina State Archives, and the Cabell Memorial Foundation.

An earlier version of "The College in the Dartmouth College Case" in Chapter 7 appeared in the *New England Quarterly,* 47 (December 1974), and is adapted for use here with the kind permission of the editors.

Mr. Kenyon C. Bolton III of Cambridge, Massachusetts, provided valuable assistance on Washington Allston and generously allowed me to reproduce his photographs of "The Buck's Progress."

Several colleagues at Berkeley—Michael Hindus, Gordon Link, William Gienapp, and especially William Rorabaugh—shared their time and expertise.

Finally, my wife, Sheila, went through much with patience and affection for the sake of this work.

CONTENTS

THE RIGHTS OF YOUTH

CHAPTER ONE

The Influence
of the First Lapse

AN ADHERENT OF the germ theory of history might trace the seeds of American student unrest to the first two "exorbitant children" sent to Harvard from England who "raised a riot" just prior to the first commencement.[1] If the seeds were planted this early, however, they were a century and a half in taking root. Historians who have written about student disorders of the past invariably have focused on the nineteenth century or plotted a rising curve of disruptions between the years 1760 and 1860.[2] There was a significant difference between the misbehavior of colonial undergraduates and the sustained resistance which arose at the turn of the nineteenth century. The riots and rebellions in the years 1798 to 1815 were really the first major wave of student revolt in American history. To appreciate this change and why it came about it is necessary to look briefly at colonial student disturbances and to consider how certain post-1776 trends in education and society may have contributed to the rise of rebellions at the end of the eighteenth century.

From its beginnings in the seventeenth century, American higher education was collegiate in nature—a place to live as well as to learn—designed to cultivate the whole man—body, mind,

1

and soul — rather than to train the intellect alone. Student behavior was therefore a central academic concern. Throughout the colonial era and well beyond the Revolution there was no student disciplinary problem as such. Undergraduates were relatively quiescent until the 1760s, when the first small wave of campus unquiet reached the colleges. The first student rebellion at Harvard, America's oldest college, came in 1766, 130 years after its founding.[3] In the same year a decade of turmoil at Yale finally culminated in the resignation of President Thomas Clap.[4] By 1776, discontent had surfaced at the College of Rhode Island (Brown), King's College (Columbia), Dartmouth, the College of New Jersey (Princeton), the College of William and Mary, and of course again at Harvard and Yale.[5] Although this was the first stirring of students in American history, it was hardly a major revolt. These disorders were small, nonviolent, short-ranged in their goals, and easily put down. They had little effect either upon the colleges or the rest of society. They were not the antecedents of later revolt.

By far the most serious student disorders occurred at Yale, the center of fierce religious and political struggles growing out of the Great Awakening. So many students were influenced by the New Light teachings of the English evangelist George Whitefield that the Yale trustees passed a law in 1741 which declared "that if any Student of this College shall directly or indirectly say, that the Rector, either of the Trustees or Tutors are Hypocrites, carnall or unconverted Men, he Shall for the first Offence make a publick Confession in the Hall, & for the Second Offence be expell'd."[6] When the Cleveland brothers were expelled in 1745 for attending a New Light worship service, their classmates protested by reprinting John Locke's *Essay on Toleration,* indicative of the curious relationship between the Awakening and the Enlightenment.[7]

Yale's student evangelicals of the 1740s were a different breed from her rioters of the fifties and sixties. The reason was that around 1750 President Thomas Clap, impressed by the growing political power of the New Lights and alarmed by the creeping

Arminianism of the Old Lights, reversed himself and swung the college over to the New Lights.[8] Thereafter student opposition seems to have come from the Old Light side. This is significant for while describing the two groups is extremely difficult, it seems they reflected social and economic divisions to some extent, with Old Lights being associated with "the large landholders and conservative merchants."[9] Later student rebels would also be predominately upper class.

The context of religious and political struggle surrounding Yale's disorders greatly enhanced their significance. As would be true in a later period, partisans used unrest for ammunition. Clap's enemies pointed to student riots as indictments of his re- gime. "Can you wonder, Sir," asked one critic, "that there has been of late Years, such loud Murmuring and Complaints of the Scholars against the College and Government . . . so frequent Tumults and insurrections? . . . *Oppression will make a wise man mad,* how much more a Company of unwise and giddy Youth."[10] No better example could be found of the colonists' highly tolerant attitude toward civil disorders. They viewed mobs and riots as natural reactions toward tyranny and misgovernment. Responsibility was more often placed on public officials than on rioters.[11] This assumption was shared by both Clap's adversaries and his defenders. Rather than blame the students for Yale's disorders, which might cast doubts on Clap's administration, the president's allies traced the troubles to outside agitators — "restless and designing men" who "stirred them up, led them on, with a Design to bring a Disgrace and Scandal upon the College."[12] There was probably some truth to the charge.[13] But blaming outsiders could be carried to an extreme, as when Clap refused to admit that the students had stoned his house and insisted that the mob must have consisted of townsmen disguised in academic gowns.[14]

The tendency to fault college officers or "designing men" for college disorders minimized the role of the students. Boys will be boys. This attitude was best expressed by Chauncey Whittelsey, who as a tutor had helped Clap suppress the Great Awakening. Writing when the college had been sacked, the tutors driven off, and attendance reduced by two-thirds, he said, "I am almost ready to weep; Alma Mater is truly in a deplorable Situation, and I fear will be ruined." Yet he did not blame the students but felt sure that if he and his correspondent were tutors once again order would be easily restored: "perhaps I am mistaken, and human Nature is different in Yalensian Youth, from what it once was; but I rather think the influence of the first Lapse is nearly the same at this Day as it was then."[15] For Whittelsey student revolt was not the product of radicalism or the conflict of generations but of human nature and original sin and consequently not very alarming.

Another reason why student protest was viewed with equanimity was because of its association, after 1765 at least, with the popular cause of colonial resistance to Great Britain. In 1772 President John Witherspoon of Princeton explained that "the spirit of liberty" had led his students into "outrage and sedition."[16] College authorities had no wish to snuff out this spirit. As a member of the Harvard Corporation observed,

> The young gentlemen are already taken up with politics. They have caught the spirit of the times . . . They have sometimes been wrought up to such a pitch of enthusiasm, that it has been difficult for the Tutors to keep them within due bounds . . . Their Tutors are fearful of giving too great a check to a disposition, which may, hereafter fill the country with patriots; and choose to leave it to age and experience to check their ardor.[17]

The public seems to have approved of student demonstrations in support of colonial rights, including hanging public figures in effigy, burning commons tea, and declaiming on liberty at commencements dressed in homespun in honor of the nonimportation agreements. "How happy ought we to esteem ourselves," commented a newspaper after one such episode, "when we see some of our youth who will probably fill some of the highest stations in their country when their fathers have fallen asleep, so early declaring their love to their country."[18] Activism was patriotic.

In view of this adult approbation, it is remarkable that students did not do more to advance the cause of colonial rights. Even wearing homespun failed to become an annual custom. Contrary to the general rule that "students have played an important role in revolutionary movements throughout the ages," American students were in the tail end of the movement for independence.[19] When John Trumbull, student and tutor at Yale from 1763 to 1773, satirized colonial undergraduates in the characters of Tom Brainless and Dick Hairbrain, he rightly portrayed them as coxcombs and fops rather than as rioters or revolutionaries.[20] The Revolution was "a remarkable example of a political change which was accompanied by little generational unrest."[21]

Student disorders of this period were mirthful affairs. In Harvard's 1766 rebellion the undergraduates composed a mock-epic "Book of Harvard" which described the insurrection in Old Testament prose. By this account, Asa Dunbar — grandfather of America's apostle of civil disobedience, Henry David Thoreau — told the college officials, "behold our Butter stinketh . . . give us, we pray thee, Butter that stinketh not." The unamused Harvard governors dealt firmly with the insurgents, but they also alleviated many of the student complaints and made the Harvard Corporation more youthful in composition and more responsive.[22] Yale's "Wilkes and Liberty" carouse of 1769 commemorated the popular English radical John Wilkes, a hero in America, who had been imprisoned for libeling King George III and who was then repeatedly elected to and expelled from Parliament. Since Wilkes's libel had appeared in the forty-fifth issue of his *North Briton,* the number "45" became a well-known symbol for resistance to tyranny. During the Yale demonstration, the students drank 45 glasses till they reached the 45th degree of drunkenness, which supposedly came at precisely 45 minutes after midnight, when they commenced "BAWLING in concert just 45 times, sometimes Wilkes and Liberty, sometimes No. 45, but for the most part their joy was too great to admit of articulation."[23] At Princeton, in 1770, the students intercepted a letter from the merchants of New York to those in other colonies announcing their plans of abandoning the nonimportation agreements. The students used the occasion for a demonstration. With the college bell tolling in the background, they assembled on the green in full academic gown to watch the public hangman burn the letter as a warning, they said, to all "betrayers of their country."[24]

Undergraduates were almost pitifully tame. The worst mischiefs at Princeton in the early 1770s, according to Philip Fithian, consisted of

> writing witty pointed anonymous Papers, in *Songs, Confessions, Wills, Soliliques, Proclamations, Advertisements &c*—Picking from the neighbourhood now & then a plump fat Hen or Turkey for the private entertainment of the Club "instituted for inventing & practising several kinds of mischief in a secret polite manner"—Parading bad Women—Burning Curse-John—Darting Sun-Beams upon the Town-People—Reconoitering Houses in the Town, & ogling Women with the Telescope—Making Squibs & other frightful compositions with Gun-Powder, & lightening them in the Rooms of timorous Boys, & *new comers.*[25]

After the Revolution, there was not an immediate upsurge of student resistance. Yale had a minor riot in 1786, Harvard in 1791, but for the most part disorders were on a par with those of the colonial era. Professor Eliphalet Pearson's "Journal of Disorders" was a record of the worst Harvard disturbances:

> December 9, 1788. Disorders coming out of chapel. Also in the hall at breakfast the same morning. *Bisket, tea cups, saucers,* and a KNIFE thrown at the tutors. At evening prayers the *Lights* were all extinguished by powder and lead, except 2 or 3. Upon this a general *laugh* among the juniors . . .

December 15, 1788. More disorders at my public lecture, than I ever knew before. The bible, cloth, candles, and branches, I found laid in confusion upon the seat of the desk. During lecture several pebbles were snapped, certain gutteral sounds were made on each side of the chapel, besides some whistling.

May 29, 1789. In the evening Russel, Adams I, Blake first and second, Sparhawk, Ellery, went to Bradish's and there supped with one Green, an Englishman . . . About 3 o'clock next morning the company left the house, and on their way to College grossly insulted the President by shouts and yells, challenges, curses, threats of laying siege to, undermining, and burning his house. Abbot found Green and Sparhawk conducting Russel, naked, to his chamber.[26]

This was merely misbehavior, far from open resistance. In his Harvard diary for 1786, young John Quincy Adams noted the extreme timidity of his classmates in confronting the college authorities. "It was much like AEsop's fable of the mice, who determined to have a bell tied round the cat's neck; they were all desirous that it should be done, but no one was willing to undertake the performance of it."[27]

This reluctance forced students to employ covert means of protest. One technique in particular was used both before and just after the Revolution. During Harvard's 1791 rebellion an emetic was placed in the breakfast, temporarily halting all campus proceedings.[28] Similarly, in 1764 eighty-two Yale undergraduates had been stricken with "violent Vomitings," which the alarmed citizens of New Haven attributed to a French "Poyson plot" till President Clap exposed the student culprits.[29] Chemical warfare like this, of limited duration and hard to trace, showed the furtive nature of student protest through most of the eighteenth century. It is significant that there were no such incidents in the more serious student resistance at the turn of the century.

The Revolution brought other changes, however, which were large factors in the coming of revolt. The decline of the colleges,

confusion about their purposes, falling academic standards, erod-
ing customs, and deteriorating student-faculty relations all resulted directly or indirectly from the Revolution. The war itself
damaged and impoverished many colleges. Those that had been
requisitioned for hospitals and armories were left in poor condition. Those with ties to the Church of England — William and
Mary, King's College, and the College of Philadelphia — were
especially hard hit by the loss of English endowment. All of the
colleges suffered from the monetary instability and economic de-
pression that followed the war. Yet at the same time a host of new
institutions were founded which further thinned the available resources. Between 1782 and 1802 nineteen new colleges were set
up, more than twice as many as in the entire colonial era. As one
critic said, "The multiplication of colleges may tend to the diffusion of knowledge, but it likewise tends to disperse the rays . . .
The same funds, which now faintly move through the veins of our
numerous colleges, would give life and animation to one university."[30]

With neither a foundation in adequate systems of primary and
secondary schools nor a firm national commitment to higher education, these new colleges had shaky beginnings. When academic
standards slipped in these booster colleges, the traditional programs of older institutions were endangered as well.

The Revolution forced a new look at the very purposes of higher
education. Noah Webster, Benjamin Rush, and other theorists
urged that a less classical and more utilitarian education was best
adapted to a republican government. Their opinion was rein-
forced by the pedagogy of the Enlightenment.[31] Although no dra-
matic curricular revolution took place, there was a gradual shift
toward greater emphasis on the sciences, mathematics, modern
languages, and moral philosophy. In 1796 President Samuel Stanhope Smith of Princeton wrote to Benjamin Rush, "the time is, I
believe, now come or nearly so, that I can propose to the trustees

that the study of languages, except modern ones, shall cease after the Freshman class . . . and that three entire years be employed in the different branches of art and science."[32]

Dissatisfied with the classics but afraid to abandon them altogether, most colleges offered a hodgepodge of different subjects. As one champion of the classics complained, "the student's library was a strange medley of extracts, compilations, and abridgements, plays, travels, and romances, which, however they might have become the chamber of a fine lady, suffered not a little, when compared with the classical dignity of their predecessors."[33] Students apparently favored modernizing the curriculum. Daniel D. Tompkins (Columbia 1795), later Vice-President for eight years under President Monroe, was certain that "the study of the Moderns is of more advantage than of the Ancients, especially to Modern Youth."[34] He also argued against the traditional compulsory curriculum because "students seldom possess the same inclination for any particular science or the same natural Genius."[35] In the end, postrevolutionary academic experiments proved unsuccessful. After a period of curricular confusion, most colleges retreated to the old prescribed classical course of study. While it lasted, however, this flux undoubtedly contributed to the undermining of academic authority.

The postwar decline of the college and the confusion about the proper curriculum fostered undergraduate pressure for an abbreviated college education. Students developed what a prize-winning essayist termed "a false taste in education," supposing that a complete education might consist simply of English, mathematics, and "a smathering of French."[36] The Enlightenment idea of relevant education could easily be used to justify a popular anti-intellectualism. The erudite Scotsman Charles Nisbet, president of Dickinson College, deplored the conditions he found in America. "Our students are generally very averse to Reading or thinking," he complained. The fault lay with "Quacks in sundry Parts of the

Country, who flatter Expectations of this Nature, & undertake to teach young Men everything that can be taught, by Way of Amusement, & in a short time."[37]

In a subtle way, curricular reform subverted the traditional four-year organization of instruction. Colonial colleges had devoted most of the first two years to intense study of Latin and Greek. If the classics were now obsolete, it might be asked, why must college last four years at all? Weaker institutions yielded to this question. By the turn of the century, William and Mary, Dickinson, the University of Pennsylvania, and Transylvania were granting diplomas for only one or two years of study. Even major colleges such as Princeton and Yale, though they preserved the semblance of the four-year course, actually shortened the period of instruction by admitting many students as juniors. This was less a tribute to the qualifications of entering students, which were generally low, than evidence of falling standards. Examinations and grades were virtually nonexistent. For students in the colonial era who passed through four years of prescribed courses, the absence of grading may not have mattered so much. Now that requirements were changing, however, there was danger that the colleges would become diploma mills. As one observer commented, "since at most of our colleges degrees are obtained without any exercise being performed or any examination passed, it will readily be granted that degrees are frequently conferred without merit."[38]

Rote recitation was the principal method of classroom instruction. In his Harvard diary, John Quincy Adams described a recitation on Locke:

When the tutor inquires what is contained in such a section, many of the scholars repeat the first two lines in it, which are very frequently nothing to the purpose; and leave the rest for the tutor to explain, which he commonly does by saying over again the words of the author.[39]

This, however dull, was recitation at its best. At Dickinson, Dr.

Robert Davidson, vice-president of the college, forced his students to memorize a long "rhyming geography" he had composed including an introductory acrostic on his own name:

Round the globe now to rove, and its surface survey,
Oh, youth of America, hasten away;
Bid adieu for awhile to the toys you desire,
Earth's beauties to view, and its wonders admire;
Refuse not instruction, improve well your time,
They are happy in age who are wise in their prime.
Delighted we'll pass seas, continents, through,
And isles without number, the old and the new;
Vast oceans and seas, too, shall have their due praise,
Including the rivers, the lakes, and the bays . . .

No wonder that Roger Brooke Taney (Dickenson 1795), later chief justice of the Supreme Court, recalled that Davidson's teaching was "the subject of ridicule" among the students.[40] It reminds one of the scene in which Hugh Henry Brackenridge's fictional Captain Farrago discovers an illiterate Irishman passing in an American university in the 1790s as a professor of Greek on the strength of his heavy Irish brogue.[41] Poor teaching, low standards, curricular uncertainty, and the general decline of the colleges all intensified undergraduate impatience to graduate and get out into the world.

The Revolution also fostered an egalitarianism that added to campus unrest. It was once thought that an influx of middle-class boys democratized the colleges, but a recent demographic study has challenged this myth, estimating that the probability of a white family sending a son to college around 1790 was only one in a hundred. "When comparing students who attended school in the quarter century before and after the War for Independence, only slight differences emerge."[42] American colleges were elitist institutions, though not all the students were wealthy.

If the composition of the student body was the same, however, the mutual relationships among the students were different. Colonial America had had numerous customs of social deference. Until 1773 at Harvard and 1768 at Yale, students had been ranked not alphabetically or by merit but according to the social status of their fathers.[43] After the Revolution, undergraduate relations were less hierarchical. Distinctions between the classes began to break down. President Jonathan Maxcy of Brown reprimanded the students in 1791 "for making no distinctions, in their intercourse, between the higher and lower classes."[44] In 1793 Brown's new laws tried to shore up such class differences:

> No member of an under class may go into the chapel, dining-hall, or other room . . . before any member of any class above him.
> Any student passing by one of a class above him, shall take off his hat in a respectful and decent manner.[45]

The foremost class custom was fagging—forcing underclassmen to act as servants for upperclassmen. In colonial colleges, fagging had served as an important disciplinary tool. Upperclassmen had been responsible for initiating their fags into the college customs and seeing that they obeyed the laws. By the turn of the century, fagging was becoming obsolete. It was abolished outright at Harvard in 1798 and at Yale in 1804. Most of the new colleges never sanctioned this undemocratic custom in the first place. In some institutions it lingered on in an attenuated form, as at Dartmouth where in 1794 individual freshmen could be excused from being fags on the condition that they not try to have fags once they were sophomores.[46] The end of fagging meant that the burden of keeping order on campus fell more heavily on the professors and thus increased the likelihood of disciplinary conflicts.

Professors, too, were troubled by the breakdown of social deference. Samuel Stanhope Smith of Princeton explained conditions in America to Dr. Nisbet, while the latter was still in Sctoland: "our freedom certainly takes away the distinctions of rank that are so visible in Europe; and of consequence takes away, in the same

proportion, those submissive forms of politeness that exist there."[47]
During the Whiskey Rebellion of 1793, President Nisbet, now in
America, preached to his western Pennsylvania parishioners that
"not all men were equally fitted to be Philosophers, Legislators,
and Statesmen; but that some were intended for working with
their hands," and was nearly mobbed as a result.[48]

Academics rightly feared egalitarianism as hostile toward intellect and learning. They were used to being treated with deference
and respect. Hence they generally espoused a conservative social
philosophy. In his lectures President Smith taught that universal
suffrage and social equality were contrary to "the natural order of
things."[49] The one place academics could demand subordination
was on campus where professors exacted the full measure of respect from the undergraduates. Most colleges in the colonial era
had laid out elaborate procedures for tipping one's hat to one's better. Dartmouth had not had such rules, but in 1782 it too required
that students remove their hats within six rods of the president,
that they "stand in his presence till they have permission to sit,
wait for his liberty to speak and deliver their sentiments with mod-
esty and propriety, and deliberately."[50] These were small tokens to
be sure, but they were not merely taken for granted by the students. John Quincy Adams recorded in his Harvard diary: "It is
against the laws of the college to call any undergraduate by any
but his sir-name, and I am told the President, who is remarkably
strict on all these matters, reproved a gentleman at his table for
calling a student Mr. while he was present."[51] By the end of the
century, students invariably addressed each other as Mr. and Sir.
There was leveling of age as well as rank.

Discipline was the most common student complaint. In 1789 a
Princeton graduate wrote "A Valedictory Oration, to Scholastic
Education," likening college discipline to that of a prison.

Freed from tyrannic tutor's sway,
I leave thee, sacred doom! this day,

Adieu ye reverend hypocrites!
Ye holy despots, little wits!
Hence lead me from the loathsome cell,
Where masters whip and pupils yell,
Where cruelty with bitter hand,
Envenom'd beats the little band.[52]

Actually, student discipline was quite light. For a minor offense an offender would receive an admonition or have to pay a small fine. For a greater infraction he might have to apologize before the rest of the college. Except for rare cases of expulsion, the most serious punishment was "rustication" — having to spend time away from the campus under the tutelage of a clergyman. Even this could be "pleasant and cheerful," as Harvard senior Joseph Dennie reported from exile at Groton in 1789. "No *unseasonable* morning prayers" forced him from bed, and afternoons could be spent in the company of "mortal females." When it came time for him to graduate, his parents literally had to drag him back to Cambridge.[53] But "Modern Youth," as Tompkins had described his generation, found it increasingly difficult to submit to faculty authority. "It seems almost to be an axiom among the governors of the college to treat the students pretty much like brute beasts," the studious young Adams charged. "There is an important air and a haughty look that every person belonging to the government assumes, which indeed it is hard for me to submit to."[54] On October 25, 1796, the University of North Carolina's undergraduate Philanthropic Society debated, "Whether the laws of the University are generally good or not?" After a heated discussion, it was resolved that they were good "except that the Faculty has too much authority."[55]

The climate in America following the Revolution was certainly conducive to youthful presumptuousness. The young represented the future of the new republic. From 1786 to 1798 one of the most debated pedagogical issues was how best to instill "republican principles" into the rising generations. This was the high point of the Enlightenment, and the faith in natural rights was readily extended to the young. In the University of North Carolina's 1789 charter, for instance, the trustees were empowered to formulate only those student laws *"not contrary to the unalienable liberty of a citizen."*[56] Two decades later John Randolph would assure his young ward that "although you are not yet of an age to be your own master, yet you are possessed of rights which it would be tyranny and injustice to withhold or invade."[57]

Hannah More's prediction had come true: men did speak of the rights of youth. But as late as the mid-1790s, there was not yet a "student problem" per se. Campuses remained quiet; students were inert and unorganized. No one spoke of generational conflict or of an alien philosophy dividing the old from the young. Though long-range trends contributed to student unrest, the rise of campus revolt itself came not gradually but quite suddenly, during the national crisis of 1798. The crisis both mobilized the young and altered the meaning of youthful disorders. After the turn of the century student unrest was no longer calmly attributed to the "influence of the first lapse" but was perceived as "the product of vice and irreligion." This change in perception would make a crucial difference.

CHAPTER TWO

The Genius of Revolt

IT IS SOMEWHAT hazardous to speak of a national student "movement" at the turn of the nineteenth century, as there was no Students for a Democratic Society or Student League for Industrial Democracy or other coordinating organization. Student disunity reflected conditions in the United States. Bad roads, vast distances, and slow communications kept the different areas of the country apart. Colleges were especially isolated, built away from cities on purpose to save the morals of the young. Given these conditions, is it possible to portray a general movement as opposed to numerous unrelated incidents?

College professors certainly saw student unrest as a common problem, attributed it to the same source, and took concerted action against it. Students were highly mobile, transferring institutions often, visiting others on vacations, and no doubt gaining a mutual understanding of what was going on. Apart from this, the rebellions themselves seemed to follow a general course. There were at least thirteen major confrontations at the six schools hardest hit, not counting numerous cases of attempted arson, bombings, drinking sprees, vandalism, and verbal insubordination.[1] There were roughly two stages. The first, from 1798 to 1802, might be called the emergence of student power. The second, from 1805 to 1808, was the era of great campus rebellions.

In 1798 Brown University was disrupted by what one student called "a damn partial distribution" of parts.[2] "Parts" were the graduation speaking assignments which served in the absence of grades as a rough indicator of class rank. They were also a subtle form of discipline, awarded sometimes for conduct as well as for scholarship. In *Strictures on Harvard University* (1798), William Austin, a Harvard senior, denounced parts as "the political engine of government." Dickinson College narrowly averted a riot in 1809 when popular James Buchanan, the future United States President, was denied an honor on the ground that "it would have a bad tendency to confer an honor of the college upon a student who had shewn so little respect for the rules of the college and for the professors."[3]

Although a few institutions allowed student literary societies to nominate speakers to be chosen by the faculty, in general professors resisted undergraduate encroachments in this area for two good reasons. First, whoever chose the speakers was in effect the arbiter of academic merit, and that was presumably independent of majority vote or personal popularity. Second, along with authority to assign parts went the power to control the speeches and insure that the college would not be embarrassed at public ceremonies. Students were notoriously indiscreet. In 1811 the president of Columbia attempted to halt an unauthorized, controversial address and caused a full-scale riot.[4]

So, at Brown in 1798, the faculty refused to review the assignments, though the students "hissed and clapt" Professor Asa Messer in chapel and the hallways "resounded with crashing of bottles and the hoarse rumbling of wood and stones." Defeated on this issue, the students began to protest the price of board at commons. When President Maxcy forbade student meetings and twice refused to meet with the student committee, the rebels "rose in mass & put a stop to commons for a few days." Finding that not even

threats of expulsion could break the resistance, the college government retreated. Maxcy signed a "Treaty of Amity & Intercourse
between the President of Rhode-Island College & the Party Rebellious" which promised that if the students returned to commons,
the faculty would review the price and rules, grant amnesty to the
rebels, and open legitimate channels of protest.[5] It was an early,
though qualified, grant of student rights.

The Dickinson student strike of 1798 struck at the heart of academic authority. Through a quirk, Dickinson had been organized
by courses of instruction rather than traditional classes of freshmen, sophomores, and so on. Once a student had taken all the
courses he was entitled to a degree, with the implied assumption
that classes would be spread out over a number of years. In 1798,
however, the students wanted to take them all at the same time.
They boycotted classes until officially permitted to complete their
educations in a year.[6] The exasperated president had seen this
coming for some time. "I should not be surprised to hear of students receiving their degrees without any study at all," he wrote.[7]
What was most astonishing was that the trustees acquiesced in the
demand without demur, causing Richard Hofstadter to call this
"one of the most remarkable episodes in the history of higher education."[8] The result, according to Dickinson historians, was a
marked decline of the college. But it was a victory for student
power on a fundamental issue.

The rise of student power was evident at Union College in 1800,
during the short presidency of Jonathan Edwards, Jr. Discontent
was directed at two unpopular professors. The students petitioned
for the reinstatement of a classmate who had been expelled for cir-
culating an attack upon Professor Andrew Yates "which contained
prophane language and threatened him with violence to his person."[9] When the faculty refused, the students took it to the trustees, adding the demand that Professor Yates be fired. At the same
time, the juniors petitioned for the dismissal of Professor Benjamin Allen. The trustees were shocked by the students' audacity.

The board resolved "that the students in calling in question the abilities of their professors have assumed a prerogative with which they are not invested and have attempted to judge on a subject to which they are incompetent."[10] It appointed a special committee to find out if the students had been "urged to these dangerous measures by some secret influence or prejudice." Although the student demands were rejected, Professor Yates resigned, giving the rebels a victory in fact if not in theory.

Although student rebels had won a few limited triumphs, it was unrealistic to suppose that they would gain a lasting voice on parts, degree requirements, or faculty competence. The issue on which they might hope to succeed, and on which the fate of their resistance depended, was that of discipline. Disciplinary rules determined whether students could organize and protest and what would happen to them if they did. Discipline was also the most flexible issue for student rebels. Whenever something was needed to provoke a confrontation, misbehavior could goad the faculty into handing down punishments which became automatic pretexts for protest and resistance.

Discipline was the issue in the University of North Carolina riot of 1799. As described by one of the undergraduates, "this place is not in the most thriving condition. Most of the boys that are here this year will not return next . . . our President has got a horsewhipping from a boy which he and the Teachers had expelled unjustly and we have been in great confusion in taking his part for he was liked by all the boys."[11] In one of the most violent riots of the era, the president was beaten, two professors stoned, and the others threatened with injury. As one trustee put it, the entire college was in a state of "Anarchy and Confusion."[12] As a result of the riot, most of the faculty resigned, new and stricter rules were adopted, and the state legislature cut off the university's endowment. As at Dickinson, that is, the outcome was disastrous.

In 1800 disciplinary conflicts broke out in four colleges. Little is known about those at Harvard and Brown. At Harvard new rules for maintaining order in the chapel were at stake. Four-fifths of the students signed a remonstrance threatening to withdraw and presented it to the president who "very ungraciously and ungracefully received it."[13] The outcome is unknown. Likewise, no record exists to show how Brown overcame an imminent crisis. A boycott of classes almost led to a mass exodus when the seniors marched up to the president "four by four, requesting him to dismiss us."[14]

At William and Mary a student was expelled for cursing the Williamsburg postmaster and refusing to apologize. "The students were . . . very much agitated, and did not hesitate to censure the conduct of the professors," wrote an undergraduate.[15] Some proposed to "publish the injustice of the expulsion," others to break Professor St. George Tucker's windows. A petition was sent to the faculty, but it was rejected as too disrespectful. When the students made plans to go on strike, however, the faculty backed down and reinstated the offender.

At Princeton two minor riots resulted when three seniors were suspended for scraping the tutors at morning prayers (scraping was a loud shuffling of the feet). Outraged by this decision, the students fired pistols, smashed the doors and walls with brickbats, and rolled barrels of stones along the halls. A few days later one of the disciplined seniors returned to campus and beat the tutor who had turned him in. Then three more days of rioting ensued. Order was restored only when President Smith threatened to shut down the college.[16] While student resistance saved a few malcontents from punishment, nowhere had it won the right to review disciplinary proceedings on a regulr basis or to experiment with student self-government. In this sense, the protests were all failures.

A new dimension was added to revolt at this time when academics began to blame disorders on the radicalism and infidelity of the French Revolution. President Smith recalled that one of the 1800 agitators had "attempted to excite an insurrection on jacobinic & anti-religious principles."[17] Likewise, in 1801 the students of Transylvania University conducted a public trial of a professor who had tried to suppress their freethinking. When the trustees hesitated, the students began withdrawing, finally forcing the board to dismiss him.[18] Fear of student radicalism greatly enhanced the significance of student discontent.

The year 1802 marked the peak of the first stage of revolt. Williams College was in a state of siege for nearly two weeks.[19] At Yale, according to a tutor, there was "nothing but wars and rumors of wars."[20] A riot at William and Mary was used by Federalist politicians for a newspaper attack on the Jeffersonians.[21] Here, too, the riot was linked to atheism. The students had purportedly gone "to the church, broke and destroyed all the windows, cut down the pulpit, tore out all the leaves of the bible and gave them to the wind."[22] Although President James Madison, Episcopal Bishop of Virginia (not to be confused with his cousin the United States President), explained that the only damage to the church was two or three broken windows, his disclaimers were overshadowed by the second serious event—the burning of Nassau Hall.[23]

Nassau Hall was Princeton's major college building. It was completely gutted by a mysterious fire on March 6, 1802. For months before the students had been in a state of insurrection; some of them had reportedly hinted about burning the college. Hence, though no evidence of arson was ever found, the fire was blamed on student resistance. Accounts of the disaster were carried in newspapers throughout the country. Things had gotten out of hand. Academics were consequently able to suppress student rebelliousness for a short time.[24]

There was a national crackdown on discipline after 1802. New, stricter codes of laws were written at Princeton, Transylvania, Williams, South Carolina College, the University of North Carolina, and William and Mary. A more repressive spirit animated professors. In his inaugural address, President Joseph McKeen of Bowdoin told parents to give no heed to their sons' complaints of tyranny or mistreatment: "The volatility of a youthful mind frequently gives rise to eccentricities and an impatience of the most wholesome restraint; the mildest government is thought oppressive, and the indulgent parent's ear is easily opened to the voice of complaint; imaginary fears are excited, that the genius of a darling son will be cramped, his spirit broken."[25]

What happened at Union College was indicative of the national reaction. At his arrival President Eliphalet Nott instituted what he called a monastic system of discipline. "Our students, like those of the Moravian schools," he explained, "are to be entirely separated from the great world."

> Not the least disorder is allowed in or about the edifice . . . The week is completely filled up with collegiate, the Sabbath with religious, exercises. On the latter day no student goes from the yard except to church, and even then he walks with his professor in procession, sits with him, and with him returns. Perhaps no college has ever furnished such complete security to the manners and morals of youth.[26]

Union professors justified this regimentation by pointing to the close proximity of the Mohawk River and its corrupting boatmen. "The situation of the College demands a more rigid government than any other with which I am acquainted," wrote Professor Henry Davis. "Were the College planted in the midst of sober New England people, a milder government might answer."[27] But students and many townsmen disagreed. As John Howard Payne wrote his father in June 1806, "this college is universally railed at here for the excessive and unexampled rigidity of its governors."[28] Union was only an extreme example of a national trend. As might be expected, this excessive surveillance of students at Union and elsewhere soon bred renewed resistance.

The second stage of student revolt began with the Great Secession at the University of North Carolina in 1805. It was a protest against the Monitor Act passed by the trustees which made student prefects responsible for keeping order in the college. The students' mutual compact was what professors called an illegal combination:

We the students of University of North Carolina, having sent a remonstrance to the Faculty & Trustees for a repeal of laws, which we deem injurious to the welfare of the same, do solemnly declare, & pledge our honour as gentlemen, never to take the oath so arbitrarily and unjustly imposed upon us by the late ordinance. Moreover we do promise and pledge ourselves by every obligation which we hold most dear and sacred, that if the Faculty or Trustees should select any person or persons whose names are hereunto subscribed for punishment that we will leave College until those persons selected and punished shall be restored. We also consider it to be the nature of this mutual obligation that if any person should violate the pledge of his most sacred word & honour he is to be considered unworthy the attention of gentlemen & should be rejected from all company where decency and respectability have any place.[19]

Repeal of the act came too late: most of the seceders refused to return. Ultimately, forty-five students withdrew from the university, a majority of its small enrollment. Thus the university was crippled again, as it had been in 1799.[30]

The great rebellions at Harvard and Princeton in 1807 were also marked by unanimity and mass desertions: Harvard lost forty students, Princeton more than fifty.[31] There were numerous instances of unrest at other institutions as well. Yale had a town-gown riot in 1806.[32] Archibald Alexander resigned as president of Hampden-Sydney in 1807 because "our students were in a state of much turbulence and insubordination . . . and I grew weary of governing them."[33] Williams was closed for a month by an 1808 rebellion, and a new faculty had to be recruited.[34] In the same year William and Mary had another serious uprising.[35] Minor disturbances at Union from 1806 to 1809 finally culminated in the mysterious "Illumination of the 13th of May" which so unnerved the faculty that a shake-up of the professors and disciplinary procedures ensued.[36] Dartmouth, too, had an unsettling riot in 1809.

These post-1807 disorders were anticlimactic, however, for the war had been lost at Harvard and Princeton in 1807. As a writer of the time put it, "that an alarming spirit of insubordination should have made its appearance at the same moment in two of the most respectable literary seminaries in different parts of the Country," raised the possibility that student rebellion had become a nationally organized movement. Fortunately, he went on, the governors of both institutions "have adopted precisely the same courses, have suggested the same ideas, and are actuated by the same principles," and had firmly withstood the pressures of student revolt.[37]

The policy which finally crushed student resistance was the practice of sending blacklists with the names of student activists to other colleges, instructing them to admit none of the rebels. The origin of this student blacklisting is rather obscure. As early as 1802 William and Mary officials had announced that "information of every expulsion, which may take place, shall be by the president communicated to all other public seminaries in the United States."[38] Independently, the Princeton trustees resolved in 1803 "that no person will be received into this Institution under any pretence whatsoever who may have studied at any other College or University without producing a certificate from the President or Faculty of said College or University that he has left it without censure."[39] From letters sent out in 1807, it appears that between 1802 and 1807 a general agreement on blacklisting was worked out among the different colleges. Of those responding to the blacklists sent out by Harvard and Princeton in 1807, the only institution that refused to go along was the University of Pennsylvania, which had a desperate need for students. Even academic liberals such as Bishop Madison of William and Mary agreed that drastic action was required.[40] Those institutions that had not previously adopted the policy quickly did so. Entering students at the University of North Carolina would henceforth be required to swear in writing that they had never been expelled nor deserted from another college to escape punishment; transfer students would have to bring with them a certificate of honorable dismissal.[41] Dartmouth sent out a blacklist in 1809, the University of North Carolina in 1816.[42] As late as the 1830s an educator could speak of "a general understanding amongst our colleges, that no student having been dismissed from one, should be received into another."[43] Blacklisting was effective because it meant that no activist would foment more than one rebellion, that students who needed a degree for advancement in life would be more wary of revolt, and that college governments could break up student combinations by holding out the promise of "regular dismissals."

After 1807 for all practical purposes there was no longer a nascent student movement, though there continued to be an abundance of riots and rebellions. Almost without exception there was a wave of disorders every four or five years—in 1811-1812, 1817-1819, 1825-1826, 1828-1830, 1834 and so forth.[44] What happened was that student revolt became a tradition. A college education was incomplete without one confrontation. Although later riots were sometimes more violent than those between 1798 and 1808, in other ways they were less alarming. The threat of radicalism was erased by faculty censorship. A series of religious revivals swept the colleges and reassured academics that their institutions were still secure. Moreover, American society as a whole grew so violent as to make student turmoil hardly exceptional.[45] In later rebellions some of the humor attending colonial resistance was recaptured. Harvard's 1819 uprising was described in "The Rebelliad."

When Nathan threw a piece of bread
And hit Abijah on the head,
The wrathful freshman, in a thrice,
Sent back another bigger slice,
Which, being buttered pretty well,
Made greasy work wher'er it fell.
And thus arose a fearful battle,
The coffee-cups and saucers rattle,
The bread-bowls fly at woeful rate,
And break full many a learned pate.[46]

Ante-Bellum America never experienced a massive student movement comparable to those of France or Germany. The small

size of American colleges as well as vastly different national histories undoubtedly precluded students in America from becoming a
major social force. But there was a glimmering of something in
the years 1798 to 1808 which if left alone might well have become
a student movement of sorts. It did not amount to more because it
was so thoroughly suppressed.

THE HARVARD REBELLION OF 1807

William Bentley, the Salem Republican clergyman, himself a
graduate of Harvard, noted in his diary on April 19, 1807, "the
most interesting topic of conversation is taken from affairs at
Cambridge."[47] The Harvard Rebellion to which he referred broke
out on March 30, though it had been brewing for months.[48] The
first sign of protest had been vandalism. As Professor Levi Hedge
listed the damage:

> they broke down one of the outer doors of Holden Chapel,
> forced their way into the Junior's reciting room, totally demol-
> ished one of those large windows, tumbled out the desk and
> some of the furniture of the room. They then collected the rub-
> bish into a heap midway between Harvard and Mass., set it on
> fire, and sent up such a hue and cry as alarmed the college and
> some parts of the town. The windows of the chapel have been
> repeatedly broken.[49]

The vandalism turned to rebellion when a sophomore was handed
a four-month suspension for "openly and grossly insulting the
members of the Government . . . by hissing at them as they
passed."[50] The students petitioned for his pardon, promising to
end the campus disorders in return for his reinstatement.[51] The
faculty then relented. Apparently the government's appeasement
was mistaken for weakness. As one student described the reaction
of his classmates: "the multitude upsent a shout of victory over de-

tested power; a shout ominous of future noble achievements."[52]
The faculty also reasoned that its leniency "was ungratefully and
without any foundation represented by some of the Students, as a
triumph over the Immediate Government, and a mark of imbecil-
ity."[53] Next time, it vowed, there would be no appeasement.

The ostensible cause of the rebellion was the state of the college
commons. In the ten days before the uprising the students twice
petitioned for reforms, and a committee called on the president
three times without gaining admittance. The students were actually trying to provoke a confrontation: the committee intention-
ally chose inconvenient times for its visits and reported to the rest
of the undergraduates that it had called on him twenty times, not
three.[54] When an untimely dinner of fish and rotten cabbage was
served on March 30, the students went into action. A large banner
announcing a mass meeting was unfurled over the dining hall passage. For a day the students marched in and out of the commons
without eating. There were plans for an attack upon the kitchen,
but these were thwarted when the government discovered the plot
and closed the commons altogether.

At its April 3 meeting, the Harvard Corporation declared the
conduct of the rebels to be "disorderly, indecent, an insult to the
authority of the College, and a violation of the laws." It objected
less to the walkout than to the illegal "combination." "A Government of the Students is erected against the regular Government of
the College," it said. Therefore everyone implicated in the revolt
would have to sign a written apology or suffer expulsion.[55] When
President Samuel Webber tried to read the Corporation's resolution to the students, he was interrupted by "the rude shuffling of
feet." After his announcement, "the classes met again at the ring-
ing of the bell, without leave from the President, for the purpose
of forming new combinations of resistance."[56] A statement
emerged from this new meeting reputedly signed by every undergraduate pledging that rather than comply with the Corporation's
demands the students would leave Harvard en masse. According

to Hedge, "some of the richest of them are going to Oxford and
Edinburgh, some are filing off to New Haven. They mean to take
Bowdoin College by storm, 70 or 80 are going there in a body."[57]
But this bold talk was mostly wishful thinking.

On April 15 the faculty called the students in one by one and
demanded that they sign the confession. Seventy-four signed and
ninety-nine refused. Finding that the combination could be
broken, the Corporation decided that rather than dismiss nearly
half the student body (forty-five had been absent when the rebellion broke) it would punish only the leaders. The problem was no
one knew who they were.[58] Eventually, twenty-three of the most
obdurate undergraduates were expelled. Eight of these later recanted and gained readmittance. Of those who escaped punishment, however, many refused to return. Thus in the last count the
student body was reduced by forty at the end of the term. Breaking the "combination" did not immediately restore order. A kind
of guerrilla warfare persisted for about a year afterwards. Hedge
wrote: "the town has been repeatedly alarmed in the night by fires
wantonly kindled in buildings belonging to the college."[59] Only in
the fall of 1808, by which time most of the disaffected students
had either been expelled or graduated, did the Harvard rebellion
fully end.

Known as the Rotten Cabbage Rebellion because of its origin in
the commons, the insurrection was more significant than its name
would imply. It was a good illustration of the fact that the specific
grievances involved in rebellions were often simply pretexts for
venting a general malaise. In 1807 both professors and students
admitted as much. Hedge wrote that the state of commons "though
the ostensible is not the real cause" of the rebellion. Great pains
had been taken recently to improve the fare, he said. The rotten
cabbage was simply "the spark to set the combustibles on fire."[60]
One of the students agreed that "complaints against Commons
were . . . a pretence" since "many scholars concerned themselves
in it who did not board in Commons."[61] The common historical

approach toward popular uprisings is to see them as expressions of specific social and political complaint by otherwise inarticulate masses.[62] But students were neither a voiceless nor, potentially, a powerless class. Student rebellions were not so much a rational form of protest as an expression of deep-seated malaise.

What the rebellions were really about therefore is rather difficult to say. A senior who opposed the revolt was struck by the irrationality of his classmates. Of one insurgent who grew so distraught over the disintegration of the combination that "he went and stood upon a tomb, and thought that if he was on a bridge, he should leap into the river," the senior asked, "Is our College to be destroyed by such persons? Are the days of witchcraft returned?"[63] A leader of the revolt blamed the disorders on student resentment of faculty arrogance. "Let the Students be once convinced that the Government is not continually struggling to support its dignity and authority, but that they are under the conduct of men . . . who wear their dignity as a natural and easy appendage, and not as a retreating soldier does his arms, by continual defensive exertions."[64] William Bentley had a similar interpretation. "The College to meet these serious evils," he said, "is entirely in the hands of young & inexperienced men who have no weight from years, or fame, or address."[65] There were other concrete issues besides the rotten cabbage which may have contributed to the discontent. One of these was the faculty's refusal to abolish Hebrew. In 1806 the freshmen had petitioned for elective Hebrew; when this was refused they tried to destroy the Hebrew grammars and some Hebrew type.[66] After the rebellion, the Corporation modified the Hebrew requirement to exempt students after the freshman year if their parents so desired.[67] Another source of dissatisfaction may have been rising costs. Tuition and board rose from $128 in 1805-1806 to $167 in 1806-1807 and $180 in 1807-1808, an almost 50 percent jump in two years.[68] Yet none of these causes nor all of them together really explains the revolt.

The inability of the rebels to maintain a united front was a tacit admission that conditions were not intolerable. That may be why nonconforming students were so persecuted. Consider, for instance, Joseph Tufts, the senior from Charlestown, Massachusetts, whose mock heroic *Don-Quixots at College* ridiculed his self-important classmates. He was ostracized and accused of placing his own selfish ambition of speaking at the commencement exercises above the fate of the student rebellion. "This poor youth," gibed one of his detractors, "has probably been under considerable apprehension, lest the disturbance in college might prevent him from displaying his sapience, at the next exhibition, where, perhaps, he had a part, the fruit of long and toilsome fishery."[69] Tufts was the leading scholar in his class, and he did give the Valedictory Address in 1807. From his complaints in later life, however, this award appears to have been scant compensation for his misery as a student. "I suffered almost every thing, that an enraged mob can inflict. Such an effect had this upon my feelings, that for years after, there was not a day when I did not think of it. And I often think of it to this day . . . Had it not been for these miscreants the course of my life would have been far more comfortable and happy."[70]

This personal side of student revolt is hard to recover but highly important. For participants on both sides these were events of lasting significance. In 1811 two Brown students were "denounced as informers and threatened with *tar and feathers*."[71] In 1817 the pious students at Princeton were locked in their rooms by the rioters to keep them from giving testimony to the faculty.[72] Understandably, the orderly undergraduates hated their tormentors. "Since the filth & dregs have been purged out," wrote a student from Princeton of his classmates being expelled, "we have had quite peaceful times."[73] Amos Kendall testified against Dartmouth rioters in 1809, and years later he and his persecutors were exchanging insults by mail.[74] The extreme peer group loyalty demanded of students suggests that campus revolt was basically a manifestation of generational consciousness.[75] That specific issues were merely pretexts for provoking confrontations would tend to confirm this conclusion. Student protest was a sign of deep and complex generational unrest. Such demonstrations "become ceremonies of solidarity whose value, for many participants, lies as much in the experience of 'one-ness' as in any practical object they may seek to achieve."[76] The causes of this generational unrest remain to be explored.

THE PRINCETON REBELLION OF 1807

On March 31, 1807, only a day after the Harvard revolt, another major disturbance broke out at Princeton. This was the climax of student resistance in this period, as those who witnessed it were well aware. "The cause in which the governors of the College of New Jersey are engaged," wrote President Timothy Dwight from Yale, "is the common cause of all colleges."[77] For months students and government alike had been primed for a showdown. One student after another had been suspended for "dissipation" and other minor crimes normally meriting a milder punishment. According to one source, the undergraduates had "twice attempted to burn the College."[78] Finally, in order to precipitate a crisis, the students sent a petition to the faculty, demanding the reinstatement of three suspended students and a retraction from President Smith and Professor Maclean of certain unspecified accusations they had made concerning the offenders. There was an obvious threat in the petition's request for an "immediate answer" that would determine the "future proceedings" of the students.[79]

The faculty refused to consider the petition on the familiar ground that it was the result of a "combination" formed to resist the authority of the government. At prayers, Smith and trustee Richard Stockton lectured the students on the illegality of their behavior. The students responded by scraping their feet. Finally Smith gave them an ultimatum: they would either come forward as the roll was called and remove their names from the petition or they would be expelled. At this point one of the rebels stood up and cried that they would retract nothing. Then 120 "shouting and yelling" students rushed out of the hall, leaving only 25 behind. When each of the remaining students had removed his name, Smith announced the suspension of the rest. That evening the rebels occupied Nassau Hall and began to set up barricades. The town militia was called out, but when they tried to enter the students drove them back with broken stairway banisters and stones.[80] Rather than risk serious injury, Smith closed the college so that the trustees could meet and devise an official response.

The rebels were elated by their seeming victory. They stayed in town and organized a revolutionary "committee" designed to co-ordinate strategy and present a united front to the trustees.[81] They were fully confident of success. Joseph C. Breckenridge declared that unless the trustees satisfied the student demands, "I believe not a single man whose name is annexed to the paper will enter college next session . . . If they do in despite of reason expel us; in the spirit of prophecy I predict that they will sign with their own hands the death-warrant of this institution."[82]

But the trustees were adamant. Like the Harvard Corporation, they reduced the controversy to a single issue: "we must either govern our own college or resign it to the government of inconsiderate boys or passionate young men."[83] To uphold their authority, they were willing to dismiss the entire student body. One trustee wrote, "such a spirit of insubordination has been excited . . . that it will be very difficult if not impossible, to govern the college, without, in a great measure, changing its inhabitants — I have therefore little concern tho' we should lost one half the present students; & would rather lose the whole than take them back without a change in their sentiments."[84]

This spirit dominated the trustees. At their first meeting on April 8 they refused to receive a student delegation as being part of an unlawful combination. The next day they decided to confront the rebels individually. The students, thinking that they were being invited to plead their case, chose Abel P. Upshur as their first spokesman. Before he said a word, however, the trustees told him that he would be expelled unless he renounced the combination, which he declined to do. He eventually managed to denounce the tyranny of the college governors, but when he left the meeting he was expelled. Those who followed faced the same choice. The combination began to crumble when some of the students broke under the pressure and renounced the resistance. Those who refused to yield were blacklisted.

The rebel committee replied with a forceful broadside pleading for student unity. It granted that "our prospect for reinstatement we cannot but esteem unpromising," but it exhorted the students to "adhere to your deliberate resolve, to evince to the world that you are capable of acting for yourself, that age should not sanction impertinence, that youth has its privileges, and that the genius of revolt shall come forward to support them whenever the hand of presuming authority shall attempt to level or abridge them."[85] With the combination breaking up, the exhilaration of closing the college was soon forgotten. The brother of a student could imagine that "for the first two or three days after the college was dismissed, no doubt more heroes stalked the streets of Princeton than did in Paris after the memorable Revolution of France — But now without any great effort of fancy, I can see them moping about with broken spirits and relenting hearts."[86] Joseph C. Breckenridge's response was truly pathetic: "Faculty of the College! tyrants of my tender years! . . . hoary-headed despots! who actuated by the unhallowed spirit of revenge, have essayed to trample on the tender victims of your resentment!"[87]

In the end, nearly seventy of the rebels straggled back to college, but at least fifty-five refused to return. Although the great rebellion was over, the victory of the trustees was hollow. It proved that student resistance could not succeed, but not that riots and rebellions could be prevented. Princeton was plagued with disorders for years to come.

Two actions taken by the Princeton trustees were particularly significant. First, on April 10 they issued a remarkable document addressed to the parents which stated that the "infinite command of money" which students enjoyed was the principal cause of resistance. Parents were directed to limit students to $188 per year for college expenses and $250-$280 per year for allowance. They were asked to swear in person or in writing that they would neither exceed these sums nor honor any debts contracted by their sons buying on credit. They were also requested to disburse their funds through the newly-created college bursar, who would control student spending. Violations of these rules, the trustees warned, "shall be deemed a sufficient cause to dismiss such student from the College."[88] The regulation was clearly intended to undermine the rebels by cutting off their funds, forcing them to return to campus or return home.

The new law also said much about the academic perception of student unrest. It was the wealthy young "bloods" who were blamed for the disturbance. This contradicts a recent theory which has held that an influx of poor students after the Revolution caused the breakdown of order and discipline in the colleges.[89] The reverse was actually true. The American Education Society was founded in 1815 to provide scholarships for ministerial candidates from poor families partly to uplift the discipline and morality of the colleges.[90] Poor students valued their education more highly than the bloods as their only means of advancement. Moreover, they were more tractable than their wealthy peers because they were used to hard work and parental discipline. A few years later one educator proposed that

> by introducing into them [the colleges] a much larger number of the sons of persons in moderate circumstances, — of our farmers and mechanics, — of such persons as bring up their children with modesty and unassuming manners and industrious habits, and who do not spoil them by allowing them to have too much money, the whole mass of the students would be likely to profit by their example, and the general tone of our colleges in respect of morality be improved.[91]

Campus revolt was seen primarily as an upper-class pattern of behavior.

The second action of the trustees was to attack the student literary societies which functioned something like an underground university during the rebellion. Literary societies were well-established extracurricular institutions. The two Princeton societies, the Cliosophic Society and the American Whig Society, both went back to the 1760s.[92] They were highly independent. They met in college buildings but owned their own libraries and furniture and governed themselves by their own rules. Like the social fraternities which emerged in the mid-nineteenth century, they gave students fellowship, secrecy, and ritual. By contrast, however, they were basically intellectual in orientation. Many students regarded their weekly debating and reading of essays as the most important part of their education. As one ex-Whig wrote just prior to the rebellion: "I have just written to my uncle and requested his permission to leave College . . . I am expelled from the AWS. You may therefore assure my uncle . . . that no improvement can be derived here which I might not obtain elsewhere in much less time."[93] In their disciplinary capacity the societies were potentially an important restraining influence, and the faculty frequently appealed to them for help in keeping order. In 1806 and 1809 the societies considered cooperating with the government but decided against it because it might jeopardize their independence.[94]

Apparently the societies attempted to carry on their extracurricular education after the trustees had closed the official institution. On May 8 the trustees resolved:

> That no society or association of students belonging to the College shall at their stated or occasional meetings admit to the same any person who has been or may be expelled, dismissed, or suspended from the College for irregular conduct and not restored. That the admission of any such persons by said society or association shall be judged a departure from the obligations due to the Institution, and that on proof of such offence the society or association so offending shall be dissolved, and their room of

meeting shall be taken possession of by the Faculty of the College, and appropriated to such use as they shall judge proper. *And that no organized association of the students be permitted to assemble statedly or occasionally at any place beyond the limits of the grounds belonging to this corporation.*[95]

For a while the societies and the government were on the verge of a major confrontation. As William Meade, later Bishop of Virginia, wrote on May 21: "the trustees, not content with expelling the non-retractors from College, wished to force the societies to do the same also, threatening to dissolve them in case of a refusal. They, however, did refuse in a very resolute manner, — and College and societies were at the point of dissolution at several times."[96] Whether the trustees finally backed down or a compromise was reached the records do not say.

The involvement of the societies in the rebellion gave student resistance a legitimacy it might otherwise have lacked. On this point the records of the Philanthropic Society at the University of North Carolina are pertinent. One can almost read the course of the Great Secession in the debates:

"Ought children to evade the commands of their parents in any respect?" Determined 9-4 that they ought.

"Were the students of this University justified in sending a remonstrance to the Trustees?" 7-4 that they were.

"Is a man justifiable for escaping punishment to be unjustly inflicted upon him?" 6-5 that he is.[97]

By comparing a list of those expelled from Princeton during the rebellion with a letter containing the names of the most influential members in the societies, one finds that the leaders of the revolt were among the most respected students.[98] According to young Meade, who had been expelled himself and then recanted, "many have returned, but the finest young men have refused to return."[99]

One other curious circumstance is highly noteworthy. The societies themselves were disrupted by the underlying malaise. Both

Whigs and Clios suffered schisms in the winter of 1806-1807 which finally resulted in the formation of a new student group, the short-lived Euterpean Society, named presumably for the Greek Muse of Music, Euterpe, the relevance of which is hard to fathom. Significantly, the Whig chronicler for the year 1807 saw a direct relationship between the confusion within the societies and the subsequent campus revolt. "The storm passed on to rage with augmented force in another direction," he explained, "and if within the sphere of our history, it would be no difficult task to trace the connection between this and that which afterwards burst with such violence in our parent institution."[100] Although his meaning is unclear, he likened the "principles" of the Euterpeans to those of the Adelphics of 1805—another abortive attempt to create a third society. According to the Whig chornicler for 1805, the creators of the Adelphic Society were motivated by vanity: "vanity from a desire of having their names ranked among the founders of a new institution."[101] In 1807, the Euterpeans were said to be similarly inspired by "the idea of becoming the founders of a third institution, which they vainly hoped should some day rival those two which had so long existed with such honor to themselves and which claimed the support of so many distinguished names of our Country."[102]

The clerks may have been trying to make an important psychological point. The original founders of the Whigs were James Madison, Hugh Henry Brackenridge, Philip Freneau, Aaron Burr —in short, the founders of the American nation.[103] At a symbolic level, bolting from the societies created by the Founding Fathers was tantamount to redeclaring independence, not from England this time but from the Founders themselves. It was a way of disassociating from the leading figures of the adult generation. Students rose up against college professors because they were convenient father-figures, symbols of the older generation. Insofar as this was true, the key to unlocking student discontent may well lie beyond the colleges altogether—in the attitude of the rising generation to the general course of national events.

CHAPTER THREE

The Sons of the Founders

"OUR POST-REVOLUTIONARY youth are born under happier stars than you and I were," scoffed Jefferson to Adams. "They acquire all learning in their mother's womb, and bring it into the world ready-made. The information of books is no longer necessary, and all knowledge which is not innate, is in contempt."[1] The thought came naturally. Turn-of-the-century college students were not simply young men of sixteen or eighteen but a distinct generation — the Sons of the Founders — of whom great things were expected, as they were surely aware. They were named for Revolutionary War heroes — William Steuben Smith, George Washington Rodgers, Washington Irving — or for ancient great — Peter Augustus Jay, Lucius Manlius Sargent, Lucius Quintius Cincinnatus Elmer — or for a combination of the two — David Washington Cincinnatus Olyphant — to mention just a few. Born during or just after the Revolution, they grew up in an affectedly republican society. As John Adams counseled his daughter on the upbringing of his grandsons, "the young gentlemen, I hope, think of Greece and Italy."[2] Institutions were changed on their behalf. David Ramsay wrote that primogeniture was abolished in South Carolina "to republicanize the rising generation."[3] State universities were created, while pedagogues debated how best to instill republican values into the young. In a famous phrase, Dr. Benjamin Rush prophesied that his plan of education would convert American youths into "republican machines."[4]

But the product of all this effort, in the eyes of some, was a disappointment. The rising generation was insubordinate, dissipated, and rebellious. In 1807 John Randolph said they "early assume airs of manhood; and these premature men remain children for the rest of their lives." With a "smathering of Latin, drinking grog, and chewing tobacco, these stripplings set up for legislators and statesmen."[5] Dr. Benjamin Waterhouse warned the students of Harvard that "I have been a Professor in this University twenty three years, and can say, as a physician, that I never observed so many palid faces, and so many marks of declining health, nor ever knew so many hectical habits, and consumptive affections, as of late years."[6] If age proposes, youth disposes. With all of this attention focused on the young it was natural for students to take themselves quite seriously.

What delimits a distinct generation is not merely an artificial span of years but also the experience of a socializing event. Members of the generation may respond to it differently, but it defines their frame of reference. For the Sons of the Founders the crisis of 1798 was the closest thing to a socializing event. The year 1798 has been singled out as "the high tide of revolutionary democracy."[7] It was the year of the XYZ Affair, the Alien and Sedition Acts, the Bavarian Illuminati Conspiracy, and the Quasi-War with France.

The socialization process was not entirely spontaneous. Federalist politicians took advantage of the panic to organize Associations of Young Men to serve as a kind of defense league. The Young Men made quite a mark on the nation. On May 7, 1798, twelve hundred Young Men marched through Philadelphia to the President's house to offer their lives for the country. That night they mobbed the residence of Benjamin Franklin Bache, the Republican newspaper editor.[8] On May 9, set aside by President Adams for a national fast, Federalist youths wearing the Black Cockade fought in the streets with Republicans wearing the Red. The light horse soldiers were called out, a guard was posted in front of the President's home, and the streets were patrolled all night. Adams had been warned that a massacre was planned by Frenchmen and Republicans for the day of the fast, and he was so alarmed by the turmoil that he ordered a chest of arms from the war office and distributed it among his servants to await the attack.[9]

Not all of the Young Men were actually young in years, however young in heart. Brockholst Livingston, a Republican, pointed out in the newspaper that the chairman of the New York Association of Young Men was a "stripling of forty-eight years" and that another member, a James Jones, was a spry lad of nearly sixty. Upon reading the article, Jones flew into a rage and caned Livingston who thereupon challenged him to a duel. They fought in the Hoboken fields where Jones became the first and certainly the oldest martyr to the movement of Young Men.[10] In theory, the Young Men were supposed to be between the ages of eighteen and thirty. If some were older, others were possibly younger.

Republicans were certainly convinced that the youth of the nation seemed Federalist. Abraham Bishop wrote, "well did Mr. Adams calculate in the awful days of 1798, on our young men. His measures required the aid of men, who had never heard of our Revolution."[11] Mercy Otis Warren, one of Adams's critics, recognized the "powerful effect" he had on "the rising generation, the young men," but blamed it on their inexperience.[12] Jefferson himself commented on the young men's Federalism but hoped that "it has been from delusions which they will soon dissipate."[13] Benjamin Austin, the Massachusetts Republican, dedicated two revealing essays "To the Young Men," beginning in the 45th number of his newspaper column, explaining to them that this was the symbol of Wilkes and Liberty, which they were too young to know. He bemoaned the fact that "by the most unaccountable fatality, those, who assumed the name of *federalists,* acquired an influence over the minds of the *young* American citizens." He attributed this influence to the intolerance of the Federalists but also, in an essay "Billy Dapper and Charles Steady," Federalist and Republican respectively, to the social and economic power Federalists could exert on the young.[14] It is somewhat ironic that the elitist Federalists inaugurated this youthful political involvement. The Young Men are a good example of what Joseph Kett found in other areas: that "from the 1790's onward . . . teenagers became truly conspicuous for the first time in American history."[15]

College students participated in the crisis by sending patriotic addresses to the President, which, with the President's replies, were printed in papers across the country. Seven student bodies sent letters of support—Harvard, Dartmouth, Williams, Dickinson, Princeton, North Carolina and Brown—and two others—Yale and Union—may have done so.[16] Students at the College of William and Mary, on the other hand, sent a protest critical of the President to the Virginia congressional delegation. In a few cases these addresses were initiated by professors or politicians but more often the lead was taken by the students themselves. This petitioning of the government was unprecedented for students. Nothing like it had occurred at the Great Awakening, the Revolution, or the ratification of the Constitution.

What stands out in these addresses is their strong sense of generational consciousness as revealed particularly in their repeated references to the Founding Fathers. Students at Dickinson praised "the virtue and patriotism of our fathers" and vowed to prove that "we inherit their noble example." Harvard undergraduates proclaimed, "We wish to convince mankind that we inherit the intrepid spirit of our ancestors . . . We were not the sons of those who sealed our liberties with their blood, if we would not defend with these lives that soil, which now affords a peaceful grave to the moldering bones of our forefathers." Princeton scholars longed "to manifest to the world . . . that the youth of Nassau Hall will

glory in defending the independence of their Fathers."[17] Behind
the rhetoric lay an important psychological truth. As a postrevolutionary generation, overshadowed by the Founders, America's
young needed a cause which would prove their manhood and establish their identity. With heroes for fathers, the sons were un-
likely to repudiate their elders directly. Rather, they would try to
outdo them. Youth movements are by no means exclusively leftist
or revolutionary but frequently ultranationalist in character.[18]
The Sons of the Founders were a generation of this type.

President Adams's replies were attacked by Jefferson for their
conservativism, and have been blamed for creating the climate
leading up to the Sedition Act, but they have never been analyzed
for their effect upon the young.[19] Adams played upon the idea
that young men need a cause. He told the Dartmouth students,
"those of you who feel an inclination to a life of danger and glory
may find employment for all your activity and enterprise of your
genius." To Harvard students he declared, "if your cause should require defense in arms, your country will have armies and navies in
which you may secure your own honor, and advance the power,
prosperity, and glory of your contemporaries and posterity."
Would there really be war? To the Princeton students he confided:
"to me there appears no means of averting the storm; and, in my
opinion, we must all be ready to dedicate ourselves to fatigues and
dangers."[20] No wonder the young were excited — danger and glory,
honor and a cause — their moment in history had come. In at least
three colleges, students began to drill.[21]

It is remarkable how seriously Federalists and academics took
these addresses. At Williams the occasion was used to bolster the
sagging reputation of the college. In early 1798 a prominent Federalist trustee, Henry Van Schaack, had charged that the institution was "poisoned with antifederal trash." President Ebenezer
Fitch was said to be encouraging the student address, according to
another observer, to "do away the suspicions which have persisted
with regard to his political character." And the students were

equally anxious to prove their orthodoxy, "as from the sentiments of a few individuals, their federalism had been unjustly suspected." The address had the desired effect. Van Schaack afterwards rejoiced, "the young Gentlemen have signed a spirited address to the President. You see, my friend, this country will come out right at last."[22]

The Young Men of Richmond, Virginia, and the students of the College of William and Mary, were the exceptions that proved the rule that young men on both sides were caught up in the crisis. The Young Men accused President Adams of manipulating adolescents through the war scare. They feared that this would establish "a precedent for managing by executive influence the affections of the rising generations, and conducting them to whatever may be the objects of the administration."[23] The students of William and Mary, in their pacifist petition to the Virginia congressmen, foresaw a host of evils that would befall the country as a result of war with France: aggrandizement of the executive, corruption, militarism, decline of world republicanism, and ultimately the return of monarchy.[24] Significantly, neither group was tearing down but rather upholding the values of their fathers, for in Virginia opposition to the Federalists was widespread. In fact, the students had been told that their address had gained "the Approbation of the enlightened Jefferson," which added to their self-esteem.[25]

Political involvement bred minor student disorders. When Harvard students attending a 1798 town meeting were disappointed in the outcome of an election they "expressed their disapprobation by a general *hiss!* The infatuated dupes of Jacobinic fraud [that is, the Republicans] then bawled aloud to drive all students from the house." After similar disorders a year later students were barred from town meetings altogether. They responded "by breaking the windows of the last representative. He confesses this last measure not federal."[26] When war did not come, many of Harvard's young Federalists grew impatient and identified with the extreme wing of the Federalists, the Junto, which was still trying to provoke a war with France. When the 1800 meeting of Phi Beta Kappa was disrupted by "the impertinence and froth" of the "political boys," one member complained: "sorry I am to see men so bare-faced in their support of a set of aristocrats, calumniators of our Adams as well as of all moderate men."[27] Adams discovered student disaffection for himself when he visited the 1800 commencement in the company of Governor Caleb Strong of Massachusetts and Governor Jonathan Trumbull of Connecticut. The English Orator's address was so highly critical of the President's conciliatory policies that the dignitaries walked out on his performance.[28]

Adams fared as badly on the other extreme. On the 4th of July, 1798, William and Mary students paraded the streets and burned an effigy of the President in which he was shown receiving a "Royal Address" and searching frantically through a batch of ready-made responses for an appropriate reply. The faculty was troubled by the demonstration, but the students took it in stride. "When the students concern [themselves] with the practices of government," wrote law student Joseph C. Cabell, "they sometimes indulge in temporary ebullitions of Passion . . . It would be absurd to suppose that their Passions would not rise & fall like *other men*."[29]

But the crisis seemed to call for more than words and demonstrations. It was supposed to be the occasion for this generation to find itself. For some of the young it provided careers. Of the fifty naval officers famous enough to be in the *Dictionary of American Biography* born between 1775 and 1790 — the Sons of the Founders generation — 70 percent entered the navy in the years 1798-1800. Among them were such ultranationalists as Oliver Hazard Perry ("we have met the enemy and they are ours") and Stephen Decatur ("our country, right or wrong"). Decatur was literally a Son of the Founders. He grew up in Philadelphia, the national capital, where his friends were the sons of Federalist officials. He attended the University of Pennsylvania briefly but was too restless to remain. As a teenager he had fistfights with Francophiles over the issue of wearing cockades. In 1798 he found himself. He first sailed in the navy under his father, who had earlier served in the Revolutionary War.[30]

College students apparently envied their activist peers. Charles J. Ingersoll, son of a Federalist politician, friend of Hamilton's son and Washington's ward, left the best account of how the Quasi-War excited the young. "Public sentiment," he recalled, "*especially among the youthful,* was mostly belligerent throughout the Northern and Western United States."

> Resuming my place at Princeton College, I have still the liveliest recollection of *the fiery, fighting patriotism predominant with young America panting for war* . . . Mortified that I was too young, and small of my age, to mount a sword or epaulet, I ardently desiderated those fascinating emblems of display and exploit, or a midshipman's warrant for that navy whose victories over the French were the delight of our vaunts. Some of my acquaintances, not much older, among them George Izard and Alexander McComb, became then embryo generals of our future war with England in 1812 . . . At no time during our war with England did the war fever blaze so bright as that against France.[31]

It may be hard to recapture this enthusiasm for the military. It must be remembered that an officer was a gentleman, that Napoleon was reshaping the world with an army, and that the Founders had forged the nation in a war. Not all young patriots were satisfied, however. Unlike the navy, the new army saw no action and by 1800 was being disbanded. Abigail Adams Smith, whose husband trained the new recruits, noted the discouragement of the young men: "Our encampment exhibits a scene of melancholy countenances; some say, alas, my occupation is gone . . . several young men, who had calculated upon making it their profession, are greatly mortified and disappointed, who for want of property or friends, or perhaps other talents, will now be destitute of any means of support."[32] For some, then, the crisis ended in frustration.

The Quasi-War made students impatient. Ingersoll, for instance, grew increasingly unhappy at Princeton and dropped out after minor disciplinary trouble in 1799. Although it left no hard evidence behind, the Dickinson strike suggests this unrest. The time when it occurred—only months after the students wrote in their address "we shall cheerfully leave the pleasing walks of science, when the voice of our country calls"—and the goal of the strike—being allowed to graduate after a single year—show the pressure students felt to get out into the world.

The relationship between the Sons of the Founders' ultranationalism, political activism, and student discontent can be seen in individual cases. Consider the experiences of three Harvard undergraduates of this period: William Ellergy Channing, Unitarian minister and reformer, William Austin, prominent Massachusetts jurist and author, and Washington Allston, the foremost painter of his day.

Channing was named for the most famous of Rhode Island's Sons of Liberty, William Ellery, his grandfather, to whom he was quite close, particularly after the early death of his father. While a youth Channing's home was visited by Washington and Jay, and he grew up a faithful Federalist. In 1798 it was Channing, a senior, who instigated and composed Harvard's patriotic address. Subsequently assigned to give the closing speech at the commencement, he chose for his topic "The Present Age" as a vehicle for denouncing the French Revolution and its baleful effects on mankind. Because of Republican attacks on the highly partisan speeches of the year before, however, the faculty decreed that this year's oration leave out politics. The Harvard seniors protested against this and declared that "the present crisis in America requires a political discussion of the interests of our country, free and uncontrolled."[33] The faculty insisted on censoring controversial passages in Channing's speech, but for almost a month he refused to give it at all rather than amend it. During his one-man protest a friend sent him a significant letter of support:

The government of college have completed the climax of their despotism. They have obtained an *arrêt,* which from its features I could swear is the offspring of the French Directory. Although they pretend to be firm friends to American liberty and independence, their embargo on politics . . . is strong proof to me that they are Jacobins, or at best pretended patriots, who have not the courage to defend the rights of their country.[34]

Harvard's faculty was hardly Jacobin. But to see in its cautious ban on politics "pretended patriotism" testifies to the political extremism of the students. Near the end of his oration Channing cried, "but that I am forbid, I could a tale unfold, which would harrow up your souls," and he left the stage amid his classmates' wild cheers.

William Austin, Channing's classmate, did not bear a hero's name, though he had the distinction of being born while his family was fleeing a British attack. Scion of an old and well-to-do Charlestown family, Austin carried literary identification with the Founders to an extreme. In an 1801 oration on the anniversary of Bunker Hill he proclaimed: "Your posterity, if occasion should demand, would on these very heights revive the days of '75, emulate your deeds, bleed as you bled, rear a second monument by the side of the present to the same principle, and, *in a word, renovate your own selves.* "[35] Similar sentiments appeared in his *Letters From London* (1804), written while studying law at Lincoln's Inn and hobnobbing about Lonon with six of his former Harvard classmates. "I know not who can travel with more advantage to himself, or to his country," he wrote, "than a citizen of the United States, *born since the Revolution,* for the moment he arrives, the love of his country becomes his predominant passion."[36]

Austin proved his patriotism in the crisis of 1798 by publishing a volume containing the patriotic addresses sent by towns, militia companies, and students, with the President's replies. In the stirring preface he warned France that the United States loved peace

so ardently "we will *fight* for it." After graduation he lived up to
his word by taking a commission as chaplain-teacher aboard the
Constitution, one of the warships hastily completed for the war.[37]

It seems Austin was an academic rebel at Harvard. His classmate Sidney Willard wrote that "at no time did Mr. Austin, while
at college, show any desire to excel in the prescribed studies,"
though "he employed much of his time usefully, and was among
the most distinguished belles-lettrists . . . of his class."[38] Austin
was invited to join Phi Beta Kappa but declined because he disapproved of secret societies (which at this time were associated with
Free Masonry and Illuminism). It was not simply sour grapes,
therefore, which prompted him to write *Strictures on Harvard
University, By a Senior.* This thirty-five page indictment was the
fullest exposition of student grievance written in the first two centuries of higher education in America.

Strictures on Harvard attacked the compulsory curriculum, the
system of awarding honors, the disciplinary regulations, and the
faculty's refusal to support extracurricular projects like a student
periodical. Austin attributed faculty conservatism to the fact that
most of the professors were clergymen. It was well known, he
wrote, that "the clergy, in all nations and ages, have ever been
more illiberal, than their contemporaries." His anticlericalism was
inherited from his family, which though nominally members of
Charlestown's First Church had taken to worshipping at the Bap-
tist Meeting House to escape the Reverend Jedidiah Morse's cease-
less controversies. He was far from irreligious, however. He even
wrote a book of amateur theology, *The Human Character of Jesus
Christ* (1807), which despite a deceptive title, was actually an endeavor "to explore a new but indirect argument in favor of the
divinity of Jesus Christ."[39]

The main complaint in *Strictures on Harvard* concerned the repressive spirit of the college:

Where the gesture, countenance, gait, word and action, are
narrowly watched, with a design to censure, rather than reform

. . . Where a manly independence is construed into insolence and contempt of authority; and a meek spirit of passive obedience and nonresistance is the only road to college honor . . . What are the State to expect? Courtiers or Republicans? Creatures or Men?

Austin's criterion of republican education appeared to be that the university treat its students like men.[40]

Washington Allston, an aristocratic South Carolinian two classes behind Channing and Austin, seemed determined to live out the significance of his given name. He was poet, secretary, and eventually president of the Hasty Pudding Club, founded in 1795 and dedicated to "friendship and patriotism," in contrast to Porcellain, founded in 1790, whose members honored Bacchus. George Washington, President at the time, was called "the Father of Hasty Pudding," and his birthday was the club's annual event. The name Hasty Pudding came from the most famous song of the Revolution, "Yankee Doodle." The first stanza — "Father and I went down to camp, / Along with Captain Gooding, / And there we see the men and boys / As thick as hasty pudding" — evokes generational unity in times of military crisis. According to Allston's biograhper, he was deeply affected by Washington's death in 1799 and spoke at Harvard's commemorative services. While a student, Allston's favorite haunt was a spot on the Charles River where General Washington had placed a cannon, later known as Fort Washington, where thirty years later he returned, built a house, and spent the remainder of his life. Another favorite walk was the naval yard where as a freshman he watched the construction of the *Constitution,* upon which Austin would shortly sail.[41]

Like Austin, Allston was sometimes guilty of "greatly neglecting his college duties." The cause was not dissipation; his sketches "The Buck's Progress" made fun of the blades and swells. Rather, the trouble was that his passions — poetry and painting simply fell outside the daily college fare. Although the faculty tried to encourage his talents, to study art he had to sail for Italy. At gradua-

THE BUCK'S PROGRESS

Painted by Washington Allston, November 10, 1796
Courtesy H. W. L. Dana Collection
Longfellow House, Cambridge, Massachusetts.

I. The Introduction of a Country Lad
to a Club of Town Bucks

II. A Beau in His Dressing Room

III. A Midnight Fray with Watchmen

tion he wrote his mother of his patriotic goal—"I am determined, if resolution and perseverance will effect it, to be the first painter, at least, from America."[42]

As an artist Allston was somewhat apolitical, though what allegiance he had was Federalist, as his veneration for Washington would suggest. He sometimes painted political themes. In 1798 he sketched an ugly "Bonaparte in Egypt," and a nonextant drawing depicted "The French National Assembly as a Rasher of Frogs." But he was not a slave to the Federalist line. At the height of the war scare, when Reverend Jedidiah Morse was lecturing the country on the danger of Illuminati infiltration, he played an iconoclastic prank. As recalled by his friend,

> While the excitement was at the highest the students of Harvard were surprised at seeing upon the boards for advertisement in the chapel entry a summons for the meeting of a secret society, and while they were seeking to elucidate the mystery, another paper appeared in the same place solemnly warning them against indiscreet curiosity, and denounced the most dreadful penalties against anyone who should seek to lift the veil. This was followed by a second summons in irregular verse, in which all the ingredients of a hell broth were made to boil and bubble. All these papers were ornamented with altars, daggers, swords, chalices, death-heads and cross-bones, and other paraphernalia of German romance were stamped, not drawn, upon the papers, which besides bore huge seals. All this was in ridicule of the stuff of the day, yet Allston always belonged to the Federal party.[43]

For the faculty Illuminism was not a laughing matter, as we shall see, but for students Federalism often coincided with freethinking. Austin went out of his way to visit William Godwin while in England. Channing was deeply influenced by Godwin and other radical writers while a tutor in Virginia. A leader of student resistance at Princeton, John James Marshall, son of Kentucky's Federalist senator Humphrey Marshall, and Princeton valedictorian in 1806, was described by another young man as "a Deist and a violent Federalist."[44] Such Young Federalist freethinking was a source of serious misunderstanding.

Channing, Austin, and Allston graduated at the beginning of the student protest and never actually participated in a major revolt. But later rebels shared their generational self-consciousness. Joseph C. Breckenridge, to give just one more case, figured in the Princeton rebellion of 1807. The Breckenridges were an old, wealthy Virginia family who moved to Kentucky in 1790. John Breckenridge, Joseph's father, Republican congressman and attorney general under Jefferson, died young on December 14, 1806. Upon hearing this Joseph, the eldest son, sought to return home and act as the head of the family. "This place which has been the scene of my long suffering and suspense [on account of his father's health] has become odious to me," he wrote his brother-in-law. "If I remain here I never can apply myself: I never can be content."[45] His family forced him to stay in school but his behavior grew highly erratic. First, with several friends he broke away from the Whigs and founded the Euterpean Society.[46] Then, a few months later, he was deeply involved in the campus rebellion. When he wrote home of the uprising, he took the Revolution for his model. "The faculty affirm that we had no right to form ourselves into a combination," he said. "It is astonishing to me that any set of men should be so weak as to make such an observation in a country the fundamental principle of whose government is liberty of action."[47] In a curious way, his rebelliousness purged his grief and set him on his feet again. On May 17 he requested from the faculty an honorable dismissal. In late 1808 he returned, stayed to graduate, and even married President Smith's daughter. His father's death, his rebellion against faculty father-figures, and his symbolic identification with the Founding Fathers suggest the psychological implications present in student revolt.

As a socializing event the crisis of 1798 affected college students in several ways. First, it oriented the young men toward the Federalists. The patriotic addresses indicated this, and literary evidence confirmed it. A Yale student confessed in 1802: "we have but one solitary instance of a true Jeffersonian in our class."[48] At Dartmouth as late as 1811 Amos Kendall estimated that three-fourths of his classmates were Federalists.[49] "Our students are almost all Federal," exclaimed President Fitch of Williams during the rebellion of 1802, "but for once the mad spirit of liberty and equality seized them."[50] The significance of student Federalism is that after the election of Jefferson in 1800 the young men were out of power, and their alienation from politics was a factor in their rebelliousness. David Hackett Fischer has shown the importance of young Federalists in the political history of the early nineteenth century. Although most of those he describes were older than the Sons of the Founders, the dilemma they faced was the same: whether to follow the Federalists into oblivion or to bolt the party of Washington. Neither alternative was attractive, and student unrest reflected this frustration.

James Buchanan (Dickinson 1809), William Cullen Bryant (Williams 1811), James Fenimore Cooper, Thaddeus Stevens (Dartmouth 1814), James A. Bayard (Princeton 1814), and Julian C. Verplanck (Columbia 1801) were all rebellious young Federalists. Cooper, whose early teacher "was particularly severe on all the immoralities of the French Revolution . . . detested a democrat as he did the devil . . . [and] cracked jokes daily about Mr. Jefferson and Black Sal," was expelled from Yale in 1806.[51] Bryant — famous for his poem "The Embargo" (1808), with its advice to Jefferson: "Go, scan, Philosophist, thy Sally's charms, / And sink supinely in her sable arms, / But quit to abler hands the helm of state" — left Williams after a year, denouncing it as a place "where lawless Power his nest has laid, / And stern Suspicion treads her maze."[52] Verplanck, as an alumnus, helped incite the Columbia riot of 1811.[53]

Does this mean that Jeffersonian students were orderly? In most colleges, the young Democrats were a self-conscious minority who had to watch their behavior. During disorders in 1800, Evert

Bancker, one of the Democrats, formed a committee to assist President Edwards in quelling the disturbance.[54] In 1809, Amos Kendall, another serious young Democrat, gave testimony that caused two rioters to be expelled.[55] James K. Polk, a studious, sickly young boy, was regarded as one of the most obedient students at the University of North Carolina.[56] Outside the South, Democratic students were probably less aristocratic than the Federalists. But many student rebels were Democrats, as William and Mary, the most Jeffersonian college in the country, could testify. A simple dichotomy between rebellious young Federalists and orderly young Democrats will not entirely do. Though party affiliation was important, there was something bothering youth per se.

A second result of the crisis of 1798 was to bring the Sons of the Founders prematurely close to power and then after 1800 to thrust them back again. As many Federalist leaders began to withdraw from politics they discouraged the young from political involvement. Benjamin Austin observed that with Jeffersonians in office Federalists endeavored "to inculcate an *indifference* in the minds of the young men, on the present subject of politics . . . [by making it] *disreputable* for a young man to concern himself with the affairs of government."[57] In the same year his father became president of Columbia, Clement C. Moore expressed regret "that more of the well-disposed among his young countrymen do not devote their leisure hours to the attainment of useful learning, rather than to frivolous amusements or political wrangling."[58] In 1803 President Dwight told his Yale graduates to "never look either for subsistence, or for character, to popular suffrage, or governmental appointment, to public salaries, or official perquisites."[59] In 1808 Samuel Stanhope Smith discouraged a former student from enlisting in the military by saying, "with the spirit which animates our government, it must be extremely unpleasant to gentlemen of talents & enterprise."[60] The efforts to shut off youthful political involvement may well have added to student unrest, and minor political disturbances continued.[61]

Finally, the crisis of 1798 intensified the Sons of the Founders' nationalism. While for the next decade and a half England and France were alternately allowed to violate our rights, impress our seamen, and fire on our ships with virtual impunity, American weakness, frustrating as it was to all Americans, must have been particularly galling to the young. American honor remained unvindicated till the War of 1812. The strongest advocates for war — the War Hawks — bore a striking resemblance to the Young Men of 1798, though theirs was a Republican war, fought against Great Britain.[62] Before this the young found few outlets for their patriotism. The Miranda expedition of 1806 — an attempt to liberate South America from Spain — was an adventure which captured the imagination of the young, but it was a small-scale, secret operation which ended in disaster.[63] For the most part young men who wanted to prove themselves had to do so symbolically. Joseph Tufts's pamphlet, *Don Quixots at College,* captured this misdirected idealism — the students were tilting at windmills.

Resistance allowed students to assert their manhood and maturity. The rights of youth was an issue in every confrontation — whether students should have a voice in disciplinary procedures, in awarding honors, in judging the competence of the faculty. As a minor theme, students fought for the right to address each other as "Mr." and "Sir." Student literature appealed to this yearning for manhood. The Princeton broadside of 1807 began with the bold salutation, "Sir," and exhorted wavering resisters to "evince to the world that you are capable of acting for yourself."[64] The Harvard rebels at the same time declared: "there is a point of submission beyond which no *man* can pass without ceasing to be a *man*."[65] Seen in this light, student revolt was important as a ritual, a kind of *rite de passage.* It was the manifold crises of these years that made growing up so imperative.

Campus rebellions also offered students a form of surrogate political activity, with even ostensibly nonpolitical disorders being unmistakably political in function. Students held mass meetings,

elected chairmen and committees, debated, amended, petitioned
— all as a form of practical political participation. Students wrote
of their uprisings in these terms. Describing the Great Secession at
Chapel Hill a student said: "the legislature of North Carolina cannot produce men, of such accurate judgment, reasoning and flu-
ent language, as was displayed in the debates of our honorable
body."[66] Of disorders at Washington Academy another wrote:
"No situation could be better adapted to give me an idea of the
world than in a seminary of learning. Here I see a government —
the people and the rulers. I see party spirit — factions and sometimes little civil wars. Now a truce and sometimes hostilities com-
mence again."[67]

The Sons of the Founders were reliving the Revolution. An undergraduate wrote of Brown's 1800 riot: "Nothing but riot and
confusion! No regard paid to superiors. Indeed, Sir, the Spirit of
'75 was displayed in its brightest colors."[68] But though at least one
founder saw the relationship, he took a dimmer view. In 1809 Dr.
Ramsay made the inevitable, damning comparison between the
generations: "The elder citizens have successfully contended for
the rights of men. Their sons, too little accustomed to the discipline of a strict education, seem equally zealous for the rights of
boys."[69]

CHAPTER FOUR

The Defenders
of the Faith

"REVOLUTIONS MAY BE unhappy events when we consider merely the ease and pleasures of mankind," Samuel Stanhope Smith granted Charles Nisbet, still in Scotland, "but when we consider that human society can advance only to a certain point before it becomes corrupted, and begins to decline, and that letters always decline with virtue, revolutions are perhaps the necessary scaffolding by which science and human nature must gradually arrive at their summit."[1] Such radical sentiments came easily to American academics in the years immediately following the War for Independence. By 1798, however, the American professoriate had made an aboutface on the idea of revolution. As the future president of Harvard told the Phi Beta Kappa Society,

> Since revolution has come to mean subversion, it means too much to be applied to that alteration of our political relations made by independence. We contended for preservation, not acquisition, to keep the rights we had, rather than to gain those we never had; and the separation was resorted to chiefly as a necessary means of maintaining the ancient ground.[2]

THE DEFENDERS OF THE FAITH   59

This contrast in point of view was the result of an intellectual counterrevolution which was a crucial element in the reaction of American academics to turn-of-the-century student revolt.

College professors were not only teachers but clergymen as well. Even tutors were usually postgraduate students of divinity. As guardians of the faith, academics were increasingly worried about the state of religion in America as the eighteenth century drew to a close. In the colonial era, the clergy had been the most learned and respected segment of society. Almost every colony had an established church supported by law. The clergy had been warm advocates of American independence, but the Revolution had dealt the churches a hard blow. Benjamin Trumbull accounted for the postrevolutionary religious declension in his *A Complete History of Connecticut* (1818):

> A state of war is peculiarly unfriendly to religion. It dissipates the mind, diminishes the degree of instruction, removes great numbers almost wholly from it, connects them with the most dangerous company, and presents them with the worst examples. It hardens and emboldens men in sin; is productive of profaneness, intemperance, disregard to propriety, violence, and licentious living.[3]

In the gradual secularization of society after the Revolution, state church establishments were attacked and slowly abolished.

Academics were not merely clergymen, moreover, but almost to a man Congregationalist, Presbyterian, or Episcopalian—those denominations which valued a learned clergy. After the Revolution, not only did religion decline, but the religious composition of the nation began to change, again to the detriment of the clerical-professoriate. The rising sects in the new republic were the Methodists and Baptists, whose enthusiastic lay preachers were looked upon by one college head as "the most illiterate vagrants, who un derstood neither what they say nor whereof they affirm."[4] The growth of these sects debased the social position of the learned clergy and threatened their colleges as well. In part because of their humbler origins and in part as a defense mechanism, Methodists and Baptists spread a popular anti-intellectualism. "Larnin isn't religion, and eddication don't give a man the power of the Spirit," one Methodist was supposed to have said. "St. Peter was a fisherman — do you think he ever went to Yale College?"[5] In time both Methodists and Baptists built their own colleges and educated their ministry, but the first Methodist endeavor, Cokesbury College founded in 1787 and closed in 1795, had been a conspicuous failure. As one Episcopalian scoffed, it was ridiculous to try to make a college out of "tinkers and taylors, weavers, shoemakers and country mechanics of all kinds — or, in other words, of men illiterate and wholly unacquainted with colleges and their contents."[6] From the end of the Revolution to about 1795, the learned clergy tended to blame Methodists and Baptists for the religious decline in the country. In opposition to their rivals, they stressed their own sophistication and intellectuality. But the cultural leveling which eroded their social position was an amorphous problem beyond their power to control. The higher they held their educated noses, the less they appealed to the people.

It was not Methodism that caused the professoriate's intellectual counterrevolution but a threat from the other religious extreme — the rise of militant deism in the 1790s. It was this which led the learned clergy to turn against the French Revolution and the Enlightenment.[7] Deism was over a century old in 1798. It was an Enlightenment religion, based on Reason rather than Revelation. In general it held to nothing but a single, all-powerful but nonintervening deity and an afterlife of rewards and punishments. Until the 1790s, deism in America had been a fashionable, upper-class philosophy rather than a popular movement. In the 1790s, however, the character of deism was altered in a way which made it utterly unacceptable to the American clergy, liberal and orthodox alike. First, Elihu Palmer traveled about the country spreading deist clubs and newspapers. Second, Thomas Paine's inflammatory *The Age of Reason* (1794-1795) reached the country and went through seventeen American editions by 1796. With it came the first importation of older deist works, such as Volney's *Common Sense; or Natural Ideas Opposed to Supernatural* and Voltaire's anticlerical *Philosophical Dictionary.* Both Palmer's clubs and Paine's popularization were purportedly aimed at the young and the lower classes, both of which were regarded as potentially dangerous elements of society because they lacked the experience of age or the restraint of education.

The rise of militant deism transformed the professors' general uneasiness into an organized counteroffensive aimed at supposedly subversive ideas. There was an almost irresistible tendency to blame deism for the breakdown of deference. As Reverend Samuel E. McCorkle, former professor at the University of North Carolina, charged: "it is deism — deism — deism — detestable deism . . . that has disadjusted and disorganized society."[8] The professoriate's reaction was part of a worldwide movement. The French Revolution had made intellectuals more conscious of the uses of social philosophy for good or ill. This new awareness may be traced in etymological change. According to the Oxford English Dictionary, "philosophy" as the love of knowledge is as old as the English language, but "philosophist" — what young Bryant called Jefferson in his poem — in the deprecatory sense of one who speculates erroneously and dangerously, was first used in the years 1798 and 1799. Likewise, the word "ideology" in a disparaging sense was first used in the early1800s.

American academics were inevitably influenced by this profound intellectual shift, but they were also responding to a more specific intellectual event. In 1798, in the midst of the panic over the Quasi-War with France, Reverend Jedidiah Morse propounded his theory of the Bavarian Illuminati conspiracy to which nearly all American academics subscribed. Their gullibility in this episode makes this one of the darkest days in the annals of the American academe. Their belief in Illuminism was central to the colleges' response to turn-of-the-century student revolt.

American susceptibility to conspiracy theories has been an important theme in American history.[9] At least since the Revolution, Americans have been prone to see secret cabals and plots moving events. The belief in an imperial conspiracy against colonial liberty at the time of the Revolution, in which first the king's ministers, the Parliament, and finally the king himself appeared implicated, gave hidden significance to British acts and urgency to colonial resistance. Colonists saw the course of history as a struggle between liberty and power in which power constantly strove for aggrandizement. Hence eighteenth-century libertarians preached the necessity of checks to power such as a constitution, an independent judiciary, and a vigilant free press. Hence, also, the Founding Fathers created a government of different branches which might check and balance one another so that no single faction could usurp the power of the whole. This was based on an Enlightenment view of human nature. The seeds of despotism and faction were "sown in the nature of man," as Madison explained in his famous Tenth Federalist. The lust for power, inherent in all men, might be restrained but never eradicated.

The theory of a Bavarian Illuminati conspiracy was different. Not only was it more unfounded, more irrational, than its colonial predecessor, but also the very idea of conspiracy had radically changed. Whereas there had been a bold realism about the Founding Fathers' distrust of human nature, there was a frightened defensiveness about the foes of Illuminism. In place of a threat coming from those in power, who despite their abuses had an aura of legitimacy, in Illuminism the danger was posed by left-wing subversives with no respect for civilization or morality. While the Founding Fathers had seen the seeds of tyranny in all men, the national guardians of 1798 limited their suspicions to clearly discernible enemies—foreigners, political dissenters, and "philosophers." Finally, rather than an eternal part of human nature, conspiracy as defined in 1798 was an exotic plant which if vigorously suppressed might be stamped out altogether. These differences made the Illuminati scare more frightening and ultimately more divisive than its predecessors. As one scholar has put it, "the Illuminati controversy, which raged through the states from 1797 and 1798 for nearly a decade before it subsided . . . divided intellectual America into two hostile camps, and was, in a manner of speaking, the witch hunt of the Enlightenment."[10]

At times of national crisis, it was customary for the clergy to explain to the people how their public sins had called down the wrath of the Lord. Academics stepped down from their ivory towers repeatedly from 1798 to 1800 to fan the nation's passions. "So sudden, so unexpected, so alarming a state of things," be wailed President Dwight, "has not existed since the deluge."[11] "Never before has our government been assaulted with greater violence, by foreign foes and domestic traitors," cried President Maxcy.[12] "Every civil and religious institution is threatened with ruin," warned President Fitch, "a spirit of VANDALISM, hostile to rational liberty, has already devastated the fairest parts of Europe, and menaces the civilized world with universal carnage."[13] It was on the first of these public occasions, the day set aside by President Adams for a national fast, that Jedidiah Morse, Charlestown's well-known Congregational minister and a member of the Harvard overseers, startled his congregation by announcing the discovery of a secret organization at work in Europe and the United States to overthrow the governments and religions of the world.[14]

Jedidiah Morse's reputation lent credibility to his charges. As author of *The American Geography* (1789), which passed through seven American editions, and of the article on America in the first American edition of the *Encyclopedia Britannica* (1790), he was regarded by many as the most authoritative source of information on the country. Having traveled widely and corresponded with men in all parts of the nation, he presumably knew what was going on in the remotest corners of the land. Yet his source for this new revelation was not his own investigations but the work of a Scottish clergyman, John Robison, *Proofs of a Conspiracy Against All the Religions and Governments of Europe, carried on in the Secret Meetings of the Free Masons, Illuminati, and Reading Societies* (1797), which according to Morse first appeared in America in April of 1798, an opportune moment. Riding the tide of hysteria caused by the Quasi-War, within three weeks the work had been reprinted in Philadelphia and New York. Robison, a member of the intellectual circle of the University of Edinburgh and general secretary of the Royal Society of Edinburgh, appeared to have impressive credentials. What really clinched acceptance of his exposure, for those who were ever to believe it, was the reception of Abbe Barruel's *Memoirs pour l'histoire du Jacobinism* (1797), which reached America in translation in 1799. Working independently, the two had arrived at the same frightening conclusions.

Robison and Barruel reasoned that the cause of the French Revolution and the subsequent international upheaval, which they deplored, was the radical speculations of the philosophes. They focused on the Free Mason lodges of France and Germany where thinkers met to exchange ideas. Some of these lodges, they charged, "had become schools of irreligion and licentiousness."[15] They singled out an offshoot of Masonry, the Bavarian Illuminati, and claimed that this group was ready to take over the world by using Free Mason lodges to disseminate subversive literature and form revolutionary cadres. The Illuminati really had existed, founded at the University of Ingolstadt in 1775 by Professor Adam Weishaupt, but it was only one secret debating society among many created to escape government censorship and police controls. At the peak of its strength in 1784 it had perhaps two or three thousand members in different locations, organized into a strict hierarchical structure, dedicated to saving the world by spreading enlightenment. Although it did hope to gain power by infiltrating governments and universities, it was rather vague about what it would do with the power it gained. Its real end, Robison assured his readers, was to reduce "mankind to the state of one indistinguishable chaotic mass."[16] The Illuminati had been suppressed by the Elector of Bavaria in 1786 and declared extinct, but Robison believed that "it had by this time taken so deep root that it still subsists without being detected."[17] That it was invisible was only proof of its success at secrecy. It had already reached the United States both writers agreed. At the conclusion of his work Barruel prayed, "God grant that the United States may not learn to their cost, that Republics are equally menaced with Monarchies; and that the immensity of the ocean is but a feeble barrier against the universal conspiracy of the Sect!"[18]

Morse was unable to substantiate the existence of Illuminism in America. His claim that a branch of Virginia Free Masons long since extinct were really Illuminati in disguise was easily refuted. When pressed for further proof, he and his academic allies adduced evidence of all the alarming changes in the nation:

> our unhappy and threatening political divisions; the unceasing abuse of our wise and faithful rulers; the virulent opposition to some of the laws of our country, and the measures of the Supreme Executive; the Pennsylvania insurrection; the circulation of baneful and corrupting books, and the consequent spread of infidelity, impiety and immorality . . . and lastly, the apparently systematic endeavours made to destroy, not only the influence and support, but the official existence of the clergy.[19]

Who could deny all this? Only a secret conspiracy it seemed could account for it.

The emotional appeal of Morse's theory must have blunted the critical faculties of the professors. President Nisbet wrote that "the facts" related by Robison were "clothed with complete historical evidence."[20] Professor David Tappan of Harvard praised Robison's extraordinary means of information and thorough analysis.[21]

President Smith wrote that Morse's evidence on the existence of Illuminism in the United States (easily discredited by less gullible thinkers) "ought to be universally known in America that the people might understand that insidious enemy against whom they should be forever on their guard."[22] Yale instructor Ebenezer Grant Marsh published an abridgment of Barruel's *Histoire du Jacobinism* and was urged by President Dwight to bring out a second edition. His early death lost academic counterreformers a young champion.[23] Harvard Professor Eliphalet Pearson saw evidence of Illuminism in the Massachusetts Republican talk of removing Harvard's tax exemption and subjecting its students and faculty to militia duty. He corresponded with educators throughout New England gathering precedents for a legal brief in defense of the college. The replies he received showed the widespread equation of Republicanism with Illuminism among the academic community. One Dartmouth professor replied:

> Do you indeed think an attempt will be made to subject *your* society to taxation, as we are subjected? Will the enlightened patriots of Massachusetts suffer such a thing? Is this design the result of a secret & malignant combination to destroy religion, civil government, and the useful sciences? If so, I entirely agree with you, that every honest man ought to exert himself to counteract the evil. That such a combination exists in our country, I apprehend, we have reason to believe.[24]

Most colleges were highly receptive to the Illuminati theory; no attack on Morse came out of an American university. Rather, the task of exploding the theory fell to Republican journalists who heaped ridicule on its defenders, dubbing them the "real" conspirators who would subvert the Constitution to weld a union of church and state. There can be no doubt that this episode did much to undermine the credibility of the clergy and the academic community. Impervious to scorn, however, professors continued to make Robison and Barruel a banner for the cause of orthodoxy and Federalism. When President Dwight feared that Jefferson's

election presaged "the dissolution of the United States," he encouraged Morse to go on with his plans to found the ultra-Federalist *New England Palladium,* stating that "the Palladium will be
the Standard of the party" and that its first task would be "to res-
cue Barruel & Robison."[25]

The Illuminati scare gave great impetus to the academic counterrevolution. Bejamin Silliman, a newly appointed Yale professor, published anonymously in 1802 *Letters of Shahcoolen, A
Hindu Philosopher,* a fictitious account of the pernicious influence of Mary Wollstonecraft's English feminism on American
women. In his "Theories of Modern Philosophy in Religion, Government and Morals, Contrasted with the Practical System of New
England," he attacked William Godwin, the English anarchist,
who he said "is read and admired, by all that class of citizens who
arrogate to themselves the title of Republican." "The principles of
Godwin," he prophesied, "if carried into full effect in this country,
would make the United States, what France has been: A NATION OF
RAVISHERS, ASSASSINS AND PREDATORY WARRIORS."[26] The war was
carried on in the first issue of Harvard's *The Literary Miscellany*
(1805), which carried a long "Examination of Modern Ethics,"
first published in London and republished here by Professor Levi
Hedge. "Knowledge without goodness is dangerous," was the text
of many a Pearson sermon. "Witness the Rousseaus, Voltaires,
Mirabeaus, Condorcets, Diderots, and Weishaupts," he told the
graduates of Phillips Academy, "who with an impious host of scientific satellites have well nigh banished peace, order, government, religion, and humanity from one quarter of the globe."[27]
Academics did not reject all of the Enlightenment's advances and
discoveries, of course, but they certainly stifled the spirit of speculation and succeeded in making many Enlightenment writings
anathema in America. As a literary movement, the academic
counterreformation was more destructive than productive; "it was
not a debate among intellectuals, but an all-out ideological warfare — a battle for the minds of the people."[28]

The Illuminati scare also altered the professoriate's attitude to-

ward students. The young were supposedly the prime targets of
the Illuminati: academies and universities the central area of indoctrination.[29] As a future Dartmouth trustee explained, "the
conspirators appear to have been aware of the importance of
youth . . . The directions of the insinuator teach him to seek after
young men from eighteen to thirty, those in particular who have
not completed their education."[30] President Dwight had earlier
warned that adolescents were particularly susceptible to the lure
of freethinking.[31] The professoriate had the important responsibility of saving the young. As one clergyman put it, "in such a time
as this, great attention should be paid to the education of youth,
that their minds may be early imbued with religious principles."[32]
In 1799 the General Assembly of the Presbyterian Church instructed its members to redouble their educational efforts to stem
the "vain and pernicious philosophy" which had "spread its infec-
tion from Europe to America."[33]

The young were already suspect. The Massachusetts Congregationalist Convention's 1798 address lamented "the dissipation, irreligion, and licentiousness prevalent among the youth of the
day."[34] Jedidiah Morse, too, said one could "mark the progress of
these enemies of human happiness among ourselves in the corruption of the principles and morals of our youth."[35] The growing
consciousness of the young around the turn of the century was a
natural outgrowth of the fear of Illuminism. Meanwhile, from
across the Atlantic came horror stories of radicalism among the
students of Europe:

> So late as February, 1798, the magistrates of Jena were com-
> pelled to punish a number of the students of that university,
> who had formed an association, by the name of Amicists, under
> the direction of some Illuminatee. They had been taught to
> consider the oath of their association as superseding all others.
>   The university of Halle, was in a similar situation with that of
> Jena. That public insults were offered by the students, to the
> ministers of religion, while attending to the duties of their of-

fice; that dogs were set at them while preaching, and that inde-
cencies took place in the churches, which would not be suffered
in the streets.

In the great universities of Germany . . . the students have the
appearance of a set of rude and insolent Jacobins. In some universities, where the students amount to about a thousand or
twelve hundred, they are all formed into private societies; and
that, in all the German universities, the chief study is the new
system of philosophy, by which the mind is totally bewildered,
and at length deprived of every solid principle of religion, morality, or sound politics.

Nov[ember] 1793, the pupils of the new republican schools of
the section des Areis [France], appeared at the bar, and one of
them set forth, that all religious worship had been suppressed in
his section, even to the very idea of religion. He added, that *he
and his school fellows detested God.*[36]

To insure that nothing like this happen in America, academics
began to crack down on secret student societies. At Dartmouth a
law was passed in 1799 forbidding any student from becoming a
Free Mason.[37] At Harvard and Yale even the chapters of the Phi
Beta Kappa Society were under scrutiny because their meetings
were closed.[38] Only student literary societies were beyond faculty
jurisdiction, though there was at least one famous case of attempted faculty interference. If students had been quiescent at
this time, no doubt academic apprehensions would quickly have
passed. But at this very moment students were staging the riots
and rebellions of the first American student revolt. It was no wonder, then, that in this climate of suspicion student rebels were
readily perceived by professors as Jacobins.

The accession of Jeffersonian Republicans in 1800 confirmed
the worst fears of the professors. President Smith had been an
Adams elector. President Nisbet greeted the news of the election
by exclaiming, "God give us patience to endure their tyranny."[39]
On the losing side after 1800, the academic community was gradually alienated from national politics. There was a pervasive antic-

ipation of a terrible catastrophe about to befall the colleges. The
Democratic-Republicans were tantamount to Illuminists in the
eyes of professors and regarded as the inveterate foes of higher education. Samuel Phillips, Massachusetts state senator and bene-
factor of Harvard and evangelical enterprises, saw Jefferson as
merely a dupe of the French. "If we fall under the dominion of
France," he worried, "what will become of our Colleges? Rather
than become subservient to their purposes, far better that they be
reduced to ashes!"[40] Within Harvard, according to a professor in
the Medical School:

> When Mr. Jefferson came into office, the late Judge Lowell, a
> leading man of the *Junto,* and an influential governor of this
> University . . . gave us of the college to understand, that the
> church and all our other sacred Institutions were in danger,
> particularly the University, that therefore it behooved us Profes-
> sors to rally with the clergy, and together form the front-rank in
> the Massachusetts *army of federalism,* in opposition to infidel-
> ity, Jacobinism, and *Jeffersonianism.*[41]

While the colleges awaited the attack, professors of doubtful
loyalty were forced out. Yale's solitary Republican, having sub-
mitted to a loyalty oath in 1798, was finally dismissed after the
election and exiled to the University of Georgia, where he lan-
guished "only twelve miles from the Cherokee Indians."[42] Republican professors were clearly exceptions. They were either mathe-
maticians, scientists, or physicians; none but Bishop Madison was
an ordained clergyman.[43]

Of course the attack never came—no guillotines were mounted
on the Yale Green or Harvard Square. Academic fears of the Jeffersonian Republicans were not entirely unfounded, however. The
Democratic-Republicans had subjected the colleges to fierce criticisms following the crisis of 1798. Their main concern was the
Federalist indoctrination supposedly going on in the classrooms.
As Abraham Bishop protested, "Federalists pretend we are

opposed to colleges merely because we are unwilling to have the poison of federalism infused into the minds of the youth."[44]

Beyond the issue of partisanship was the whole question of the place of colleges in American society. There was a strong antielitist strain in the popular Jeffersonian movement. In Connecticut, for instance, John Cosens Ogden was a thorn in the side of Yale not only because he charged that it discriminated against Episcopalian students and that Dwight had perverted it "to promote party, bigotry, and error," but also because he urged the state legislature to democratize Connecticut education by spending its annual grant to Yale on building common schools instead.[45] In North Carolina, the most famous case, the state legislature withdrew the university's endowment after a Republican victory in 1800, an act widely seen as evidence of Republican hostility toward higher learning. As one defender of the university complained, "our enlightened legislature discovered that education was inconsistent with republicanism; that it created an aristocracy of the learned, who would trample upon the rights and liberties of the ignorant."[46] Even after 1800 the university continued to be attacked as a bastion of Federalism, one critic charging that only ultra-Federalist professors and anti-Republican texts were employed and that therefore "the youths who went there Republicans, returned with directly opposite principles."[47] The only fully Republican institution was the College of William and Mary and it was in decline. Republicans longed for a constitutional way to gain control of education and often plotted to infiltrate northern colleges.[48] No radical plan was proposed for transforming the colleges, but the wish was there nonetheless. Jefferson's minister to Spain observed: "it is extremely to be regretted that our system of education is so corrupted; when, however, we shall have obtained a completely Republican legislature, we may hope to see an effectual & radical change."[49]

Republican attacks like these were understandable and perhaps justifiable, for the colleges did appear to be partisan institutions.

But they were also regrettable, for they placed American higher education on the defensive, both intellectually and in its relations to the outside world. The old-time college grew up acutely aware that it lived in a hostile environment.

Republican students often complained of political indoctrination. A student at Union wrote home:

> We are at present studying the Constitutions of the United and of the Several States; so that Doct[or] [James Blair] Smith has made the greatest part of the class Federals; he is lecturing dayly upon Federalism, and trys to shew that the Alien and Sedition Bills are constitutional.[50]

Dr. Smith's brother, Samuel Stanhope Smith, president of Princeton, allegedly inculcated politics "directly hostile to republican principles" and partial to "the british constitution."[51] A student transferred from Williams to Brown in 1804 to escape what he thought was political discrimination.[52] During the War of 1812 a southern student at Yale declared:

> His Excy. Dr. Dwight is most grossly infected by this raging political epidemick & instead of resisting the current of this pestilential malady he is borne willingly along . . . the Revd old Man occasionally whets his splenitick appetite in a political Sermon, unfortunately for him his prejudices are so irresistable and powerful that they "mantle his clearer reason" baffle all his powers of ratiocination and change his party hatred and dislike into pitiful individualism and personal animosity—but what of him? he is nothing to us so I'll let him rest.[53]

Academics sincerely did not think of themselves as partisans. They simply upheld religion, morality, civilization, authority, and order. It was their opponents who had divided the country into hostile factions and transformed legislators into party hacks, or at least so the professors reasoned. President Dwight assured his pupils, "we have no political parties here . . . We ask, what kind of a scholar is he? Not, to what party does he belong?"[54] His esteem for the brilliant young John C. Calhoun (Yale 1804) attested his assertion, though of course there were few Calhouns in any class.[55] Likewise, President Joseph Caldwell responded to charges of indoctrination by saying that "so far as the subscriber is able to retrace the lapse of eight years at least, he has never once mentioned to a student a single sentiment upon the politics of the day, or on the civil government of the United States," which if true made his teaching somewhat irrelevant to say the least.[56]

Such statements undoubtedly contained a good deal of self-delusion. But it was probably true that the colleges wanted to stay above partisan squabbles since they were not autonomous institutions but dependent upon the state for assistance. Even those schools now designated "private" received state funding and were subject in part to state control.[57] Openly to antagonize Republicans, especially after 1800, bordered on the suicidal. For this reason there seems to have been an academic retreat from the political arena. "On coming to Princeton, in 1813," wrote Samuel Miller, "I resolved to begin a new course in regard to *Politics.* I determined to do and say as little on the subject as could be deemed consistent with the character of a good citizen: — to attend no political meetings; to write no political paragraphs; to avoid talking on the subject much either in public or private."[58] In a similar vein, Eliphalet Pearson, now at Andover Theological Seminary, counseled his son at Yale: "I hope you will have no connection with politics . . . It is unchristian, unmanly, & very unbecoming a youth."[59] Party politics was still looked upon as an evil. Therefore President Dwight urged his students *"to allay the prejudices, and the heat, of party spirit in your native country."*[60]

In place of politics, the professoriate espoused the creation of voluntaristic religious and moral societies intended both to fight infidelity and to elevate the morality of the nation. Academics were instrumental in founding these associations. Professor Pearson was co-founder with Jedidiah Morse of the Massachusetts Society for Promoting Christian Knowledge and served as its first executive. Ashbel Green, Princeton trustee and president of Princeton in 1812, started America's first national Bible Society. Timothy Dwight pioneered the Missionary Society of Connecticut. Ebenezer Fitch led the western Massachusetts temperance and sabbatarian crusades. Eliphalet Nott was a major spokesman for the national prohibition movement. Their efforts were the parents of the national evangelical societies which arose in the 1810s and 1820s — the American Bible Society (1816), American Education Society (1816), American Sunday School Union (1824), American Home Missionary Society (1826), and American Temperance Society (1826) — later collectively called the Benevolent Empire, which exerted a profound influence on the popular morals and culture of America.[61]

A lively debate is still going on among historians as to the motives behind these organizations — whether they were founded for social improvement or for social control, that is, to keep the masses in their place.[62] An ambivalent sense of the future seems to have motivated the professoriate in the early 1800s — a fear of social disintegration certainly but also a vision of a constantly improving society, uplifted not by the impious schemes of Godwin or Paine but by the meliorative power of Christianity.[63] Evangelical societies were meant to inaugurate the millennium. Yet to overstress the idealism present at the turn of the century, without paying attention to the fears which inspired evangelical efforts, seriously distorts the historical record. Early evangelical societies represented an alliance between clergy and Federalist politicians aimed at eradicating subversive ideas. In his $5,000 bequest to Harvard, for example, a huge sum at the time, Federalist Samuel Dexter specified as its purpose that unbelievers might be proselytized and doubters confirmed in the truth of Christianity.[64] Likewise, Samuel Phillips funded the Massachusetts Society for the Promotion of Christian Knowledge "to guard against the dissemination of the least particle of infidelity or modern philosophy."[65] Alex-

ander Hamilton, the national leader of the Federalists, even cyn-
ically proposed that these reform societies be organized into a new
association, "The Christian Constitutional Society," a thinly disguised political party designed to encourage "the use of all lawful
means in concert to promote the election of fit men."[66] Although
American academics were less cynical than Hamilton, in their
intellectual orientation they were if anything even more conservative.

The colleges responded to the great shocks of militant deism,
Illuminism, and Jeffersonianism by contracting intellectually. In
place of the open, tolerant spirit of the 1780s and 1790s, the colleges grew defensive and closed. Later case studies will show how
the prescribed classics returned to the center of instruction. The
underlying philosophical system of academic thought was Scottish
Common Sense Philosophy, expounded by Francis Hutcheson,
Adam Ferguson, and other spokesmen of the Scottish Enlightenment. This was "an apologetic philosophy, *par excellence,*" originally designed to refute David Hume's atheistical skepticism.[67]
Not wishing to repudiate all of the Enlightenment's achievements,
yet demanding a sounder foundation for religion and morality,
academics relied on Common Sense because its dualistic episte-
mology offered a means of reconciling scientific empiricism in the
realm of matter with religious certitude in the realm of mind. In
the colonial era, Common Sense had been a liberating influence.[68]
After the turn of the century, however, its negative aspects came
to predominate. As drilled into generation after generation of students in the senior-year course on moral philosophy, it furnished
students with a neat system of values but at the same time robbed
them of much of the excitement of intellectual exploration. It
provided answers rather than raised questions, imparted old
truths rather than searched for new ones.[69] Students may not have
fully comprehended the mental reaction going on, but they could
certainly feel it, for they were caught in the center of the professoriate's intellectual retreat.

CHAPTER FIVE

The Progress of
Vice and Irreligion

ON JULY 3, 1809, the president of the University of Vermont sent his condolences to the president of Dartmouth on the "spirit of insubordination" which had erupted there. Remarking that there had been "repeated and alarming instances of disorders in almost all our Northern Seminaries," he speculated on the causes of student protests:

> how far they originate in defects of our *institutions* themselves; from deficiencies in modern, early parental discipline; from erroneous notions of *liberty* and equality; from the spirit of revolution in the *minds* of men, constantly progressing, tending to a relinquishment of all *ancient* systems, discipline and dignities; from an increasing desire to *level* distinctions, traduce authority and diminish restraint; from licentious political discussions and controversies.[1]

Although unusually elaborate, his plaintive list of social ills was quite typical of the academic response to student revolt.

What distinguished college riots and rebellions in the decade after 1798 from earlier campus disturbances was not so much the quantitative aspect — their unprecedented frequency and magnitude—as it was a qualitative change—that for the first time in American history student disorder was perceived as a symptom of deeper evils within the society. Student revolt was attributed to the breakdown of social order in general and to the spread of radical philosophy among students more specifically. Such fears account for the undue alarm and vigorous repression which greeted the nascent student movement. Only by studying contemporary opinion as revealed in letters and pamphlets can these important apprehensions be explored.

There is abundant evidence of the fear of student radicalism but only the slightest trace of the existence of such radicalism. Student petitions and manifestoes contained virtually no ideology. Students repeatedly denied that their resistance had subversive origins. But a number of students did read Godwin and Paine, and there are signs of freethinking within the literary societies. The issue of student radicalism emerged in every major rebellion, yet it is difficult to reach a satisfactory conclusion on the central question. Student revolt was not "radical" in the sense that undergraduates hoped to foment a general revolution. Quite the contrary: students were Federalists and elitists. Resistance was intellectually motivated, however, insofar as students resented the suppression of their freethinking and insofar as literary heroes such as Godwin's Caleb Williams inspired them to suffer persecution for the sake of "justice." The issue of radicalism placed student revolt in the center of turn-of-the-century intellectual history.

The first great exposé of student freethinking occurred at Transylvania University in the summer of 1801. "Transylvania"— meaning "backwoods"—was an appropriate name for Kentucky's university at Lexington, the westernmost institution in the country. From June 24 to July 1, 1801, the trustees of Transylvania conducted a public hearing at the behest of the students on the conduct of Professor James Welsh, a Presbyterian clergyman. Unfortunately, there are no extant copies of the petition calling for the investigation. The incident leading up to the hearing was a trivial altercation between Welsh and one of the students, Rice Jones, the campus radical. As librarian, Welsh accused Jones of tearing a map out of one of the volumes which (he added triumphantly) was overdue! When Jones denied the charge, Welsh threatened to kick him down the stairs, or actually did so, the record being somewhat unclear. During the trial it was brought out that Welsh had previously promised to beat any student who insulted him, though corporal punishment was against the laws of the college. It also appeared that the professor had long been antagonized by the students' custom of addressing their classmates as "Mr." and "Sir" and had repeatedly ridiculed the practice. Welsh's popularity may be gauged by the fact that twenty students testified against him at the trial while only four spoke in his behalf.[2]

Welsh's defense was to smear young Jones and portray himself as saving the university from student radicalism.

Q. "Have you not frequently heard Mr. Jones advocate principles contrary to Christianity?"
A. "I have, but he did not endeavour to inculcate those principles to my knowledge."
Q. "Have you not heard Mr. Jones advocate Payne, Boulanger & Voltaire in the University?"
A. "I have heard him speak with applause of them, but do not recollect that I ever heard him contest with any person about these authors."
Q. "Have you not also heard Mr. Jones advocate Godwin?"
A. "I believe I have heard him speak favorably of it."
Q. "Have you not seen a piece of poetry made by Mr. Jones on Jefferson's election?"
A. "I have."

John Johnson, president of the newly formed Transylvania Philosophical Society, also brought charges against Welsh. He complained that Welsh barged into meetings of the student literary society despite a rule prohibiting professors from attending. Whenever Johnson had spoken, Welsh had snickered and made faces. When discussions led to controversial topics, Welsh had tried to quash debate on the grounds that it would displease the trustees. When a member had alluded to Godwin's *Political Justice* during a meeting, Welsh stormed that "Mr. Jones nor any other person should support those principles in the U[niversity]."

At first the inquisition was indecisive. The trustees were too deeply divided themselves to agree either to censure the students or to dismiss Welsh. However, when fifteen of the students then withdrew from the university and others planned to do so, the trustees met in emergency session and finally resolved that Welsh must go. Student resistance was thus linked with the defense of freethinking. After the trial, reports circulated that a new club had been created at the university "for the purpose of discussing Deistical principles."[3] Despite a public denial by the students, the rumor persisted. Then at the request of the students, the trustees investigated the charge and exonerated them. As a further disclaimer, young Johnson published his inaugural address to the Philosophical Society. His address was more calculated to calm the public than call his fellow students to the barricades. For his examples of great philosophers, he chose the safely dead patriots David Rittenhouse and Benjamin Franklin rather than Godwin and Paine.[4]

Nevertheless, the Welsh trial seems to have fed Presbyterian fires. Under the banner of saving the college from deism, the Presbyterian faction of the trustees had wrested control of the university from their liberal adversaries by 1804. Given the Presbyterian trustees' own explanation of their policies — "to institute such discipline as will preserve the youth committed to their care, from the hands of those harpies who strive to make shipwreck of their principles and habits" and to redeem "the university from the obloquy under which it labored, as a seat of infidelity and cave of moral death" — the significance of the Welsh trial and the student walkout in the history of Transylvania is apparent.[5]

The issue of radicalism next arose at Princeton, just prior to the

Nassau Hall fire in 1802. During the Christmas holidays in 1801, four inebriated undergraduates had committed various acts of mischief and disorder. The usual punishment for such misbehavior was a simple reprimand, but for an unknown reason the faculty suspended the offenders. On January 2, 1802, therefore, the students began the new year by sending a petition to the faculty protesting against this "extraordinary" decision. With a reminder that the college catalogue had "avowed that we were to be governed with the tenderness of Parents," the students declared, "we wish to avert the rigours of the Inquisition."[6] In rejecting this petition as "disrespectful & improper," the faculty must have cast even stronger aspersions on the signers, for in their next petition the students complained,

> You apprehend, gentlemen, unhappy consequences from the establishment of a Jacobinical precedent. With you we detest Jacobinism. With you we love subordination. You are convinced that it is indispensably necessary to our common interests and comfort. But gentlemen, respectful remonstrance is not the weapon of Jacobinism—Jacobinism does not delight in such decorum.[7]

There was considerably less decorum, however, when this reiterated demand for clemency was rejected. Violence broke out and a "combination" of students was formed to boycott classes till the suspended students were reinstated. At this point, finally, the faculty backed down.

This background information is essential for comprehending the college government's reaction to the Nassau Hall fire. It explains why, despite the lack of proof, the blaze was blamed on the students. A day after the fire a townsman wrote:

> For several weeks past the students have been in a state of open rebellion against the laws of College. Revelling and debauchery had triumphed over all order and discipline. Hence the faculty

found it necessary to suspend several of them; by perhaps an ill judged lenity they were again reinstated, as this did not restore them to proper subordination. Some, who are not yet designated, were heard to say that College would be burnt before the session was out. This naturally raised a suspicion at first that they were the perpetrators or planners of this diabolical business.[8]

There were alternative explanations, however. One undergraduate conducted his own investigation and concluded that a faulty chimney must have caused the fire.[9] This same Princeton resident himself reported that "as Ferguson's house was last night set on fire, and again today in meeting time, by Findley's Negroe boy, as is since discovered, it may yet prove that the Students have been unjustly censured."[10]

But no doubts assailed the faculty or trustees. When he first saw the blaze, President Smith "looked up at the fire, raised his hands, [and] exclaimed, 'This is the progress of vice and irreligion.' "[11] To Jedidiah Morse he wrote that the disaster was but "one effect of those irreligious and demoralizing principles which are threatening in the end to overturn our country." Two years before, he said, a student had "attempted to excite an insurrection on jacobinic and anti-religious principles," and in a recent riot at William and Mary the students "broke into the church and took out the bible, and burnt it." "These, my friend, are some of the signs of the days which are coming upon us."[12] Presidents of other institutions concurred with his gloomy forecast. "Burning of Colleges is part of the new Order of things," wrote President Nisbet from Dickinson.[13] President Joseph Willard of Harvard attributed Princeton's disciplinary problems to the fact that its students "so generally come from those parts of the Union [the South and the West] where disorganizing and loose principles generally prevail."[14]

Although no evidence of an incendiary could be found, two southern students were expelled as a warning to the rest. The charges brought against them can be inferred from the defense of one, a young Virginian who was later reinstated. He denied "that I despise all religion" or that he had "endeavoured to propagate my sentiments among my fellow students." It was true that he had written two compositions for Dr. Smith on "religious intolerance," but he denied that these contained any irreligious expressions. "I did not come here," he concluded, "(as has already been suggested) as a missionary to propagate principles of infidelity."[15] The other expelled student, from North Carolina, who refused to bow to the trustees, was described by a classmate as a "free thinker."[16]

This view of the fire as an expression of atheism set the official response of the authorities. In a remarkable and influential address to the students on May 6, the Reverend Ashbel Green announced that "from this hour a new era commences in the government and discipline of this institution." No more illegal student combinations would be tolerated. The entire student body would be dismissed before the government would suffer "the least infringement or contempt of its authority." He inveighed against the "bad principles" which were corrupting American society, leading to "loose sentiments in regard to morals and religion," "dissipation of mind and dissoluteness of manners," and the "neglect of family government." Then he struck directly at what he supposed were the students' religious heresies. "Notwithstanding all the talk you may hear about *the religion of nature,*" he said, "be assured that it is *only talk,* and that in practice there is no such religion." Finally, he declared that "to allow skeptical and irreligious principles to be maintained in this college" would be a "sacrilegious perversion" of its original design. "We are not, indeed, going to turn inquisitors, and to search your minds, or require you to avow your secret sentiments," he assured them. "But if any student voluntarily avows opinions hostile to revelation he must leave this institution." He closed his emotional address almost like a revival meeting, asking that the students "come forward" and swear to obey the laws.[17]

Green also served as acting president while Smith toured the

South seeking contributions for rebuilding Nassau Hall. He quickly enacted a more repressive regime, including new rules which stipulated:

> No student shall possess or exhibit any lascivious, impious, or irreligious books.
>
> No student shall visit on the sabbath, nor shall any who live and board in college, go without the bounds of the college (by which are meant the front and back yards of the college).
>
> Besides the public exercises of religious worship on the sabbath, there shall be assigned to each class certain exercises for their religious instruction.[18]

These rules became models for other institutions. At Transylvania, new regulations in 1803 required that "no student shall possess or exhibit any indecent picture, nor purchase or read in the University any lascivious or immoral books," a clause not found in the 1799 regulations.[19] Green's reforms were supported by at least one important intellectual figure. Dr. Benjamin Rush, signer of the Declaration of Independence, founder of Dickinson College, and professor at the University of Pennsylvania Medical School, who had a son at Princeton, applauded the inclusion of religious studies into the curriculum and thanked Green for finally denying the existence of a "religion of nature." He even suggested that candidates for degrees be required to pass an examination in "theological science" in order to obtain their diploma.[20] This would have gone far toward making Princeton a purely sectarian institution, and this was practically what the trustees now promised the parents:

> We aim to make this institution an asylum for pious youth, so that in this day of general and lamentable depravity, parents may send their children to it with every expectation of safety and advantage. This we know will create us some enemies; but your patronage and prayers will, in every view, be more than a compensation for their hostility.[21]

In the South as well as the rest of the nation, campus disorders were seen as products of radicalism and irreligion. After the 1799 riot at the University of North Carolina, the Reverend Samuel E. McCorkle, co-founder of the institution, observed, "you notice the Jacobine defense of the students. It is that their expelled friends were 'actuated by the purest motives' . . . who will undertake to govern such men?"[22] After the Great Secession of 1805, William R. Davie, the university's other founder, a prominent Federalist political figure, pondered the "spirit of insubordination and the means of preventing it."

> I think the real causes may be found in the defects of education in the So[uthern] States, the weakness of parental authority, the spirit of the Times . . . the consequent presumption and loose manners of young men, Boys 16 or 17 years, without judgment, without experience or almost any kind of knowledge of any kind, arrogantly affect to judge for themselves, their teachers and their parents in matters of morality, of Government, of Education, in fact of everything.[23]

Even at the College of William and Mary, the nation's most liberal and tolerant institution, Bishop Madison justified new rules passed after the riot of 1802 by asserting that "the spirit of dissipation, nursed by certain destructive principles, which one or two popular writers seem to have disseminated, rendered it absolutely necessary to adopt such Regulations."[24] These men were not all Presbyterian "bigots": Davie was a deist and Madison a latitudinarian Episcopalian. Each, however, was as alarmed by the ideological implications of student revolt as his Calvinist counterparts at Princeton.

Whether an institution was Calvinist was not the decisive factor. In 1805 Harvard, still nominally orthodox Calvinist, was taken over by proto-Unitarians. Jedidiah Morse deplored this as "a revolution which will deeply and lastingly affect the cause of evangelical truth."[25] Harvard's Unitarian authorities, however, in no sense countenanced student freethinking or resistance. In fact, their Arminian theology placed even greater emphasis on morality and behavior than did Calvinism. During the rebellion of 1807, Harvard's governors blamed the insurrection on a "spirit of disorganization," which in Massachusetts was a direct synonym for "Jacobinism."[26] The college's official account of the trouble used the same phrase, attributing the rebellion to "the arts or influence of a few disorganizing spirits."[27] At the height of the uprising, Theophilus Parsons, chief justice of the Supreme Court of Massachusetts, president of the Harvard Corporation, and leader of the Unitarian coup, lectured the students "with much severity on the subject of their late conduct. He termed it 'indecent and unmanly, evincing a disposition to break through all restraints of law and authority, a contempt of all salutary regulations, which if not checked, would inevitably make Harvard the nurse of demagogues and disorganizers.' " The student who left this record of Parsons's address was a leader of the rebellion who had drafted the student pledge of resistance. According to him, Parsons's outburst only steeled the determination of the rebels:

> The terms, which he applied to our conduct, I knew as to myself and believed as to others, were wide from just. The dispositions, the principles, he ascribed to us, I could not on the strictest scrutiny find to have had any share in regulating my conduct. Conscious that my views and persuaded that those of my companions were greatly misconceived . . . I forgot to consider whether we ourselves had not injured. Certain that we were not as guilty as our governors had represented us, this resolution insensibly became that of our entire innocency.

To the end this student swore, "I am not a disorganizer."[28]

The 1807 rebellion at Princeton drew the attention of academics throughout the country. President Dwight prayed that the firmness of the trustees might "ultimately serve to strengthen the hands of discipline, & to put down that impatience of control which we also lament as a strong characteristic of the rising generation."[29] Bishop Madison added his condemnation of "the ungovernable & licentious spirit of Youth."[30] "Had a milder policy been adopted," agreed President Nott of Union, "the youth in other seminaries emboldened by a successful experiment would have been easily excited to a similar combination," and no check would have been given to "the leveling spirit of the times."[31]

During the rebellion the students were reprimanded by the senior member of the Board of Trustees, Elias Boudinot. Boudinot had been an important figure in the War of Independence, serving as commissary general of prisoners in the Continental Army, representative to the Continental Congress, and president of the Continental Congress from 1782 to 1783. He was later a United States congressman and director of the United States Mint. In 1805 he left civic life to study the Bible and promote the American Bible Society, of which he was the president from 1816 to 1821. In 1815 he wrote *The Second Advent*, a reinterpretation of the prophecies on the Second Coming of Christ in light of the French Revolution in which Napoleon was identified as the Antichrist. In 1816 he brought out *A Star in the West; or, A Humble Attempt to Discover the Long Lost Ten Tribes of Israel, Preparatory to their Return to Their Beloved City, Jerusalem,* which contained considerable anthropological data and concluded that the North American Indians were the direct descendants of the Jews.[32]

Boudinot's retreat from politics into voluntaristic evangelical reform was prompted by his fears for the youth of America. Ever since the publication of Paine's *Age of Reason*, he had been obsessed with the danger of adolescents falling under the influence of irreligious books: "I was much mortified to find, the whole force of this vain man's genius and art, pointed at the youth of America, and her unlearned citizens, (for I have no doubt that it was originally intended for them) in hopes of raising a skeptical disposition in their minds, knowing that this was the best inlet to infidelity."[33] To combat Paine, Boudinot wrote *The Age of Revelation, or The*

Age of Reason Shewn to be An Age of Infidelity (1801), a lengthy
review of Christian doctrine in fairly simple terms. His conviction
that Paine and other deists were popular reading among the
young led naturally to his assertion that student revolt was con-
nected with radicalism. In a long address to the students he
warned them that "delusive mentors" were destroying their
morals: "The clumsy sophistry of Godwin, the pernicious subtle-
ties of Hume, and the coarse vulgarities of Paine, have been exposed at once in all their loathsome deformity—From these un-
hingers of human happiness, these presumptious undoers of the
labours of Antiquity, I trust the Youths who now hear me will turn
away with abhorence."[34]

He was not alone in associating this rebellion with worldwide
revolution. One newspaper thought the conduct of the students
"perfectly consistent with the tenets of our quack politicians, our
sticklers for human perfectibility. The same mental epidemic
which has crazed Europe, and is extending its baleful ravages
throughout the civilized world, has contaminated these young
rights-of-boys politicians." Parts of the student statement it considered "worthy of a Godwin or a Holcroft, or in other words, display[ing] a spirit which ought to be suppressed."[35] It was referring
to the vow that the "genius of revolt" would arise to defend the
rights of youth "whenever the hand of presuming authority shall
attempt to level or abridge them."[36] However, this was no more
than a desperate attempt to keep the combination from dissolv-
ing, hardly prima facie evidence of radicalism among students.

With public and professors ready to pounce on everything they
wrote, it was understandable that most undergraduate manifestoes did not venture far from a dry recitation of facts and demands. There was only one serious effort to analyze the intellectual sources of student revolt, that coming ironically in a tongue-
in-cheek attack upon the Harvard rebels' *Statement of Facts
Relative to the Late Proceedings in Harvard College* (1807). Pos-
ing as a defender of the students, the writer declared that it was

obvious that the student statement must have been composed by imposters attempting to discredit the rebellion. He showed this by allegedly finding the pamphlet full of plagiarism, hypocrisy, and errors in grammar. "We think it impossible that the Students of Harvard University could ever have written or signed any such pamphlet. To suppose them capable of doing it would discredit them more than anything which their most bitter enemies could have devised."[37]

In accusing the students of plagiarism, the reviewer had some insights into the models of the manifesto. The introductory remarks were lifted from the Declaration of Independence, he said, the conclusion taken from Samuel Dexter's closing speech at the trial of Thomas O. Selfridge. With the first the epitome of the Enlightenment natural rights philosophy and the latter an exposition of the Romantic exaltation of personal honor, the student statement thus stood between two intellectual traditions, just as American thought was in transit from an Age of Reason to an Age of Feeling. All that the students took from the Declaration was a paraphrase of Jefferson's words that when one people separates itself from another "a decent respect to the opinions of mankind requires that they should declare the causes which impel them to the separation" — and hence the students gave their reasons for revolt. The other document, however, is less well known and particularly close to the Harvard community.

On August 4, 1806, Charles Austin, a Harvard senior, had set out to avenge the honor of his father, Benjamin Austin, the Republican political writer already mentioned as the author of the essays "To the Young Men," against the ultra-Federalist lawyer Thomas O. Selfridge, who had publicly called him "a coward, a liar, and a scoundrel."[38] When young Austin struck Selfridge on the head with a cane, the latter shot and killed him. This political murder, as it was called, was a cause célèbre dividing Massachusetts for over half a year.[39] Austin's funeral was attended by the entire senior class, the president, the professors, and the tutors. Chief Justice Parsons, president of the Harvard Corporation, was severely criticized for his part in the case, having seen to it that only a charge of manslaughter rather than murder was brought against Selfridge. When Selfridge was acquitted by reason of self-defense, Republicans denounced the decision for months in the press, though Austin's Federalist classmates do not seem to have protested.

During the trial, Samuel Dexter closed his defense of Selfridge by asserting that the imperatives of honor dictate that some insults or challenges must be avenged at once without wait for recourse through legal channels. "The greatest of all public calamities," he said, "would be a pusillanimous spirit, that would tamely surrender personal dignity to every invader."[40] The students later said something like this in their manifesto:

> that there is a point of submission beyond which no man can pass without ceasing to be a man; that 'there is a spirit in man and the inspiration of the Almighty giveth him understanding'; that this spirit cannot be debased; that it abhors disgrace; and is the life-spring of a good name. It cannot be described, for it baffles the power of description. It shews its nature when it is called into action. When this spirit is dead, character drops to the dust.[41]

Throughout the course of the student revolt, a strain of romanticism was interwoven with the concept of natural rights. As college authorities cracked down on radicalism and philosophy, justification for resistance could only be on romantic grounds. Later rebellions would be inspired by the poetry of Byron, Goethe, and Thomas Campbell, and a popular but exaggerated code of honor. "Honor" proved a more flexible rationale than "Justice," for while the latter is an intellectual concept capable of debate, the former is subjective and incommunicable. As the Harvard rebels put it, "it baffles the power of description." Driven from the plain of Reason, students retreated to the realm of Feeling, another step in the American retreat from the Enlightenment.

This is looking ahead, however. It remains to be seen just how prevalent student freethinking was at the turn of the century and how it related to student revolt. Historians have long taken it for granted that deism was rife in the colleges. Their assumption has been based on Lyman Beecher's famous recollection of his student days at Yale. "That was the day of the infidelity of the Tom Paine school," he recalled, "most of the class before me were infidels, and called each other Voltaire, Rousseau, D'Alembert, etc."[42] But Beecher's influential *Autobiography* suffers from several serious shortcomings as a source. It was not put together by Beecher himself but by his children, a good half-century after his college days. Moreover, as an evangelical clergyman, Beecher was prone to stress how bad things were at the turn of the century to justify the necessity of the Protestant Counter-Revolution of which he was a part.[43] To a surprising degree our knowledge of student freethinking comes from the recollections of evangelical clergymen, but this does not discredit the testimony. In some cases, the clergymen themselves had been influenced by freethinking in college, as had Reverend Adoniram Judson. Introduced to atheism by a classmate at Brown, Judson left home after graduation, changed his name, and followed a theatrical company. His family wept and prayed for him to no avail. Squarely on the road to ruin, he was saved by the providential death of his freethinking classmate.[44] It is not that clerical recollections are necessarily untrue, therefore, but simply that they stand in need of corroborative evidence before being taken at face value.

Contemporary student letters and nonclerical memoirs confirm the existence of student freethinking to a degree. John Pettigrew wrote that the young men of Chapel Hill preferred "Payn's Age of Reason . . . to all the books that were ever wrote since the creation of the World; they also say that he was sent into the World to set mankind to liberty."[45] From William and Mary, the nation's most intellectually tolerant institution, Joseph C. Cabell wrote, "there is not a man among us who would not enlist himself under the banner of a Paine or a Volney. There are some (of which I have the honor to be one) who even border on the gloomy verge of Atheism."[46] Of John James Marshall (Princeton 1806) a classmate recalled: "he was the most intrepid infidel in College and avowed his creed on all occasions. Godwin's *Political Justice* was his Bible."[47] At South Carolina College, according to William J. Grayson, "men who had never heard of Shakespeare or Milton were deep in the pages of Paine."[48] Of a Harvard radical, William White of Watertown, Massachusetts, Joseph Tufts recalled: "He was an infidel in religion and made no secret of his sentiments. He even took pains to promulgate them, and lent to . . . his classmates, the abominable works of Thomas Paine, and boasted of its effects on their minds." "For myself," he admitted, "the conversation of White was injurious to my faith, and for a number of years I doubted the truth of the holy religion of my ancestors."[49] For the College of William and Mary especially, one could give many other examples, though even there a confirmed Godwinist was an eccentric exception.[50] Clearly, an evangelical looking for student freethinking would have been able to find it.

What appealed to young men in the writings of Volney, Condorcet, and the more radical Godwin and Paine was their optimism, iconoclasm, and reaffirmation of progress and the perfectibility of man. "The progress of man," wrote the Frenchman Condorcet, "is absolutely indefinite."[51] In place of the religious millennium espoused by clerical academics, these writers defined progress in militantly secular terms. Godwin was an atheist; Volney, Condorcet, and Paine were deists. In *The Age of Reason,* Paine had called the Bible "a book of lies, wickedness and blasphemy" and described church establishments as "human inventions, set up to terrify and enslave mankind."[52] Some students were repelled by such outspoken anticlericalism. Thomas Robbins wrote in his Williams diary, "Read some in Paine's *Age of Reason.* Shocking!" He added a few months later, "Read *Age of Reason.* Part II blasphemous."[53] Other young men could read these Enlightenment writers with a good deal of discrimination. William

Ellery Channing wrote glowingly of Godwin, Wollstonecraft, and Rousseau before adding the qualification "what a melancholy reflection is it that all the writers I have now mentioned were all deists!"[54] Academics opposed not only the anticlericalism of such writers but their extreme statement of human perfectibility as well. As Samuel Miller explained, the corollary of extreme perfectionism was the denial of human depravity or the need for salvation at all.[55] In this manner Godwin and Paine struck at the very heart of the Christian religion.

When academics blamed student rebellions on freethinking they had a specific connection in mind. It was thought that Godwin's *Political Justice* was used to rationalize resistance, and it may have been. According to the reminiscences of one Princetonian, Godwin was popular "for he advocated the doctrine that promises were not obligatory if the promiser did not see fit to perform it." That is, at the beginning of each term the students were obliged to pledge obedience to the college laws, including rules against forming student combinations, "yet it was maintained by the disciples of Godwin that it was not obligatory, & to be violated at pleasure."[56]

Godwin's utilitarian *Enquiry Concerning Political Justice* (1793) was a serious and difficult work of ethical theory. It made "justice" —that which most contributes to the welfare of mankind—the criterion of human action, as opposed to custom, statutory law, or religious revelation. What students and professors were thinking of was his section "Of Promises" wherein he asserted that "promises and compacts are in no sense the foundation of morality. The foundation of morality is justice."[57] In the abstract world of ethical theory this was quite logical, though many classic ethical paradoxes have revolved around the question whether one is obliged to fulfill a promise when he foresees evil consequences arising from it —for example, returning a borrowed gun to a man about to commit murder. Godwin cut through these dilemmas by simply saying that promises are either redundant or actually evil themselves.

One's duty to act justly is in no way enhanced by promising to do so — it is one's duty whether one promises or not. On the other hand, acting unjustly because one had promised to in no way mitigates the immorality of the act. Godwin's opponents took this as an attack upon private property, government, and family. "All promises, oaths, contracts, &c, whatever blindly determines us to act in any definite way, shall not be allowed therefore, or not regarded."[58]

How many students used Godwin to justify rebellion, or were aware of the implications of doing so, it is now impossible to say. Certainly academics had no deep understanding of Godwin's philosophy. In what may have been the last association of student revolt with philosophical radicalism, Benjamin Rush wrote to Ashbel Green, deploring some new Princeton disorders:

> There appears to me to be but one mode of preventing such gross violations of the laws of the College in future, and that is to prevent or abolish the obligation the students enter into not to inform of each other. This obligation is founded in a deep-seated immoral principle . . . Alas! how extensive has been the influence of Godwin's works in the United States.[59]

Rush had things backwards, making Godwin an advocate of mutual obligations. Whether Godwin and Paine were to blame or not, there is no doubt that they were casualties of this turn-of-the-century national crisis and the first great student revolt. Student freethinking gradually declined after the turn of the century. No faculty book burnings or inquisitions brought this about, but rather faculty pressure caused students to censor themselves. In 1805 Princeton's American Whig Society banned "any composition, orations or debates, inconsistent with the tenets of Christianity or operating against the belief in its truths and influence."[60] In 1813 the Whigs purchased the complete Paine but voted "to send that volume of Payne's works containing the age of reason to a bookbinder that that portion of it may be taken out."[61]

This was a sad day in the history of the American college. It was not that censorship was uniquely American; in 1811 Shelley was expelled from Oxford for writing *The Necessity of Atheism*.[62] Nothing was intrinsically wrong with the intention of upholding Christianity. Outlawing Godwin and Paine may not have irreparably harmed the American radical tradition, as the Declaration of Independence and the Bible contained arguments enough for human rights. Rather, censorship was wrong because it taught students that ideas were to be feared and mistrusted. After 1815, one finds no more allusions to Godwin and Paine in student letters. Student rebellions in turn ceased to be blamed on undergraduate radicalism. Thus turn-of-the-century student revolt had come to an end, though actual student rebelliousness had not. The intellectual warfare in the colleges was over. The college governments won and the students lost.

CHAPTER SIX

The Downfall of
Republican Education

THE HIGH TIDE of Enlightenment pedagogy in America
came in 1795 when the American Philosophical Society held a contest for the best plan of "republican education" suited to the spirit
and institutions of the national republic. Most of the proposals
called for a more utilitarian education dependent upon two specific reforms: deemphasizing the "dead" languages and adopting
a modified elective principle — allowing students some choice in
the selection of courses. As significant as the proposals themselves
was the general spirit of the contest: educational reform was in the
air. The winning essays were published in 1799, but by this time
they had already become anachronisms. Curricular reform was
too closely associated with deism and revolution to be respectable.
Thomas Paine himself had said that "there is now nothing new to
be learned from the dead languages" and that "the schools of the
Greeks were schools of science and philosophy, and not of languages."[1]

In the illiberal aftermath of the Quasi-War and the Illuminati
scare, it was inevitable that colleges would turn in a conservative
direction. For example, the study of modern languages, the alternative to the classics, received a major setback in the widespread

abolition of instruction in French.[2] But the timing of this pedagogical reaction was significant: to a remarkable degree, experiments in republican education were repudiated just following
major student unrest. Revolt had an adverse impact on the colleges. As the following case studies will show, student resistance
both badly damaged respective institutions and served as an un-
witting agent of educational reaction.

WILLIAM AND MARY'S LICENTIOUS VORTEX

The College of William and Mary, second only to Harvard in antiquity, boasted of being the nation's most progressive institution. It
introduced the study of natural philosophy in 1712, experimental
philosophy in 1756, and political economy in 1779. During the
Revolution it became a truly "republican" institution when in
1779 Governor Thomas Jefferson proposed an education bill
which abolished the chairs of ancient languages and divinity and
replaced them with professorships of law and police, chemistry
and medicine, and modern languages. Although he failed to wrest
an adequate endowment from the legislature, his liberal curriculum went into effect. After 1779 William and Mary had the most
utilitarian course of study in America. Its emphasis on science,
mathematics, politics, and literature reflected Thomas Jefferson's
advanced ideas about the kind of education most conducive to the
progress of mankind.

William and Mary was equally innovative in its requirements
for admissions and degrees. Knowledge of Latin and Greek was no
longer a prerequisite for entrance. Students were allowed to take
courses in any order or even all at once. As a result, it was possible
to earn a degree in a single year. The elective principle was
adopted for the first time in American history, with students free
to decide for themselves which subjects were pertinent to their
needs. There were no compulsory courses. In administration as

well as curriculum the college was a forerunner of postrevolutionary educational reform.[3]

The spirit of the college was as liberal as its laws. The president, Bishop James Madison, was a latitudinarian Episcopalian, ordained Bishop of Virginia in 1790. Bishop Madison's faith in science and human progress had not been shaken by the French Revolution or Illuminism. He read Condorcet and Godwin with certain reservations, but he was no friend of the organized reaction against French philosophy. Indeed, he wrote his ally Thomas Jefferson that "Morse is a blockhead," and was openly sympathetic to the Democratic-Republicans.[4] Another liberal member of the faculty was St. George Tucker, professor of law from 1800, an ardent Republican and an avowed deist, author of a public letter refuting the existence of Illuminism in Virginia.[5]

The faculty ran a rather loose ship. A Frenchman traveling through the United States in the years 1795-1797 was dismayed to find that the students had almost no faculty supervision. They were not even required to live in the college dormitories but were dispersed "through the different boarding-houses in the town, at a distance from all inspection."[6] In this tolerant and easygoing atmosphere, the students read widely and thought for themselves, as they had proved by writing their dissenting address to the Virginia Congressional Delegation. In 1798 Joseph C. Cabell was proud that the students "continue to display the same freedom & liberality of opinion, the same independence of investigation, the same defiance to old-fashioned precepts & doctrines that they formerly did."[7] Another former student who had just graduated wrote that each young man acquired "the spirit of skepticism as soon as he touched the threshold of the college." "That it leads to Deism, atheism, &c," he confessed, "I will acknowledge, but on the same grounds we may object to reason."[8] But there were many now objecting to "reason" on precisely these grounds.

About this time Bishop Madison began to worry about the college's reputation for freethinking. He sought to reassure the public that the students were still sound in their thinking. At the death of ex-President Washington, he urged the students to wear black crepe as a sign of mourning. One student complained:

> Another consideration which he observed had some weight with him (a consideration which seems to me to have too great an influence over all his actions) was a desire to contradict as much as lay in his power, those reports which have been for some time so industriously circulated throughout the State, that this [college] is so far led away by Jacobinical, disorganizing principles as not only to be enemies to the Union, but even to have forgotten the services of those who most distinguished themselves in the cause of American Independence.[9]

Despite the Bishop's prompting, many of the students refused to commemorate Washington's death because of the ultra-Federalist partisanship of his second administration.

In 1801 William and Mary radicalism became a national issue when Theodore Dwight charged that Napoleon's agent in the United States was secretly republishing Godwin's *Political Justice* for subversive purposes. Since Godwin was reputedly "used in the Virginia College, for the instruction of their youth," he said, "we can at least conjecture who is at bottom of the plan for republishing it."[10] This was not the last time that Federalists scrutinized the college for material supposedly damaging to Jefferson. Bishop Madison rightly laid the attack to "the virulence & meanness of the disappointed party," but he dared not ignore the charge. In an anonymous rebuttal, he denied that *Political Justice* was a William and Mary text.[11] He also began to crack down on student freethinking. When Winfield Scott entered the college in 1805, the Bishop greeted his class with a condemnation of "Hume, Voltaire, Godwin, Helvetius, etc. etc."[12] As early as 1801 Joseph C. Cabell noticed a change. "It really is remarkable," he observed upon returning to the campus to read law with Professor Tucker, "that the taste of students here in favor of particular books and opinions varies as often as the fashions in the polite world. The Christian Religion is not as formerly a subject of general discussion, the science of metaphysics no longer engages the affections of the young men, political investigation has become less fashionable, and Godwin's *Political Justice* is read [by] only two or three of the students."[13]

The Bishop's defensiveness arose from a realization that the College of William and Mary was ailing. There were several causes, no single one of them wholly to blame. For one thing, the Revolution had cut off a sizable English endowment. In place of the $17,000 to $18,000 it had enjoyed before the war, the college now had only $3,000 per year plus the tuition it received from the students.[14] Its location in Williamsburg was also detrimental. As the population of Virginia shifted westward, the college was stranded near the coast. In 1779 the state capital had been moved from Williamsburg to Richmond. What this meant for the college, according to one student, was that Virginia's young men began "to consider Richmond as the seat of the greatest information & improvement." "If this be the case," he went on, "poor Williamsburg, which was once regarded as the asylum of Science, must be an object of secondary consideration, & Learning will not long continue to be her leading characteristic."[15] In the 1780s Jedidiah Morse had caused a great stir when he wrote of the city, "everything in Williamsburg appears dull, forsaken, and melancholy — no trade — no amusements, but the infamous one of gaming — no industry, and very little appearance of religion."[16] Conditions had improved after his visit, however. If William and Mary had been a strong institution, Williamsburg could have held its own with Richmond. Richmond had no college. The trouble was that too many Virginians were sending their sons north for an education.

The college also suffered from Williamsburg's not undeserved reputation for high living. In his novel *The Valley of the Shenandoah: or, Memoirs of the Graysons* (1824), George Tucker, class of 1797, recalled only the mellow charms of Williamsburg's polite society. Other contemporaries, however, were impressed by the decay of the Tidewater aristocracy and how it infected the undergraduates with dissolute habits. David C. Watson lamented the "proneness to dissipation & extravagance" among the students and their "want of application to serious business."[17] William T. Barry, later a United States congressman, was shocked by the condition of the college when he arrived from Kentucky with a B.A. from Transylvania to study law with Professor Tucker. Few students could escape the "licentious vortex," he wrote, and most were "very dissipated." "Parents are afraid to send their children here," he continued, "lest their morals should be perverted." He even censured the young ladies of Williamsburg for "a certain looseness of manners and conversation . . . too near the border of licentiousness."[18] It was not simply that Barry was a rustic; others were of the same opinion. In 1802 a student said simply, "the dissipation here is intolerable."[19] "Aristocracy in every form is hideous," wrote a critic a decade later, "but in no shape is it more horrible or dangerous than when stripped of its power and splendor, it is left to wallow in idleness, vice, and corruption."[20] Tea parties, midnight dinners, and balls kept the undergraduates away from their books.

Far more dangerous, the students were addicted to dueling. Four times—in 1802, 1803, 1806, 1809—and probably more often, students were disciplined for fighting duels.[21] The participants were sometimes wounded or even killed. Evangelical educators in other colleges saw these duels as part of the battle between religion and atheism in the colleges. President Dwight related the following tale:

> There came a youth from the west of Virginia to one of the colleges of that state, who had been brought up in a religious family, but found himself placed in contact with infidels, and often engaged in arguments with them on the truths of religion. He generally succeeded in worsting his opponents, and soon raised much hostility against himself in consequence. Some of his com-

panions determined to involve him in a duel, and succeeded in having a challenge presented and accepted. The youth chosen to fight him was an expert marksman; and a duel was resorted to expressly for the purpose of killing him who they could not refute. This they accomplished.[22]

The story sounds somewhat apocryphal, but student duels did undeniably give the college a bad name. One worried mother refused to send her son there because "so many young men have fallen in fighting duels that I am frightened for the safety of the lad."[23]

William and Mary's decline may never be perfectly traced for nearly all of the official records of the college for these years were destroyed in later campus fires. Nevertheless, by examining personal letters, newspaper articles, and the few surviving records, an overall picture of the problem can be drawn. It reveals an abrupt decline between 1801 and 1803 especially, brought on in large part by the riot of 1802.

The riot of 1802 broke out when two students were punished for taking part in a duel in which one of them was wounded. The student body protested against the punishments by sending a remonstrance to the faculty alleging that the sentences were "unwarranted for want of sufficient evidence" and based only on "a vague report."[24] When this petition had no effect, a group of unidentified undergraduates "broke the windows of every professor (Mr. Andrews excepted) together with those of the church and Chapel, tore up, in great measure, the bibles & prayer books, and finally broke open Boucher's shop door, and committed every act of impropriety they could think of."[25]

The riot was widely publicized. On April 3, 1802, an article appeared in the *New-York Evening Post* which declared that classes were "entirely discontinued" and the college "completely broken up." Every act of vandalism was described in detail. Professor Tucker was said to be resigning on account of the abuse he had received. Rather prematurely, the article concluded, "thus dies one of the oldest and wealthiest seminaries of learning in the United States." The intent of the article was to discredit President Jefferson. According to the writer, the riot could be ascribed to "the modern or Jeffersonian system of religion." He charged that "party-politics, instead of science, appear long since to have been the primary objects of instruction in that University—and from that foul source have flowed many of the heretical doctrines of the present day." Although the article was anonymous, the identity of its author leads to interesting speculation. The editor of the *Evening Post* was William Coleman, the protégé of Alexander Hamilton, who frequently published editorials dictated by his mentor. It is possible that Hamilton, leader of the Federalists, was directly responsible for the attack.[26] But Jefferson was undaunted. He defiantly chose for his presidential secretaries two young men who according to a clergyman "broke up William and Mary's College, and were afterward expelled from New Jersey College for atheism and infidelity."[27] Twenty years later, when the opening of the University of Virginia was marred by student disorders, his gesture returned to haunt him.

Within two weeks, this indictment of William and Mary had appeared in newspapers throughout the country. In Boston it was printed under the caption "Experiments in Natural and Political Philosophy, in the Virginia University."[28] Forced once again to write an anonymous rejoinder, Bishop Madison declared that classes were meeting as usual, that only five or six of the seventy-two students had been involved in the riot, that Judge Tucker was not resigning, that the college was proud of its alumnus Thomas Jefferson, and that party politics was never inculcated in the classroom.[29] "A Late Student" also defended the college, attributing rumors on the riot "to the penetration of declining Federalism." He deprecated both the disturbance and the duel but noted that this was neither the first nor the worst college riot in the country. He upheld the professors' religious character, though he was forced to concede that Judge Tucker was a deist (albeit a respectable one). Finally, he applauded the college's democratic ethos.

At William and Mary, he said, the students considered "the *People* and not the Magistrate, as sovereign" and believed that "*the powers that be are not . . . spotless in virtue, or infallible in wisdom.*"[30] His comments may have done more harm than good.

The riot did great damage to the college's public image. Henry St. George Tucker called the disturbance "a blow, from which it will never recover." Henceforth he would never recommend "any person to send their children here."[31] A year later a student reported that such disorders "were generally considered a death-blow to her; and there can be no doubt that she has suffered much by them." The riot had provided "unbounded scope to the inveterate malice of her enemies. Falsehood has been hatched after falsehood, and circulated with all the . . . diligence which the rancorous malignity of her enemies would suggest."[32] These gloomy prognostications were supported by the facts. The riot caused a sharp drop in attendance. There had been about sixty students per year throughout the colonial era, sixty as late as 1800 and 1801 according to student letters, and seventy-two at the time of the riot by Bishop Madison's account. In late 1802, however, there were only thirty-five students in attendance. Three years later there were still but forty-five, "the smallness of the number," in the words of a student, "occasioned by the riots and dissipation last course."[33] These figures indicate that while the college may also have suffered from demographic trends, the riot was a major factor in its decline.[34]

The riot caused a revolution within the college as well. "A Statute for the wholesome Government of the College" was put into effect to curb dissipation and restore order. It authorized the faculty to suspend students without formal proof of their guilt so long as strong suspicion of their misconduct existed. Students who refused to testify at faculty disciplinary hearings would either have to sign a declaration of innocence or be assumed guilty and expelled. The names of dismissed students would be sent to other colleges and published in the newspapers. Attendance at lectures was made mandatory, and professors were required to keep a daily roll. The doctrine of *in loco parentis* was reaffirmed by requiring the students to live under close supervision in the dormitories. So ended the free and easy atmosphere on campus.[35]

The implementation of these new regulations had the unhappy result of forcing Professor Tucker to resign. Tucker was a district court judge who taught his classes in the intervals of riding his court circuit. The reason usually given for his resignation is his appointment to the Virginia Court of Appeals, but the evidence indicates that he wished to keep on teaching and in fact continued to instruct his students at his home after leaving the college. It was the new regulations rather than his appointment which caused his leaving. One of his law students explained,

> in consequence of some new regulations made by the Visitors . . . Mr. Tucker has resigned (a few days ago) his Professorship, as he did not like to conform to the regulations . . . However, this does not affect the law students; they attend Mr. Tucker as usual . . . and will continue to do so for as long a time as if he had continued Professor.[36]

In his letter of resignation, Tucker blasted the new rules, charging that they showed a want of confidence in if not downright contempt for the professors. Such petty rules, fit only for "the superintendents of the little truants of a country village," were entirely inapplicable for "a professor of liberal science, honoured with the important trust of assisting the studies of those, who might be destined to fill the most conspicuous stations, and the highest offices in the state." To be required to monitor the living quarters of the students was "to perform the duties of a beadle . . . which must degrade the professor in the eyes of his pupils, and of the public, & the man in his own eyes."[37]

Forced to choose between the regulations and the professor, the Board of Visitors retained the former. Why it did so is difficult to understand. Tucker was certainly the most prominent member of the faculty. His *Dissertation on Slavery: with a Proposal for its*

Gradual Abolition in Virginia (1796) was widely acclaimed for its plan to emancipate the children of slaves. His annotated five-volume *Blackstone's Commentaries* (1803) had established his fame in jurisprudence. He was even a minor poet of local note. His name had drawn many students to the college — William T. Barry from Kentucky, for instance. His resignation, therefore, was a serious blow. It showed that not all academics favored the increasingly repressive paternalism of the colleges. It also indicated the great concern the college government attached to keeping order. Bishop Madison justified retaining the rules by saying "the spirit of dissipation, nursed by certain destructive principles, rendered it absolutely necessary to adopt such Regulations."[38]

Yet the new rules did not restore order, as duels and disturbances continued, reinforcing rumors about the college. Bishop Madison tried to desert ship by applying to Jefferson for the office of collector of the port of Norfolk.[39] After Madison's death in 1812, the presidency of the college fell to Reverend John Bracken, who was described by Jefferson as a "simpleton."[40] Perhaps his appointment was a concession to critics, for Bracken was the closest thing to an evangelical on the faculty. In rapid turnover he was replaced in 1814 by an abler, younger man, Dr. John Augustine Smith, who though not an evangelical was in tune with the conservative trends in education. He had the reputation of being a strict disciplinarian.[41] He threw out Rousseau's *Social Contract* as a text as "certainly objectionable" and replaced it with his own work on moral philosophy heavily influenced by the Scottish Common Sense philosophy of Dugald Stewart.[42] He even tried to reverse Jefferson's 1779 secularization by begging the Protestant Episcopal Church to restore a chair of divinity in the college. But the church refused, preferring to establish its own theological seminary in Virginia, free from the contamination of William and Mary's dissipation, just as other denominations were founding seminaries for like reasons.[43]

Thus, in less than a decade, the college changed dramatically.

Students were discouraged from reading radical literature. The easy, informal relations of the 1790s were replaced by a strictly regulated regime. An undistinguished faculty lectured to only a handful of undergraduates. An aura of failure pervaded the campus. Although Jefferson's liberal curriculum remained intact, Jefferson himself had long since given up on the college and started plans for the University of Virginia. William and Mary's "republican" education was now an anachronism, less a harbinger of the future than a remnant of the American Enlightenment, vitiated by the decline of the college. And a major cause of the institution's decline, Dr. Smith was convinced, was the irremediable problem of student unrest.[44]

DARK AND TRYING TIMES AT CHAPEL HILL

The University of North Carolina was the first state university in America. The same claim is sometimes made for the University of Georgia, since it was chartered earlier, but the University of North Carolina actually opened first, in 1795 as opposed to 1801, and was by far the more important of the two. Being the first state university did not make it what would now be considered the first public institution. At this time there was almost no distinction between public and private education.[45] Rather, the University of North Carolina was the first proof that state governments were willing to assume the responsibility for higher education. North Carolina's revolutionary constitution of 1776 had stipulated that "all useful learning shall be duly encouraged and promoted in one or more universities."[46] In fulfilling this pledge, the legislature was highly cognizant of the precedent it was setting. The legislature gave the university vast tracts of land by the Escheat Act of 1789 and the Confiscation Act of 1795. Practically speaking, these acts had the disadvantage of leaving the university somewhat land poor and embroiling its trustees in prolonged legal disputes. But the acts were nevertheless important symbols of the state's commitment to higher education.

The university was created by an alliance of Federalists and Presbyterians who varied somewhat in their plans for the college. The leaders of each group — William R. Davie and the Reverend Samuel E. McCorkle — "typified the conflicting currents and viewpoints clamoring for recognition in the early days of the University."[47] Davie, a Revolutionary War hero, national Federalist leader, and former governor of North Carolina, was the father of the University. As a state legislator, he pushed through its charter and insured its liberal endowment. As a trustee, he had a major voice in selecting its instructors and curriculum. McCorkle, the state's most prominent Presbyterian minister and indeed the only clergyman on the original board of trustees, was an equally important figure. As the head of Zion-Parnassus Academy, he supplied the university with its first student body — six of the first seven graduates came out of his academy. As the university's first professor of moral and political philosophy and the choice of many trustees for its president, he drafted the first course of study and the code of student laws.[48]

Davie and McCorkle were diametrically opposed in their religious beliefs and hence in their conceptions of education. There is actually scant evidence of Davie's religious convictions, if he had any. He is usually thought to have been a strongly anticlerical deist. Told that Bishop Charles Pettigrew and other religious leaders were calling the university "a very dissipated place," Davie blurted angrily, "nothing it seems goes well that these *Men of God* have not some hand in."[49] McCorkle, on the other hand, was an outspoken defender of divine revelation and an adversary of Paine.[50] His opinion of deism was unequivocal: "it is deism — deism — deism — detestible deism . . . that has disadjusted and disorganized society. It is deism that has burst all restraints and let loose the passions of men."[51] As might be expected, there was no love lost between the two. Davie's opposition caused McCorkle to decline the presidency in 1796. Their major clash came in drafting the university's first curriculum. This issue more than any other would give the university its identity.

On January 13, 1795, at the request of the trustees, McCorkle presented a code of laws and curriculum which with a few modifications was immediately put into effect. He called for a traditional four-year course of study requiring knowledge of Latin and Greek for admission and concentrating on the classics and the Greek Bible in the freshman and sophomore years. Although he nodded in a liberal direction by making room for a weekly lecture on "Agriculture, Botany, Zoology, Minerology or Commerce," there was no place for elective studies in science, philosophy, or modern languages. There were strict regulations for religious observance. Besides the standard requirements of Sabbath worship and daily chapel prayers, there was also a compulsory Sunday evening examination "on the general principles of religion and morality." The faculty was given broad discretionary powers to determine what constituted student misbehavior. It is possible that McCorkle even proposed corporal punishment, for he later condemned the notions that youth "are to be governed wholly by reason" and "that any use of the rod is barbarous and Gothic" as tenets of "our modern Jacobine deistic plan of education," as though he had been overridden on that point.[52] The rest of his plan went into effect. McCorkle's curriculum and rules placed America's first state university on a very conservative footing.

Opposition to this traditional curriculum was not long in coming. Davie wanted the university to be progressive, to stress science and general utility, a desire shared by most of the faculty. On April 10, 1795, the first tutor of mathematics, Charles W. Harris, complained that "there is much wrong in the old manner of educating":

> The notion that true learning consists rather in exercising the reasoning faculties, and laying up a store of useful knowledge, than in overloading the memory with words of a dead language,

is becoming daily more prevalent. It appears hard to deny a young Gentleman the honours of a College, after he has with much labour and painful attention acquired a competent knowledge of the Sciences, of composing and speaking with propriety his own language, and has conned the first principles of whatever might render him useful or creditable in the world, merely because he could not read a language 2000 years old. Tho' the laws at present require that Latin and Greek be understood by a graduate, they will in all probability be mitigated in this respect.[53]

The source of his advanced pedagogical ideas, he explained, was "a book entitled the rights of women," by a "Miss Mary Wollstonecraft."

On December 1, 1795, Davie presented the trustees with an alternative course of study which a week later was substituted for McCorkle's. The leading idea behind the new curriculum was that "the student may apply himself to those branches of learning and science alone which are absolutely necessary to fit him for his destined profession or occupation in life."[54] In other words, the elective principle was in effect, as at William and Mary. Likewise, science rather than the classics dominated the course. To allow nonclassical students to earn a degree, Davie proposed two kinds of diplomas—one in Latin for those who had learned *one* ancient language and one in English for students of science and belles-lettres alone. A college degree therefore no longer meant a knowledge of the classics. The acceptance of Davie's plan and McCorkle's resignation in mid-1796 was a clear victory for "republican" education. America's first state university would pursue the utilitarian philosophy of the Enlightenment.

From this point, however, the university entered a stormy period in which it labored simply to stay afloat. In the first place, there was an extraordinary turnover of faculty. Professors either went too far in espousing Enlightenment philosophy or endorsed Jeffersonian Republicanism. In the same year that McCorkle resigned, the university's first president, Dr. David Kerr, was removed for reputedly becoming "an outspoken infidel" and a "furious Republican."[55] His successor, Charles W. Harris, so influenced by Wollstonecraft, also resigned in late 1796, accused of becoming "the disciple of infidelity." ("I had expected something better of Harris," wrote a former Princeton classmate to another member of the faculty. "There is no knowing, however, where Philosophy will lead men.")[56] Professor Samuel A. Holmes was also dismissed, charged with instilling skepticism and defiance of authority into the students.[57] By 1800, the only surviving member of the early faculty was Reverend Joseph Caldwell, a Princeton graduate who became professor of mathematics in 1796. Caldwell had at first been repelled by the backwardness and freethinking of North Carolina society, but his irenic disposition had maintained the confidence of the university's warring factions. He had little respect for his early colleagues. One of his correspondents replied that the faculty sounded like "as motley a group as I have ever heard of — Presbyterians and Arminians — Infidels and Roman Catholics — Bless me what a collection. *The age of reason has surely come.*"[58]

The second problem facing the university was student unrest. Early disturbances at Chapel Hill were limited to drunkenness, swearing, gambling, and fighting among the undergraduates. In 1798 the students grew bolder in defying authority. One wrote that "there has been nothing going forward here but expulsions and suspensions."[59] None of these early disorders was really a riot. In the summer of 1799, however, the students rose up against the professors in what seems to have been a dispute over the disciplinary authority of the faculty. The president was horsewhipped, two professors were attacked, and the others were at least threatened with injury. This was an intolerable situation for the professors, and the entire faculty resigned. Those prevailed upon to stay lived in fear for their lives. As one of them explained,

Past transactions have given us reason to believe that they would not be scrupulous in attempting to put their threats against us

into effect. All that we have done or shall do is arm ourselves
with the instruments of defense and a resolution to use them
should there be any occasion . . . I shall stand at the post assigned to me and shall not hesitate to sacrifice any man's life for
the safety of my own.[60]

This was not education but warfare. The institution was shut
down temporarily while a stricter code of discipline was instituted.
When it reopened, there had been a sharp drop in attendance.
One trustee lamented, "the University totters, the Reputation of
it is gone."[61]

After the riot, the legislature turned against the university. Late
in 1799 a bill was introduced to cut off the appropriations of the
university. Although this failed to pass the Senate, another bill
was passed in December which suspended both the Escheat Act
and the Confiscation Act until the next convening of the legislature. In the election of 1800, Republicans won a large majority in
the state. One of the first acts of the new legislature was to repeal
both of the endowment acts, leaving the university to fend for
itself. This has usually been blamed on Republican antielitism.[62]
But the trouble with a purely partisan interpretation of repeal is
that the basis was laid in 1799, when Federalists were still ascen-
dant in the legislature. Moreover, voting on repeal was not strictly
along party lines.[63] Perhaps repeal should be ascribed to a general
anti-intellectualism. A tutor at South Carolina College wrote of
this episode, from information he received while visiting Chapel
Hill:

A few years ago the Pres[ident] the Professors and the Tutors
were all Federalists. The first graduates for 2 or 3 years (at least
the likeliest scholars of them) were likewise federalists. In a
short course of time a number of these graduates obtained seats
in the Legislature and discovered talents that the rude, illiterate
mass of old members either envied or feared. Under the ostensible motive of discouraging Federalism in the College (but
really as Mr. H. says for fear of losing their influence in the
Legrs.) these old members carried a measure for taking away

from the Univ[ersity] all the escheated property that had not yet been appropriated.[64]

William R. Davie blamed the vindictive act on "a sort of Gothic ignorance and political fanaticism [which] are the fashionable order of the day."[65] When he was unable to salvage his own political career from the tide of democracy, he retired from politics and left the state altogether in 1805.

Unquestionably, the action of the legislature proved that the university was unpopular not just in the state capital but also with the public. One recent study has traced this dislike to religious sectarianism, stating that "by 1800 Presbyterians so thoroughly controlled the school that pressure was brought upon the legislature by other denominations and by deists to annul the land grant."[66] The problem with this interpretation, apart from a total lack of evidence to support it, is that the defection of McCorkle, the leading Presbyterian clergyman, and his repeated criticisms of the university, lead to the opposite conclusion. Offered the presidency again after the riot, he disdainfully refused. In doing so he denounced "the modern French Jacobine system of Education" infesting the institution. He deplored the abolition of his Sunday-evening religious examinations and found evidence of Jacobinism in the riot. "It seems as if religion [had] abandoned the University," he lamented.[67] Bishop Pettigrew, leader of the Episcopalians, would have agreed. It was not sectarianism but infidelity that was blamed.

The truth seems to be that a major cause of the legislature's aboutface was the student riot of 1799. In a letter to the General Assembly urging reconsideration of the annulment, Acting President Joseph Caldwell reviewed the legislators' thinking. After going over again the old fears that the university would lead to a monarchy or create an aristocracy, he devoted much of his defense to the behavior of the students:

You are industrious to search out every boyish trick which you can come to the knowledge of, and you do not fail to paint every act in the deepest colors of criminality and corruption. The whole body is indiscriminately reviled by you as a herd of undisciplined people who are universally intent on mischief and outrage. Now gentlemen, we all know . . . that young men collected together under the rules of morality and college discipline, are apt to feel the restraints irksome and tedious to which they are subjected . . . can it be possible that any reasonable man on this account should think it necessary to abuse or destroy such an institution entirely, as wholly injurious, and unattended with any benefit? . . . How dreadful, how unjust, how hard it is that calumny must be forever watching as with a lynx's eye the disorders of a few wrongheaded young people.[68]

Looking back a few years later, Caldwell still blamed the riot for the university's decline:

The lapse of three or four years [after 1799] was necessary before public confidence could be restored, and the number of students could be made to ascend by slow degrees to fifty. These were dark and trying times. The youth of our state had given the strongest reasons to conclude from their conduct as students, that they were incapable of being governed.[69]

The riot not only harmed the university's reputation but also led to basic changes there. More by default than design, Professor Caldwell became head of the institution, serving as acting president till he was voted full rank in 1804. Although a Presbyterian clergyman, Caldwell was not a militant evangelical counterreformer of the Jedidiah Morse stamp. True, he warned his students of "the frigid determinations of reason" and Godwin's "visionary theory of benevolence," but he never accused his student rebels of being Jacobins or tried to marshall the undergraduates into religious societies in hopes of fostering a campus revival.[70] Caldwell's problem was to find support for an unpopular college. His solution was to pursue a middle course between McCorkle's ultra-Presbyterianism and Davie's enlightened utilitarianism. Shortly after he became president, the trustees dismantled Davie's liberal plan of study. Latin and Greek were restored in freshman and sophomore years.[71] The English diploma for nonclassical studies was also abolished, though nondegree students were still admitted, in contrast to Princeton where "irregular students" were barred outright in 1809. These changes stripped the university of its distinct identity. Henceforth it would be indistinguishable from the other colleges: another Princeton, only less eminent.

Whether as America's first state university or as one of the experiments with "republican education," the University of North Carolina had to be accounted a failure. As "A Gentleman at Raleigh" described it in 1806, "the institution now languishes; Mr. Caldwell's anti-republican love of literature, and not the emoluments of his office, induces him to preserve in existence by his influence even the shadow of a college. He is assisted by only one tutor; the funds do not permit the employment of more."[72] Fortunately, the North Carolina Court of Conferences ruled in *University* v. *Foy* (1805) that repeal of the revenue laws was unconstitutional, a legal precedent later used by Daniel Webster in the famous Dartmouth College Case. This forced the state to return the appropriations, but no one could mend the estrangement between university and legislature.

North Carolina's troubled venture into state education set a poor precedent for other states. Though more and more state universities were founded, "the states rarely assumed responsibility for the institutions they called to life."[73] Perhaps there never had been a public commitment to higher education at this time.[74] If North Carolina's pioneer endeavor had been a great success, however, it is at least possible that the course of American higher education would have been vastly different. As it was, growing up amid public hostility and indifference, the university gave up its original ambition of leavening society and simply tried to withstand the leveling tendencies of the times. In North Carolina, culture and learning were on the defensive.

PIOUS IGNORANCE AT PRINCETON

The College of New Jersey, as it was still called — Princeton — was the child of the Great Awakening of the 1740s. It was founded in the first place to promote piety. Harvard and Yale had supposedly fallen into a spiritual torpor; the English evangelist George Whitefield had said of them, "as for the Universities, I believe, it may be said, Their Light is now become Darkness, Darkness that may be felt."[75] Hitherto evangelical New Side Presbyterian clergymen had been trained in William Tennent's Log College, but the conservative Old Side Presbyterians had refused to accredit his school. To escape the charge of being ignorant "enthusiasts" as well as to provide a formal training for its clergy, the New Side founded Princeton in 1746. From 1741 to 1758 the Presbyterian church had been split in two. The Old Side, called pharisee-teachers by their opponents, stressed centralization, dogma, and control. The New Side demanded a clergy who had known the new birth. One side represented the letter, the other the spirit, of the Gospel. Not only did Princeton from the beginning contain an unstable tension between piety and intellect, but after 1758 when the two sides of the church were rejoined in a "union without love," the college had to find a means of reconciling the conflicting claims of each side.[76]

The arrival of President-elect John Witherspoon from Scotland in 1768 marked a compromise between the two sides and symbolized the coming of the Scottish Enlightenment to the college. Witherspoon not only redirected the college during the quarter century of his presidency but also played an important role in national affairs, being the only minister to sign the Declaration of Independence. His mission as an educator, as he perceived it, was "to unite together piety and literature — to show their relation to,

and their influence one upon another—and to guard against anything that may tend to separate them, and set them in opposition
one to another."[77] He widened the outlook of ministerial candidates by adding eloquence, belles-lettres, moral philosophy, Hebrew, French, and history to the curriculum. "There is no branch
of literature without its use," he explained. "If it were possible for
a minister to be acquainted with every branch, he would be more
fit for public usefulness." This faith in the compatibility of human
reason and Christian revelation was a defining trait of the American Enlightenment. It gave Witherspoon confidence in his efforts
to extend the design of the college to accommodate the needs of
the new country's rising political and professional leaders without
fear of cutting Princeton's ties to the Presbyterian church. Thus,
whereas about half of Princeton's graduates before Witherspoon's
arrival had entered the ministry, during his administration this
proportion fell to 23 percent; and of his graduates from 1777 to
1794 only 13 percent were ordained.[78] Public service was slowly but
surely overtaking piety, but no one as yet had complained.

Witherspoon's successor in 1795, Samuel Stanhope Smith, was
the epitome of the clerical man-of-letters. When the Presbyterian
clergyman Archibald Alexander first met Smith at the General
Assembly of 1791 he was forcibly but doubtfully impressed: "I saw
a person whom I must still consider the most elegant I ever saw . . .
The thought never occurred to me that he was a clergyman, and I
supposed him to be some gentleman of Philadelphia."[79] Alexander
would later side with Smith's opponents. The students were equally
struck by their president: "the Doctor I think is very much of a
gentleman, he lives elegantly."[80] But Smith's hauteur alienated
many people. As one of his recent graduates explained, "Smith
has been long known to be an aristocrat and he is not of such con-
ciliating manners as to have avoided the creating some personal
enemies."[81] When Yale's Benjamin Silliman visited Princeton in
1803, he found Smith "noble and commanding," but added
"there was a stately gravity about him which did not encourage
freedom, and I felt much constrained in his society."[82]

Intellectually, too, Smith was controversial. His serious scholar-ship was unrivaled but he was also a dilettante. Throughout his life he toyed with ideas with little fear of arming or alarming his enemies. As a Princeton tutor he had espoused Berkeleyan ideal-ism till converted to Scottish Common Sense by President Wither-spoon. Later he carried on a flirtatious literary correspondence with his cousin by marriage, Susan Shipton Blair, until it caused a minor scandal.[83] Affecting indifference to such criticisms, he wrote to Mrs. Blair: "A man may hold opinions either as certain or dubious: And if they differ from the opinions of too great a major-ity of the people, prudence & duty require him to hold them in si-lence . . . *Truth* held in secret has its pleasures."[84] What the trust-ees wondered was just how many secret things the President be-lieved.

Smith's enemies used his intellectual indiscretions to undermine his position. In 1804 reports reached the trustees that in his lec-tures Smith had said that polygamy and concubinage were not really moral evils. One of his students was engaged as a spy to re-port the truth. It turned out that Smith was speculating with a kind of moral relativism, carefully pointing out that some Old Testament patriarchs had apparently engaged in such practice. Still, the matter did not rest easy with the trustees. Doubts about Smith's soundness were increased a few years later when someone told the trustees that he had recommended to his pupils the alleg-edly Arminian works of the Scottish philosopher Thomas Reid. Smith compounded his difficulties in his later years by engaging in new theorizing on the most abstruse and controversial of all theo-logical questions — predestination and free will. When his specula-tions were attacked, he lashed out at his critics. "Some of my opin-ions are too philosophical for several of my brethren who are so deadly orthodox," he wrote Benjamin Rush.[85]

Yet he also felt compelled to justify his scholarship on religious grounds, almost to apologize for it. His major work, *An Essay on the Causes of the Variety of Complexion and Figure in the Human Species* (1787), was a pioneering exploration in cultural anthropology which reaffirmed the unity of mankind and undercut racial arguments for Negro slavery. In the expanded 1810 edition he wrote,

> If any person shall enquire why a writer who has so many other duties to fulfill more immediately relative to the sacred functions of his profession, should devote so much time to studies which seem only remotely connected with the offices of piety peculiarly belonging to a christian minister, I hope it will be a satisfactory answer; that infidelity, driven from her moral grounds of objection against the gospel, has lately bent her principal force to oppose the system of nature to that of revelation . . . While others, therefore, are successfully defending the interior fortresses of religion, I thought that I might render a valuable service to the cause, by cooperating, in some degree, with those who are defending her out works, and carrying their attacks into the enemy's camp.[86]

Obviously, in the religious climate following the crisis of 1798, Smith was on the defensive. His position was made more uncomfortable by the fact that he too deplored the leveling and divisiveness and irreligiousness of American society—to him too society seemed out of joint. But Smith was a man of the Age of Reason and not of the nineteenth-century reaction to it. Witherspoon and Smith had flourished at a time when the danger to religion had seemed to come from uncontrolled emotion. Now that Reason was the enemy, he was not the man for the times.

The significance of Smith's dilemma was that he was a leading proponent of "republican education." In 1796 he had proposed that study of the dead languages cease after the freshman year. Although he failed to achieve this, he won an important concession from the trustees in 1799 when a special category of students was created—called "irregulars"—to study only those scientific and literary courses they deemed useful to their professional careers. The plan resembled that of William R. Davie at the University of North Carolina, though irregular students would not receive a special diploma but only a certificate of proficiency in the studies they had mastered. It was a step toward the elective system and the bachelor of science degree.

The Achilles' heel for both Smith and his reforms was the students' violence, most of which has already been described. Two riots in 1800, the Nassau Hall burning in 1802, "a great deal of confusion in College" in 1804 with the students "once or twice very near rebelling," the great rebellion of 1807 which saw two more attempts to burn the college, serious disorders in 1809 when yet another case of arson was reported—this record was perhaps the worst of any college in this time.[87] Throughout the period the student unrest was attributed to radicalism and irreligion. Smith himself had been one of the first to ascribe resistance to this source and he continued to do so. In 1808 he wrote hopefully to an alumnus: "the remains of Jacobinism appear to be totally extirpated, and our system is, the moment it shews its head, to drive it off before it produces any corruption."[88]

What were the students so unhappy about? William Garnett, a young Virginian, left a detailed list of his grievances after he dropped out in 1804. He said that the students were publicly humiliated for trivial reasons. Treated like children they lost respect for themselves and acted accordingly. Compilations and abridgments were assigned rather than original sources. And monarchist principles were inculcated, while republicans were stigmatized as Jacobins and disorganizers. When Smith learned of Garnett's criticisms, he made disparaging remarks about his character which almost led to a duel and a newspaper war.[89]

Smith's anger carried over to Thomas Ruffin, one of Garnett's friends. Ruffin's father wrote him, "I am much hurt at Docr. Smith's conduct towards you . . . I have no doubt but Smith is a man possessing uncommonly strong passions, which for want of Vital Religion are indulged to a dangerous excess." That is, the parent, like the trustees, thought Smith too rationalistic and not evangelical enough. He counseled his son "to be silent on his *Ty-*

ranical whims." Rather than find him too harsh on discipline, however, he agreed with the trustees in finding him too soft. When a large bomb went off on campus he wrote:

> I was astonished that such conduct should take place at that seminary, but much more so that the transgressors should escape punishment; and can only account for it in one way, (which however may be erroneous) viz, that the principals were great favorites of the Professors, and rather than make an example of them, the whole were permitted to escape. Should this be the case, I shall entertain a more unfavorable opinion of Smith than before, which I am sorry to say was not a good one.

Such was Smith's parental support.[90]

These insurrections had a disastrous effect upon the college. There had been about 200 students in 1806. In late 1807 there remained only 112. This figure remained about the same until 1810 when attendance fell below the hundred mark. Since tuition and board were the main sources of revenue, the drop in attendance forced a cutback in offerings. In 1806 the total income from students was about $11,500; in 1808 it was only $6,500. After an increase in tuition, it was still only $8,500 in 1812.[91] Less tangible but ultimately more harmful, the trustees and the Presbyterian community lost confidence in the college. Professorships which came open were left unfilled, and no new programs were added.[92]

Presbyterians were having second thoughts about ministerial education and losing faith in Witherspoon's Enlightenment alliance between science and religion. In New England, Congregationalists were setting up a separate theological seminary at Andover to make up for the loss of Harvard. The idea that clergymen should receive a special education in isolation from the corrupting influence of other students appealed to Presbyterians as well. After the 1807 rebellion, Samuel Miller predicted "our General Assembly will, doubtless, in a few years, institute a seminary of its own, unless Princeton College should be placed on a better footing."[93] The attitude toward science had also changed. The Reverend Archibald Alexander told the General Assembly: "the great extension of the physical sciences and the taste and fashion of the age, have given such a shape and direction to the academical course that I confess it appears to me to be little adapted to introduce youth to the study of the Sacred Scriptures."[94] Support for a seminary came from unexpected quarters. Benjamin Rush endorsed it becaue it would "prevent candidates for the ministry being infected with the follies and vices of young men educated for secular professions or ridiculed by them for their piety." He added that "no one of the Latin nor Greek poets should be read in these schools, by which means a pious ignorance will be preserved of the crimes of heathen gods and men." "Nor," he went on, "should moral philosophy be taught."[95] Rush's phrase — "pious ignorance" — perfectly expressed the shrinking ideal of ministerial education. The seminary builders were most concerned with negatives — what the students would not read, not learn, not do.

Aware that abandonment by the church might well destroy the college, Smith and the trustees vainly tried to stem the seminary movement. In a statement to the General Assembly of 1806, Smith pointed out all the advantages from financial assistance and special instruction which students of divinity enjoyed in the college.[96] In a special address "On the Utility and Necessity of Learning in a Minister of the Gospel," Smith demanded of his opponents: "is not the duty of those who propose to devote themselves to the ministry of the gospel, to bestow great pains in the acquisition of literature and science?"[97] To make the college safer, the trustees abolished Smith's "irregular studies" in 1809. By this time Smith himself seems to have lost faith in this plan, perhaps blaming it for student unrest. In 1806 he counseled an entering student that being an irregular student "is by no means a respectable station in this Seminary."[98]

Although Smith and the trustees failed to prevent the establishment of a separate theological seminary, they succeeded in having it erected adjacent to the college. From this time on, however, the seminary was the favorite of the church and the college was its "wayward stepchild."[99] The founders of the seminary had a conception of the ministry that was antithetical to Smith's. In his inaugural address for the seminary's first professor of theology, Archibald Alexander, Samuel Miller declared:

> O my fathers and brethren! let it never be said of us, . . . that we take more pains to make polite scholars, eloquent orators, or men of *mere learning,* than to form able and faithful ministers of the New Testament. Let it never be said, that we are more anxious to maintain the literary and scientific honours of the ministry, than we are to promote that honour which consists in being *full of faith* and of the Holy Ghost.[100]

It was an obvious repudiation of Smith and all he stood for. It was a far cry from Smith's conception of a religion "more charming & consolatory for being associated with the pictures of taste."[101] The establishment of the seminary on these ideals marked a small but significant shift in American culture. By this time, according to one historian, "disciplinary problems . . . appear to have added force to the growing suspicion that Smith's intellectual and theological ideas were not reliable."[102] His days were clearly numbered.

The opening of the seminary was used to justify a thorough housecleaning of the college. First Professor John Maclean was asked to resign. Maclean was a chemist brought to the campus by Smith as part of his republican-education reforms in the 1790s. Then Smith himself was forced out. They were not simply victims of college politics but of powerful sectarian impulses in American education. A contemporary noted that Smith was "considered too rational and catholic for the purposes of this Seminary." "These Presbyterian gentlemen," he charged, "are driving back with full sail into the ignorance and bigotry of the dark ages."[103] Gone, too, were Smith's reforms: irregular studies and science. Eighteenth-century gentlemen like Smith inevitably saw these changes as regressive. As Smith complained, "I too often see austerity, gloom, and harsh suspicion, where candor, taste, and benevolent sentiments once prevailed."[104] The Enlightenment was over at Princeton.

DISAPPOINTED CONFIDENCE
AT JEFFERSON'S VIRGINIA

By 1810 republican education had nearly been routed. Not only had it failed at Princeton, William and Mary, and the University of North Carolina, but even institutions such as Columbia which had never dropped the classics were raising their standards and requirements in the ancient languages.[105] Dissatisfaction with the traditional curriculum reemerged in the 1820s in the guise of the "parallel" course of study, a resurrection of Davie's dual plan of English and Latin studies. Though most of these efforts also failed, for a time they amounted to a considerable educational reform movement. The parallel course was adopted at Miami University (1825), Hobart College (1825), Amherst (1826), Union College (1828), Hampden-Sydney (1828), Columbia (1830), Wesleyan (1831), and the University of the City of New York (1832).[106] The story of these endeavors belongs for the most part to a later period — to the battle between traditional culture and Jacksonian democracy rather than to the Enlightenment struggle between Reason and Revelation.

There was one departure in these years, however, which really belonged to the earlier period — the University of Virginia. The university's founder, Thomas Jefferson, had long deplored the domination of higher education by Federalism and "priestcraft." Having failed to revitalize William and Mary, he devoted the last years of his life to enshrining republicanism in his own university. "It is in our seminary," he proclaimed, "that the vestal flame is to be kept alive; from thence it is to spread anew over our own and the sister States."[107] Jefferson later listed the university, the Declaration of Independence, and the Virginia Statute of Religious Freedom as the three great accomplishments of his life for which he wished to be remembered. The founding of the university was thus the last experiment in republican education, and it too came upon the rocks of student revolt.

At its conception the university was a seeming paradox: an intolerantly liberal institution. Jefferson has been taken to task for forsaking his faith in free enquiry and creating the university as an instrument of his party, to inculcate Republicanism as he understood it. Jefferson insisted that the Board of Visitors censor "Tory" textbooks and guarantee that the professor of law always be "a strict constructionist, states' rights advocate of the old Dominion school." In truth, "the aged Jefferson had soured."[108]

The university was designed on a grand scale. An annual grant of $15,000 from the Virginia Literary Fund insured that the college would enjoy financial support. Its students were expected to meet high standards. No one under sixteen was to be admitted. The elective principle would allow students to choose their own course of study and to come and go as they liked. Lectures rather than recitation made up the class work. Since this required a competent faculty, Jefferson imported many of the professors from Europe when American scholars of equal repute could not be obtained. The university was to be a center of advanced study almost like a graduate school. There were eight independent "schools": Ancient Languages, Modern Languages, Mathematics, Natural Philosophy, Natural History, Anatomy and Medicine, Moral Philosophy, and Law. One subject was missing, however. "In our University you know there is no Professorship of Divinity," Jefferson explained to Thomas Coooper. "A handle has been made of this, to disseminate an idea that this is an institution, not merely of no religion, but against all religion."[109] The hostility of the religious community was to prove a formidable obstacle in the early years.

Having closely observed the fate of other colleges, Jefferson was most apprehensive about the problem of student discipline. He recognized that college riots were both more frequent and more serious now than in his own days at William and Mary before the Revolution.[110] To the famous Harvard educator George Ticknor he wrote, "the rock which I most dread is the discipline of the institution, and it is that on which most of our public schools labor."[111] Reasoning that uprisings at other colleges were caused by their strict and puritanical regulations, he worked out an alternative for his university deriving from his principle that that government is best which governs least. In the same letter to Ticknor he said, "we may lessen the difficulty by avoiding too much government, by requiring no useless observances, none which shall merely multiply occasions for dissatisfaction, disobedience, and revolt." He went even further and planned the first experiment in student self government in American history. This policy is particularly significant because historians have suggested that student self-government was the logical solution to student unrest. Jefferson proposed that a court be set up at the university with powers equal to those of other state courts on which a board of student censors would sit in judgment over their peers. There would be a university jail—less ominous than it sounded, designed to protect students from the ignominy of public incarceration. And, as in European universities, a proctor with the authority of a justice of the peace would police the campus, freeing professors from the degrading duties of a "beadle," as St. George Tucker had put it. The university's government would be more respected because it would have more power; it would be less resented because it would be run by the students themselves.

Aware of the precedent being set, students viewed the opening of the university as the dawning of a new day. Edmund Hubbard, one of the original undergraduates, wrote that "everything that I saw surpassed my most sanguine expectations—and I felt as if I should have been suddenly transported into some climate more suitable for Literature than what I had formerly been accustomed to." His correspondent at Presbyterian Hampden-Sydney enviously compared his own college with the new university:

> In the one we see that close and contracted spirit in the admin-istration of the affairs of the institution without the least dispo-sition to accomodate; while in the other we see a liberality of disposition, a true characteristic of the principles on which our [national] institutions are founded, or to come to the point, the traits of the yankee [Puritan] character developed in the one & those of the imagination in the other.

But Hubbard found too many of his classmates unworthy of this opportunity. A good number, he wrote in a later letter, were idlers, gamblers, liars, and cheats.[112]

Although some form of university government was quickly needed, the plan of student self-government broke down. Part of the fault lay with the legislature, which neglected to create the court, proctorship, or jail which Jefferson sought. Part of the blame lay with the faculty for offering no guidance. But the stu-dents themselves must bear the brunt of the responsibility, for they either would not or could not govern themselves. Campus disor-ders broke out on June 22, August 5, and September 19 of the very first year. The students were angry that the administration had re-fused to give them an additional summer vacation. On the night of September 30 a bottle of urine was thrown through a professor's window. The next evening, October 1, fourteen students disguised in masks met on the lawn where they were spotted by two members of the faculty. When the professors tried to detain them, the stu-dents cursed them and resisted. A brick was thrown at one, while the other was attacked with a cane. In the noisy confusion one stu-dent cried, "Down with the European Professors!"

The next day, even before the faculty had met to take action, the students presented them with a resolution signed by sixty-five of the students avowing that they refused to testify against each other concerning the riot. The entire altercation was blamed on the professors who had supposedly ganged up on one of the students. "The whole language of the remonstrance was highly objectionable," in the opinion of the faculty. Two of the European professors handed in resignations, stating that they had lost all confidence in the signers of the remonstrance. They were backed by the rest of the faculty who wrote to the Board of Visitors threatening "to resign unless an efficient Police were immediately established in the University."[113]

On this same day, the students were called before the Board of Visitors, which happened to be in session at nearby Monticello. Never before or after could there be such an august disciplinary board. Three former Presidents were present — Thomas Jefferson, James Madison, and James Monroe. According to an undergraduate there at the time: "Jefferson rose to address the students. He began by declaring that it was one of the most painful events of his life, but he had not gone far before his feelings overcame him, and he sat down."[114] He was followed by Chapman Johnson, head of the Bar in Virginia. He called on the rioters to come forward and all fourteen did so, including Jefferson's own nephew. Of this one of the professors observed, "the shock which Mr. Jefferson felt when he, for the first time, discovered that the efforts of the last ten years of his life had been foiled by one of his family, was more than his own patience could endure, and he could not forebear using, for the first time, the language of indignation and reproach."[115]

As a result of the riot, four students were expelled and several others admonished. Naturally, the disturbance fueled suspicions of the university. One clergyman from Fredericksburg wrote, "I regard it as a School in infidelity — a nursery of bad principles . . . You have probably heard some intimations of the disturbances, which prevailed there lately."[116] Attendance continued to fall far below the three hundred Jefferson had predicted. Those who came usually stayed only a year and left without a degree because they were unable to meet the academic standards. Although the

two European professors who had threatened to resign were per-
suaded to stay, one of them left a year later in similar circum-
stances. Only the curriculum and elective principle remained un-
scathed.

The greatest change coming out of the riot was abolition of student government. The Board of Visitors immediately composed a
strict code of student laws. Jefferson himself wrote an accompany-
ing statement to the students. Henceforth, he said, the civil magistrate would be called in to restrain and punish student offenders.
In this manner "habits of obedience to the laws" would become "a
proper part of education and practice."[117] His words to the students summarized the reaction of all four "republican" institutions to disorders: "coercion must be resorted to where confidence
has been disappointed." Time would show that coercion worked
no better. The violence which shook the campus in the 1830s and
1840s ultimately ended in the death of a professor. It was fortunate that Jefferson did not live to see this. His confidence in shaping American youth had suffered enough disappointment.

CHAPTER SEVEN

Little Temples of Prayer

THE DOWNFALL OF republican education coincided with the spread of the evangelical movement in the colleges. This was a part of the Second Great Awakening. Academics hoped that this religious awakening would save their schools from vice and irreligion. When student rebellions infected a college, revivals were prescribed as the cure. The first of these student revivals was at Yale in 1802, followed by others at Williams in 1805-1806, 1812, and 1815, at Middlebury in 1805-1806, 1809, and 1811, at Dartmouth in 1805 and 1815, and at Yale again in 1808, 1811-1812, and 1815. Soon an institution was not considered "safe" until it had fostered at least one such revival.

In the nation, the revivals were accompanied by an outpouring of religious literature and the founding of voluntary reform societies. Likewise, in the colleges there was a tremendous growth of student religious associations. Only Harvard and Yale had had such organizations in the 1790s, but after the turn of the century new groups were established at Dartmouth (1801), Brown (1802), Williams (1804), Bowdoin (1806), Middlebury (1808), Dickinson (1811), and Princeton (1813). These societies met in secret at first to escape persecution from rowdies. But these small bands of devout undergraduates had a disproportionately great influence. After an 1806 revival at Williams, for example, five of the pious students held the legendary Haystack Meeting at which they vowed to devote their lives to missionary work in foreign nations. In 1808 they created the Society of Brethren, perhaps America's first intercollegiate student organization. The founding of the nation's first Foreign Missionary Sending Society was a direct result of their efforts. Two of the Brethren sailed for Calcutta in 1812, the first in a long line of American missionaries.[1]

There was a direct relationship between campus evangelism and the problem of student revolt. Some historians have even implied that academics espoused revivalism primarily as a tool for restoring discipline.[2] Although this is too cynical a view of academic motivations, it is true that revivals brought temporary respite from rebellions and were therefore seen as antidotes to disorders. The subject of student revolt of necessity includes this important religious backlash.

Ironically, the effects of revivals were often as disruptive as student resistance at its worst. The psychological trauma of conversion might impair the health of anxious undergraduates. It might also lead to the physical "exercises" and "enthusiasms" witnessed at Cane Ridge and other frontier camp meetings. Most academics disapproved of these excesses but were not always able to prevent them. Revivals also brought different student factions into conflict. A Williams alumnus recalled: "the moment a sinner began to have serious thoughts the wicked would load him with ridicule and abuse."[3] In fairness to the "wicked," it must have been rather frightening to watch one's fellows writhing under a conviction of sin and feel pressured to act the same. During an 1812 revival at Williams a stalwart band of young sinners stubbornly "warded off their convictions by drinking secretly, and by card playing."[4] Finally, revivals were controversial and met resistance in many communities. In such cases, the battle for control between reformers and conservatives was sometimes of lasting significance in the history of higher education. Not every college passed through the throes of a revival or the midwifery of an evangelical president. Those that did, however, would never be the same.

YALE'S UNFASHIONABLE EDUCATION

Controversial as it is, there is no substitute for Lyman Beecher's account of the arrival of Timothy Dwight at Yale in 1795. Beecher (Yale 1797) recalled:

> Before he came college was in a most ungodly state. The college church was almost extinct. Most of the students were skeptical, and rowdies were plenty. Wine and liquors were kept in many rooms; intemperance, profanity, gambling, and licentiousness were common . . .
> Most of the classes before me were infidels, and called each other Voltaire, Rousseau, D'Alembert, etc. etc.
> They thought the Faculty were afraid of free discussion. But when they handed Dr. Dwight a list of subjects for class disputation, to their surprise he selected this: "Is the Bible the word of God?" and told them to do their best.
> He heard all they had to say, answered them, and there was an end. He preached incessantly for six months on the subject, and all infidelity skulked and hid its head.[5]

Beecher may have underestimated the accomplishments of Dwight's predecessor, Ezra Stiles,[6] but there is no denying that Yale enjoyed a powerful religious awakening under President Dwight. Yale's 1802 student revival, the first in a major institution since the 1780s, led to others in 1808, 1811-1812, and 1815. Because Dwight's Yale became a model for other evangelical colleges, it is important to examine the formula of Dwight's success and to evaluate the nature of his achievement.

Dwight's Yale had fewer disciplinary problems than Harvard, Princeton, or other colleges. He attributed his success to the "parental character" of the college government.[7] Rather than rely exclusively on printed rules and formal trials the government privately admonished wrongdoers to reform. If this failed, the government enlisted parents to try to effect a change. If nothing worked, the recalcitrant student was summarily dismissed. The obvious advantage of the system was that there was little need to interrogate classmates and no opportunity for undergraduates to protest — there being no set procedures the faculty was bound to follow. By ridding the college of troublemakers with dispatch, collective resistance was avoided. Yet Yale was by no means immune from unrest. Three years before Princeton created its bursar, Yale placed out-of-state students under the care of a patron to insure that no unauthorized debts were incurred. In 1810 a rule was passed preventing the questioning of a student by his fellows as to whether he had testified to the faculty about campus disorders. There were forty pages of student rules on the books in 1817.

But Yale students never rebelled against Dwight or his authority. Rather, their riots were aimed at New Haven's "town boys" and sailors. There were town-gown riots in 1799, 1806, and 1812.[8] Why did the college escape these outbursts? The principal reason is that Dwight was a popular and inspiring college head. An intense, impressive man, with impaired eyesight as proof of his own youthful intellectual exertions, Dwight presented education to his students as a heroic, manly endeavor. "The faculties of the mind," he said, "like those of the body, acquire strength, only by exercise." "Fashionable education" — novels, plays, voyages, biographies, and even some histories — enervated the mind and left it prey to "modern philosophy." Intellectual greatness, on the other hand, could only be acquired by "the most vigorous mental exertions" — "hard study, a thorough investigation of mathematical science, and a resolute attention to the most powerful efforts of distinguished Logicians; in a word, *an old-fashioned rigid, academical education.*"[9] Dwight's enthusiasm was catching. "He is a truly great man," young Benjamin Silliman wrote of his teacher.

"When I hear him speak, it makes me feel like a very insignificant being, and almost prompts me to despair; but I am reencouraged when I reflect that he was once as ignorant as myself, and that learning is only to be acquired by long and assiduous application."[10]

Dwight was also fortunate in having America's most pious student body. Evangelicals like Jedidiah Morse and Eliphalet Pearson sent their sons to Yale and kept a close eye on their behavior. Young Samuel F. B. Morse, the famous painter and inventor of the telegraph, knew quite well that Montaigne's "Essays" were "wicked and bad books for me or anybody else to read." In 1808 he promised his parents to "make those only my companions who are the most religious and moral."[11] When young Pearson remained on campus during a vacation, his father warned him:

> called to no daily regular exercise, and left without the kind inspection of Mr. Day, you will be in danger of indulging in sloth, idleness, & dissipation, three enemies of all excellence. This danger also will be greatly increased by the great number of scholars from a distance, particularly from the southward, who will remain on the ground; many of whom will be sauntering about from room to room, chattering about trifles, insinuating false & injurious ideas and maxims, proposing diversions & amusements, and thus enticing the unwary into erroneous & hurtful practices. Of all such characters I must solemnly charge you to be awfully aware, and shun as a pestilence their pestiferous company. Set your face resolutely against every species of vice & irregularity, and select for your companions the most studious, wise, and pious.

The death of young Pearson's tutor shortly after this made the situation of the son extremely precarious, according to the father. Soon thereafter in fact young Pearson fell from grace by using profanity and carrying a pack of cards![12]

Intellectually, Dwight's Yale offered an unending indoctrination against French philosophy. The president used every weapon he could find, fair or foul. In his 1797 analysis of "The Nature and Dangers of Infidel Philosophy," he concluded that if modern philosophers had their way: "the seat of Justice would be the nest of plunder and robbery, and the edifices of learning cells of studied iniquity, where methodized sin would be the science . . . The private dwelling would be converted into a brothel . . . and the purity, the happiness, and the hopes of mankind, would be buried under a promiscuous and universal concubinage." On other occasions, he charged that modern philosophers "bewilder the mind, by using terms without any meaning at all, or a very loose one," or that they "rarely attempt to argue; but generally attack with ridicule." Had his message been exclusively negative, it might have fallen on deaf ears. But rather than dampen the idealism of his students, he rechanneled it into Christian reform. Human progress came only through religion, he asserted. Christianity had "clearly and essentially improved the condition of men in a great number of ways"—by condemning the slave trade, elevating women, providing for education and poor relief, advancing science, and creating international rules of war." This is an evangelical age, he advised his graduating seniors: "This divine spirit, this breath from heaven, has breathed upon your own land. The dead here awake . . . Catch this divine influence yourselves!"[13]

For all his emphasis on religion, Dwight was not really theologically oriented. Regarded by some as a spokesman for the New Divinity Movement, he inherited this position rather than earned it, being the grandson of Jonathan Edwards, the movement's patron saint. Dwight simply was not overworried with logical consistency and metaphysical paradox. The thrust of his preaching was essentially pragmatic: what mattered was that listeners were saved, not so much how it happened. He stressed the "human agency" in salvation and the social obligations of the saved. "The law of God consists in two commands," he told his students, "to love him with all the heart, and our own neighbor as ourselves. These counsels every one of you has repeatedly broken; but there are two other commands, by which you can obtain eternal life. They are these, believe in the Lord Jesus Christ, and repent of your sins."[14]

The highpoints of Dwight's years were the four revivals. They were part of a much larger movement in Connecticut and the nation, and not all the credit belongs to the president. But his "affecting" preaching, his weekly Meetings for Inquiry, and his spiritual counseling all contributed to this end. In the spring of 1802 more than eighty undergraduates grew solemn and grave and concerned about the future of their souls. Within a few weeks sixty-three new members were added to the college church.[15] With membership still restricted to the elect, this meant that they had undergone a conversion, which often entailed intense, morbid introspection.

The process of receiving grace involved two general steps. First, the soul sank under the weight of its sins and a sense of total depravity. Then, after days or even weeks of psychological suffering, the afflicted gained an assurance of his salvation and felt a joyful release from the bondage of sin. When assurance did not come, however, a revival could be both physically and emotionally damaging. In 1802 one student was temporarily "distressed," but the revival as a whole was free from bizarre physical exercises or antinomian heresies. In 1808, however, Dwight nearly lost a student who was confined to his bed and thought to be on the verge of death after weeks of religious despair. The president rushed to his pupil's side when he learned of his state and directed his mind to the all-powerful love of God. This was no time for theological nicety on the question of predestination versus human means. Dwight recited Gospel promises of salvation and prayed for the deliverance of the lad. As he prayed, the student felt "a sweet serenity" steal over his soul and soon enjoyed the full joy of salvation.[16] In less capable hands, these traumas proved far more dangerous.

Ideally, revivals were supposed to bring peace and order to a college. That is what made the 1802 revival so memorable. Mills Day wrote home that "the utmost order and regularity prevails."[17]

At first a few students had ridiculed the spread of "enthusiasm" in the college, but they were quickly silenced. According to tutor Benjamin Silliman, "Yale College is a little temple: prayer and praise seem to be the delight of the greater part of the students, while those who are still unfeeling are awed into respectful silence."[18] Classes and instruction continued. Dwight himself boasted that "the state of Yale-College is, in the view of the Instructors, more pleasing and desirable than at any former period within their knowledge."[19]

The other criterion for evaluating a campus revival was the number of ministers it produced. Thirty-five of the 1802 student converts became clergymen, almost one-third of the class. For the entire period 1805 to 1815, however, when there were three revivals, less than 18 percent of the graduates entered the ministry, as compared with 25 percent for 1778-1792, 30 percent for 1745-1777, and 50 percent before 1745.[20] Yale, like Princeton, in other words, was undergoing a secular trend which all of Dwight's revivals could not reverse.

The revivals had their greatest impact in shaping Yale's future faculty. The college was almost completely inbred. Jeremiah Day, Dwight's successor in 1817, Benjamin Silliman, founder of the *American Journal of Science,* John L. Kingsley, co-author of the *Yale Report* of 1828, Eleazer Thompson Fitch, professor of divinity, Chauncey Allen Goodrich, professor of rhetoric, and Nathaniel William Taylor, of the Divinity School, all Yale alumni, were either students or tutors or both under Dwight. For half a century these men carried on Dwight's religious ideals. Silliman taught from 1802 to 1853, Kingsley from 1801 to 1851, Taylor from 1822 to 1858, Goodrich from 1817 to 1860. They had all been deeply affected by the revivals. Silliman had been converted in the revival of 1802, Goodrich and Fitch in that of 1808. Dwight's handpicked men, they bore his unmistakable impress. Taylor, the greatest Calvinist theologican of ante-bellum America, had lived in Dwight's home as an undergraduate and served as his amanuensis.

His espousal of religious revivals and his wish to make Calvinism palatable to nineteenth-century democracy were both in Dwight's tradition of pragmatic Calvinism. It was fitting that when Taylor entered Yale Divinity School it was as Dwight Professor of Didactic Theology, a chair endowed especially for Taylor by the son of Timothy Dwight.

Dwight's recruitment of Benjamin Silliman is also revealing. He wanted to add a professor of chemistry to the faculty but could find no qualified American and feared that "a foreigner, with his peculiar habits and prejudices, would not feel and act in unison with us — and that, however able he might be in point of science, he would not understand our college system and might therefore not act in harmony with his colleagues."[21] Silliman was only twenty-two at the time and totally untrained scientifically. Nevertheless, he was chosen because he was attuned to Yale values. He was sent to the University of Pennsylvania Medical School and to Europe to master his subject. As Nathan Reingold has remarked, "the college wanted a person of unimpeachable orthodoxy and apparently it sincerely believed that any reasonably able person could acquire scientific expertise."[22] Academics were selected as men first and minds only secondarily. In this way, Dwight put together the distinguished evangelical faculty that guided Yale through the 1850s. Yale, the stronghold of conservative education in ante-bellum America, was the product of Dwight's fervent belief in the value of religion and "unfashionable education."

THE COLLEGE IN THE DARTMOUTH COLLEGE CASE

Perhaps the evangelicals' most significant battle for reform occurred at Dartmouth College in Hanover, New Hampshire, where the struggle to control the college led to the famous Dartmouth College Case. Dartmouth had been originally an evangelical institution. It was founded by Eleazer Wheelock, a New Light missionary, as a school for Indians. In 1769 the school for Indians turned into a college for whites, but the evangelical impulse persisted. The college was named for the Englishman William Legge, second Earl of Dartmouth, who was a friend of the Methodists and known as the "psalm singer."[23] But during the Revolution Dartmouth was slowly secularized, like the rest of the country. The elder Wheelock passed away in 1779 and was replaced by his son John, who was not even a clergyman. The light of Dartmouth religion flickered and went out.

In 1815, thirty-six years later, the trustees of Dartmouth sought to rekindle the flame by firing the president, John Wheelock. He thought that Dartmouth belonged to him and not them. He appealed to the Republican party in the state legislature for help. In 1816 it responded by passing an act which would have placed the college under state control and changed its name to Dartmouth University. But the trustees refused to give up the college and took the case to court. For a while two rival institutions existed — the college and the university. Finally, after repeated appeals, the Dartmouth College Case reached the United States Supreme Court. In 1819 Chief Justice John Marshall handed down his precedent-setting decision in favor of the trustees, upholding the immunity of a private corporation from public interference.

While historians have often presented a blow-by-blow account of the controversy, they have failed to explain what caused it in the first place — before it became a political and judicial issue. The origins of the well-known case are shrouded in obscurity, and scholarship on this question is at a dead end. None of the several interpretations hitherto put forth to explain the college divisions has proved satisfactory. President Wheelock was not a rebel Republican fighting a conservative Board of Trustees. Nor was the denominational difference between them — he a Presbyterian and they Congregationalists — decisive.[24] These two churches, never far apart theologically, had been closely united in 1801 by the Plan of Union. As a historian of the college concluded, the denominational difference "was not sufficient to provide much of an issue." At present the standard interpretation is that there were "no serious theological or political differences between Wheelock and the trustees." The cause of the conflict has been reduced to a single issue: the autocratic personality of President Wheelock. "The objection to Wheelock," wrote the Dartmouth historian, "was based on his personal characteristics and in no way on his political or religious beliefs."[25]

In fact, John Wheelock makes a good villain on whom to blame the college strife. He had a proprietary attitude toward the institution. The Wheelocks were the wealthiest family in New Hampshire. They had based their college dynasty on a kind of economic blackmail, threatening to call in their loans whenever their will was opposed. By this means they ruled Dartmouth for nearly half a century before the younger Wheelock was deposed.

Although the college grew in his hands, he was not a great president. He was highly unpopular with the students.[26] And he was a contemptible scholar. His only pretension to scholarship was a tome entitled a *Philosophical History of the Advancement of Nations with an Inquiry into the Cause of their Rise and Decline,* sent to England in 1800 in hopes of finding a publisher but returned unpublished with a withering critique which called it "a confused mass of facts, assertions, quotations and stories totally distinct in the different points they were to establish, irrelevant in their objects to each other and to any common established opinion, principle or sentiment," composed in "language that was not that of any man who could ever have written anything for the press."[27] This rebuff ended his intellectual ambitions. Wheelock was no simpleton, however: he was a formidable opponent in intrigue. His domineering personality and constant machinations undoubtedly exacerbated Dartmouth's inner divisions. But it is inadequate to attribute the rupture within the college to this alone, for it fails to explain why the break came when it did, or what distinguished his supporters from his opponents, and leaves the entire controversy somewhat devoid of content — a tempest in a teapot.

The key to unlocking the divisions at Dartmouth and Hanover is the religious competition which first surfaced when Roswell Shurt-leff (Dartmouth 1799) was appointed Phillips Professor of Divinity in 1804. College and community were closely tied together in religious affairs. The professor of divinity was supposed to be pastor of the Church of Christ at Dartmouth College, where students and townsmen alike worshipped. While the chair of divinity had been vacant for more than a decade the duty of preaching had been assumed by Professor John Smith, Wheelock's staunchest supporter, giving the president control of both college and church. So when Shurtleff was appointed in 1804 and asked by the congregation to serve as minister, Wheelock balked and demanded that Smith continue to preach. The two sides were unable to reach a compromise and split apart in 1805. Wheelock and his friends met in the college chapel with Professor Smith as pastor. Shurtleff's followers, the majority, worshipped in the Hanover meetinghouse. It was the president's importunate demands that the trustees bar Shurtleff and the students from the meetinghouse and their stubborn refusal to do so which finally led to the break in 1815.

The importance of the church schism has never been denied. As one historian put it, "thus in a sordid squabble within an obscure church began a quarrel which was to end in the Supreme Court of the United States, with all the nation looking on."[28] Even the most recent student of the subject, who almost entirely ignores the religious aspects of the conflict (and erroneously dates the schism from 1811), admits that the split in the church was "nominally" the cause of the college break.[29] To recognize the centrality of the schism is one thing, however, and to understand it is another. Historians have never found anything more in it than one more example of Wheelock's autocratic rule.

Professor Shurtleff, as the center of opposition, was obviously an important figure. As Phillips Professor of Divinity, he tried to reawaken the spiritual life of the college from its long slumber. "With Professor Shurtleff," wrote one student, "I am highly pleased. His instructions are enlightening, weighty, and *evangeli-*

cal."[30] Shurtleff's reading of Jonathan Edwards's *Sinners in the Hands of an Angry God* to the students during an 1815 awakening seems to place him in the tradition of Edwardsian Calvinism, though he repeatedly denied being part of the New Divinity movement, which was regarded by most as fanaticism.[31] Little is known of the young professor's theological beliefs, but there is a neglected collection of his letters in the Massachusetts Historical Society which contains an account of the highly significant religious revival he promoted on the campus in the winter of 1805-1806. In this event we get our first glimpse of the substantive issues separating Shurtleff and his followers from the president.

The revival began in the Hanover community and spread to the college with a searing effect. Everything about it was disruptive. As often happened in revivals, there were marked emotional excesses. "Elias Weld was stricken with religious impressions, and thrown into a delerium . . . John Kimball was next slain by the divine law; & while borne down with grief was suddenly thrown into an ecstasy of joy . . . Farrar was about the same time awakened — He was for some weeks sinking under the weight of his sins, & a sense of divine wrath."[32]

The disruption was aggravated by the opposition of many students to whom such intense emotional experiences were incomprehensible and even frightening. Shurtleff wrote that the revival "excited the attention of all college. The enemies of vital piety were alarmed. It is said that Senior Greenwood was Captain General of the opposition. But no ridicule or contempt was sufficient to prevent a very general attendance at the conferences [campus religious meetings]."

The tragic climax of the revival insured that it would not soon be forgotten. Eliphalet Hardy, a student, sought out Professor Shurtleff on a Friday and poured out to him "the deceitfulness & depravity of his own heart." Perhaps Shurtleff's inexperience made him ill-equipped to deal with the ensuing situation or maybe there was nothing he could do. By Tuesday Hardy was much "re-

duced in bodily health . . . Wednesday evening he began to be
wild—Thursday he was distracted—refused all victuals & drink,
from an apprehension that there was a combination to poison
him." Finally, when Dr. Smith of the Medical School was called in
to examine the student, he criticized Shurtleff's handling of the affair, predicted that "the conferences would prove destructive if
not stopped," and demanded that the students be allowed to study
"without being terrified by enthusiasm." A week later the young
man died.

The significance of the revival was that it pitted Shurtleff and
Wheelock against each other on an important religious issue. The
place of emotionalism in religion had deeply divided New England Calvinists since the Great Awakening. To Wheelock and his
friends, apparently skeptical and even hostile toward the revival
from the first, Hardy's death must have fulfilled their worst expectations. To the evangelicals in the community and Professor Shurtleff, on the other hand, the death was simply the work of God and
in no sense a repudiation of the awakening. In his funeral sermon
Shurtleff denounced those "who endeavored to handle this event
v[ersu]s religion & who were then present."

> Let none presume to resist the Spirit of God by imputing his
> operations to phrenzy & enthusiasm. None, except unbelievers,
> can assert this, without being guilty of that sin which the Son of
> God hath said shall never be forgiven.

Was President Wheelock among those Shurtleff denounced?
Had he resisted the religious revival? The evidence is inconclusive
but strongly suggests that he did. One student remarked that the
president never attended the conferences. "Professor Shurtleff has
conferences twice a week," he said. Neither "the president nor any
of the government, except the tuter attend."[33] Outside the college
it was believed that the revival had been hindered by Wheelock
and Smith. "In promoting a revival of heart religion," wrote a
supporter to Shurtleff, "you will have but little assistance from the

other officers of the college. Should the D.D. [*illegible*] in Theology [Smith], be frightened lest young men go distracted and die, and think it better to have no reformations; and though the President should coldly philosophize and indirectly oppose your pious efforts, still when God hath determined, it should be a day of his almighty power."[34]

One other bit of evidence adds to the importance of the revival. The student converts apparently stopped worshipping in the chapel and became members of the meetinghouse.[35] This suggests that different attitudes toward emotional, evangelical, revivalistic religion were a major issue separating the two sides in the schism. It also implies that while the president may have opposed the revival at first because he disapproved of its irrationalism, the very fact that its converts joined the opposition church gave him sufficient grounds for obstructing the spread of evangelical religion in the college. There can be little doubt that after 1806 he insisted on controlling the church in order to keep it out of the hands of men he considered fanatics. As for Shurtleff, despite the antagonism he had aroused, he kept his post. He was accused of being "superstitious, enthusiastic, a methodist, etc." and rumors circulated that he was "inculcating the pecularities of Hopkinsianism" into the college.[36] Within a decade, however, his would be the winning side in the college.

The battle between religious reformers and the president carried over into disciplinary problems. If campus revivals were a sign that a college was safe, disorders were a warning that it was in danger. Like other colleges Dartmouth had frequent student disturbances, but it also had a small band of pious students who tried to uplift student morality. In one important episode, the devout students worked to advance the cause of temperance by urging the abolition of treating — convivial drinking — when exhibition parts were announced and on the day the speeches were performed. When the church-going students prodded the college government into banning treating, the campus rowdies responded by staging the "treating riot" of 1809 and a mock exhibition ceremony in which they tried to drown out the official proceedings by "yelling, singing doggerel songs, and firing the old cannon," leaving the impression that dissipation was rampant in the college.[37] Rather than reform the campus, however, the president seemed to wink at student misdeeds, confirming the trustees' fear that he was soft on discipline.

The trustees took Dartmouth's disciplinary problems far more seriously. In removing the president from office, they blamed him for the lax and partial discipline of the institution:

> The Trustees have evidence . . . that he frequently temporizes with those under censure; throws the blame of the painful measures adopted toward them, on the other Executive officers. General measures, unwelcome to the students, by prohibiting their vices, or restraining their passions, have been by him attributed to others. In some instances he has by his own authority, relieved from censures, and in others, connived at their opposition and breaches of known regulations of the Institution . . . And in this way has the President, *for the sake of conciliating toward himself a few vicious young men,* paralyzed and weakened the Executive arm of the Institution.

His motive in exonerating student wrongdoers, the trustees claimed, was "to make friends, and to obtain additions to [his side of] the Church, and partizans in the quarrel."[38] Thus the church schism, the religious revival, and the problem of student dissipation were all intertwined. The picture of Wheelock's chapel crammed with young ruffians comports well with that of Shurtleff's meetinghouse sheltering the converts of the revival.

In 1809, the year of the treating riot, control of the Board of Trustees definitely passed for the first time to the anti-Wheelock faction. Of the next four appointments to the board, three were Congregational ministers and the fourth, Charles Marsh, was a founder of the Society for the Promotion of Temperance.[39] Among the new anti-Wheelock trustees was Seth Payson, an old

Illuminati-baiter, who was obsessed with the danger of foreign revolutionaries infilitrating the country. His book on the Illuminati was the most elaborate exposition on the threat to the colleges. The first safeguard against such encroachments, he said, was for all Americans to "attend to the education of your children, and let it be your principal care to impress their minds with religious and moral truth."[40] It was this sense of mission, this zeal, which gave the trustees strength to stand against Wheelock's entrenched power.

In the fall of 1809 another student incident occurred — a body snatching by an undergraduate for dissection in the Medical School — that drove another nail in Wheelock's coffin. The Dartmouth Medical School, the fourth in the United States, opened its doors in 1798. It was founded almost single-handedly by Dr. Nathan Smith, a young and struggling physician who was a pioneer of medical education in New England.[41] At first the "medical school" was only a series of lectures paid for by student fees, but in 1803 the state legislature granted the college $600 for medical apparatus, in 1804 the trustees voted Dr. Smith a salary of $400, and in 1809 the state gave Dartmouth $3,450 for construction of a medical building completed in 1811. Smith soon boasted of having fifty medical students, and seventy-two physicians were graduated in the first fifteen years.

The Medical School was certainly a feather in Wheelock's cap. Besides new students, it brought the new science of chemistry to the college. Nearly half the nonmedical juniors and seniors attended Smith's lectures on chemisry and anatomy, though they had to pay an extra fee. Chemistry was somewhat suspect at other colleges, associated with foreign radicals like Lavoisier, Joseph Priestley, and Thomas Cooper. But Wheelock's enthusiasm for the subject was unbounded. After attending one of the medical lectures he gave his famous prayer: "Oh, Lord, we thank Thee for the oxygen gas, for the hydrogen gas, for the mephitic gas, we thank Thee for all the gases."[42] In addition to the hot air it caused, however, the Medical School brought problems for which the trustees were not thankful.

The body snatching episode shook the Medical School. A student who was sent to Boston to purchase a corpse for dissection stole the body of a boy from the graveyard of a nearby town instead. The dissection of convicts and strangers and blacks was a well-accepted practice, but the disinterring of a loved one could arouse extreme hostility in a community, as it had in a similar incident twenty years before when Columbia Medical School had been mobbed and several persons killed in riots.[43] In the case of Dartmouth, the crime was soon discovered and the tracks traced back to the college. An angry party of stout men armed with a search warrant entered the school and found the hidden body, badly mangled, and took it for reburial. The subsequent uproar was best described by Amos Kendall:

> This shocking development threw the surrounding country into a state of terror and excitement. People ceased for a time to bury their dead in the public burying-grounds. Town-meetings were held and violent resolutions adopted. Dr. Smith, the head of the anatomical department, rode out to attend one of the meetings, in the hope of allaying the excitement . . . But the people not only refused to hear him, but thrust him violently out of the meetinghouse, and he remounted his horse and fled to escape further outrage. Threats to burn the college buildings were freely uttered, and indeed they were in imminent danger.[44]

It was doubtless no accident when Dr. Smith's barn was burned in April 1810.

By May of that year Smith was talking of resigning. Writing to a former student, he alluded to the political ramifications of the incident:

> I have at length determined to leave Hanover . . . The political parties are so very jealous of each other in this state and so near a balance that I have nothing to expect from either, as some ig-

norant persons might be offended at any grant or assistance voted by the legislature to promote what they term "cutting up of dead bodies." No one will choose to advocate the measure and I expect they will, if not deemed too unconstitutional, revoke the grant made last year [for construction of a medical building], and, if that can not be effected, they will enact laws which will inflict corporal punishment on any person who is concerned in digging or dissecting.

He added his disenchantment with the factional conflict at the college.

If the thing should take this course it will afford me a good pretext for leaving the college and state, a thing which will not be disagreeable to me . . . The conduct of people and parties has cooled my ardor for laboring in my avocation in this place and determined me to sell my talents in physic and surgery to the highest bidder.[45]

As things turned out, Dartmouth got its building but lost its professor. Dr. Smith resigned in 1813 and went on to found Yale Medical School.

The loss of Smith was a blow to Wheelock who relied on him as an ally. Smith was no friend of evangelical reform. He had denounced the 1805-1806 revival as "enthusiasm." He seems to have gained a bad reputation among religious circles, for before his Yale appointment he had to assure President Timothy Dwight that he had returned to the fold. Writing to another man he said:

Respecting Dr. Dwight's former objections to me, I freely acknowledge that they were well founded and such as a wise and good man would always consider as all important. My earnest prayer now is to live to undo all the evil I have done by expressing my doubts as to the truth of Divine Revelation.[46]

What caused his change of heart is unknown. Possibly Paris was worth a mass, though his biographer believes his conversion was sincere. While he was at Dartmouth, nonetheless, there is no question that he was in the president's camp. Dr. Nehemiah Cleveland, president of Bowdoin, where Smith later taught, described Smith's relationship to the Dartmouth factions: "Dr. Smith had been the steadfast friend of the venerable Wheelock and though no partisan, he had deeply felt for him in those troubles which saddened his last days."[47] Smith's resignation, traced back to the body snatching, hurt Wheelock badly.

The study of medicine was not an issue in the Dartmouth College Case. The trustees had no wish to damage the Medical School and seem to have hoped that Dr. Smith would stay. But the anti-Wheelock faction must have frowned on some of the goings-on in the Medical School. Lectures on chemistry, opposition to revivals, violations of holy ground — all these things were vaguely profane. Student discipline *was* an issue, and the medical students were among the most disorderly. In 1811 a Dartmouth undergraduate made this distinction when he wrote: "the most sober and respectable part of the Inhabitants say the students were never so dissipated as at present. This opinion, however, might much more properly be applied to the medical students, than to the members of College."[48] To tighten discipline (and possibly weaken the influence of the medical professors) the trustees voted in 1811 to exclude the medical faculty from sharing in the supervision of the students.[49]

The year 1809 was thus a crucial one in Dartmouth history. In addition to the treating riot, the body snatching, and the rise of the anti-Wheelock trustees, the president began to lose control of the faculty. His old ally in the church schism, John Smith, died in 1809 and was replaced by one of Shurtleff's friends, Ebenezer Adams, who prided himself on being a strict disciplinarian.[50] The election of Zephaniah Swift Moore as professor of languages continued this trend. Even in the selection of tutors, the president charged, the trustees picked candidates on partisan grounds, nominating in 1811 a graduate who "had taken a leading and active part in the college difficulties, siding with S[hurtleff] against

the president. Nay, who was openly so implacable in his hostility
. . . as to have intemperately declared, that he would never accept
a diploma, if it must bear on its margin the name of Wheelock."[51]
The Medical School was Wheelock's last stronghold. Dr. Cyrus
Perkins, appointed in 1810, was his last faculty ally. While the
Dartmouth College Case was being litigated, Perkins firmly supported the legislature and rival university and resigned when the
trustees finally won.[52] After Dr. Smith's move to Yale in 1813, the
trustees began to appoint a medical faculty more to their liking.
In 1814 Dr. Reuben Mussey was brought in as Smith's replace-
ment. Loyal to the trustees and the college in the upcoming years,
Mussey stayed at Dartmouth till 1838. He was cast in the evangelical mold, described as "a total abstainer from the use of both tobacco and alcohol . . . a vegetarian [and] *very religious.*"[53]

Contemporaries realized that religious differences were involved
in Dartmouth's divisions but had difficulty defining the two
groups.[54] The voluminous writings produced by the controversy
were polemical in nature—full of false accusations and subter-
fuge. One of Wheelock's supporters contended that the trustees
were part of a conspiracy hatched at Andover Theological Seminary, the center of evangelical Calvinism, to convert Dartmouth
"into a sectarian school."[55] A Wheelock pamphleteer denounced
the trustees for purging the college of everyone not wearing "their
badge of orthodoxy."[56] The president himself condemned the
trustees for masking their sectarian conspiracy behind "zealous
professions of piety, and . . . of regard to the order and well-being
of society."[57] Shurtleff and the anti-Wheelock trustees, in turn,
saw the conflict as the result of a conspiracy of religious liberals—
called variously Socinians, Unitarians, Arminians, Bostonians, or
just plain liberals—against the traditional Calvinist orthodoxy of
New England. "Should the president prevail against us," wrote an
anti-Wheelock trustee to the president's successor, "I have no
doubt that the college would be converted into a seminary of So-
cinianism."[58]

What has kept other historians from advancing a religious interpretation has been that each side, accused by the other of being religious conspirators, wisely underplayed the religious nature of its own motives in public statements. Throughout the conflict the Shurtleff faction especially denied that its opposition to the president was theologically motivated. This was hairsplitting, however, for while revivalism and temperance reform are not in fact theological issues, they were nevertheless religious concerns of great importance in this period.[59] Wheelock made much the same distinction when asked by the New Hampshire legislature what religious differences separated him from the trustees. He replied somewhat evasively that while they agreed on "speculative" issues, they diverged on certain "practical" matters.[60] In other words, though both nominally Calvinists, they came down on different sides when forced to take stands on revivalism or temperance reform or student discipline. Though this was a subtle distinction, it was quite apparent to participants. As one student best described the two sides: "the professors are men of sound minds & orthodox principles. The President is generally orthodox, but he gives too much reason for the Arminians to claim him, & by the Bostonians he is called 'liberal.' "[61] What divided the two factions was a difference in mood — a sense of alarm at the dangers facing the country as well as a great faith in the meliorative power of religion. While Wheelock's faith was grown lukewarm, the trustees were on fire.

With the faculty safely in their camp, the trustees completed their takeover by dismissing Wheelock in 1815. Whereas he had been one of the first lay college presidents in America, his successor, the Reverend Francis Brown, was an orthodox Calvinist clergyman with close ties to the meetinghouse. A few years before Wheelock had fought his appointment as a tutor because he had taken communion in Shurtleff's church.[62] The religious community recognized the high stake it had in the conflict. The trustees-Shurtleff faction was supported by "all the orthodox clergy in this & the neighboring states."[63] When the case was in litigation, the

Congregational clergy set aside days of prayer to ask that the college now "a nursery of piety" would not revert to being "the reverse."[64] Timothy Farrar, one of the alumni converted in the 1805-1806 revival, served on the legal team defending Shurtleff and the trustees.

To the participants in the college and the community, then, the significance of the Dartmouth College Case was not the political battle between Federalists and Republicans or the contest between state legislature and United States Supreme Court or simply Wheelock's authoritarianism. It was, rather, the question who would control the religious future of Dartmouth and Hanover. The Supreme Court's 1819 decision in favor of the trustees was thus a victory for the movement of evangelical education.

DICKINSON'S UNFERTILE GROUND

Hurrying away from his presidency at Middlebury College, Vermont, where he had lately been overshadowed by a popular professor of mathematics full of anecdotes of Napoleon and France, the Reverend Jeremiah Atwater looked forward with a sense of mission to assuming the presidency of Dickinson College in Carlisle, Pennsylvania. Atwater was a graduate of Yale and an early protégé of Timothy Dwight. His striking angular face and tall lean figure made him the epitome of a Puritan. He firmly believed that the teacher must be "subservient to the cause of Christ" and that the primary end of education was "bringing forward young men for the ministry."[65] By this criterion his regime at Middlebury had been a success. The college had been a model of decorum and had experienced three religious revivals. To refashion Dickinson with its large contingent of southern students into another Middlebury, however, would be no easy task.

It was not an instance of evangelical replacing liberal. Dickinson's first president, the Reverend Charles Nisbet, had been one of the most violent critics of the French Revolution and French philosophy. But Nisbet was a true old-world scholar more than a petty schoolmaster and had not even formulated a code of rules for the undergraduates. After his death in 1805, discipline had remained lax. Atwater's first impression confirmed his worst fears: "the young men their own masters, doing what was right in their own eyes, spending their time at taverns & in the streets, lying in bed always till breakfast & never at the College but at the time of lecture."[66] His efforts to change things provide one of the best illustrations of the thrust of evangelical reform. The storm raised by his attempt, on the other hand, showed again the powerful and disruptive impact of the Protestant counterrevolution on American higher education.

Reform for Atwater did not so much mean curricular change or even doctrinal instruction as it did the enforcement of strict discipline. "My whole confidence of success," he wrote to trustee Benjamin Rush, "depends on introducing some of the regulations of the New England colleges, particularly those relating to the all important point of discipline, without which a college is a pest, a school of licentiousness."[67] It was this obsession with order, in part the legacy of student revolt, which vitiated evangelical reform, subordinating its intellectual side to a petty moralism.

In his inaugural address, Atwater spelled out his philosophy of education. "If we wish to form men good citizens," he declared, "we must first teach them to fear God." The institution's course of study was designed to achieve this end. Ancient languages would be emphasized so that students might read "the original of the sacred scriptures." Mathematics would be suspect because "it leads to skepticism on religious subjects." Science was allowable only so long as it supported the dictates of revelation. Piety would be the primary thing: "we shall expect . . . *always* in *all* situations, a most sacred regard to morals and religion." "God forbid," he told the clergy in the audience, that Dickinson should ever become the nursery of "dissipation, impiety and infidelity."[68]

Atwater's first goal was the construction of a dormitory where the students could be properly supervised. This ambition clashed with founder Benjamin Rush's long-held prejudice against boarding schools.[69] Rush believed that student housing corrupted the morals of the young by encouraging juvenile vices. But Atwater was adamant. "I know not how we shall succeed in having them under proper discipline without having them lodge in the College under the inspection of tutors," he declared.[70] In the end Atwater won. He then looked to Yale for a suitably pious tutor but finally settled for a devout young graduate from the University of Pennsylvania who soon became his comrade in adversity.

Atwater's second accomplishment was to compose Dickinson's first code of laws for the students, passed by the trustees on December 20, 1810. Four classes were created and required to give each other "those tokens of respect and subjection" which promoted a "due subordination among the students." Besides attending worship on the Sabbath, each class would be given "certain exercises for their religious instruction." Like McCorkle at Chapel Hill or Green at Princeton, he was adding compulsory religious doctrine to the course of studies. Every species of frivolity and immorality was prohibited, and an elastic clause covered any crimes not listed in the formal laws. To insure that wrongdoing would not go undetected, "the principal, a professor or a tutor, shall have authority to break open and enter any college chamber at all times at discretion." Each student was assigned a room which he was not allowed to change. At every step the students would be under the thumb of the faculty.[71]

Finally, Atwater erected those student religious societies that were so central a part of evangelical education. Here he met opposition from the trustees. As he complained to Ashbel Green, who was about to inaugurate his own presidency at Princeton:

The enemy has disputed every inch of ground which has been gained in favour of religion. The utmost efforts were made to prevent the introduction of a praying society &, even to this day, it is the common topic of ridicule with a great portion of the persons here. The same may be said with respect to Theological Library & magazine . . . Their wish is, that the College may have nothing to do with religion. A great part of them apparently care not, whether the students ever attend religious exercises on the Sabbath & I cannot . . . get a single person to feel much interest in carrying into execution the laws which oblige the students to attend public worship.[72]

Eventually Atwater added an "association for distributing tracts," but this was his last victory.

The president had been fortunate in getting this far. The trustees who lived in the Carlisle area (as opposed to those in Philadelphia) were outspoken in their anticlerical bias, among them the well-known Judge Hugh Henry Brackenridge, author of the satirical *Modern Chivalry,* whom Atwater called "virulent against any thing that savors of religion."[73] Why these men agreed to the appointment of Atwater in the first place is hard to explain. Faced with his crusading efforts, they soon found a champion of their own.

On June 17, 1811, in a surprise meeting of the Board of Trustees, Thomas Cooper was elected professor of chemistry and minerology. Cooper was a religious deist and political radical who had fled England during the government repression of 1794. As a Jeffersonian newspaper editor, he had been prosecuted under the Sedition Act and imprisoned for six months in 1800. Jefferson praised him as "the greatest man in American in the powers of mind and in acquired information, and that without a single exception."[74] Not only did Cooper bring to Dickinson his first-rate scientific training but he also helped the college procure the valuable scientific equipment of his friend Joseph Priestley, the famous English chemist, who had also emigrated to the United States in the mid-1790s, only to be hounded as a subversive.

When he learned of Cooper's election, Atwater was morose. His first thought, interestingly, was of discipline. "Where should we be in case of insurrection among the students," he cried, "Yet what is more likely to cause insurrection than the present disjointed state of things?"[75] His fear that Cooper would corrupt the students was not immediately realized; Cooper even attended church at first to appease the president. It was inevitable, however, that two such committed antagonists would clash. That their confrontation came over discipline rather than curriculum was a comment on the hierarchy of values in American colleges at this date.

In February 1812 two students had a duel, and Atwater and Cooper had their first major falling out in the investigation that followed. Cooper wanted no part of the trial but was dragged in by the president. The disciplinary committee met in the evening, and Atwater suspected that Cooper was slightly inebriated when he arrived. During the interrogation of the students, Cooper "would not consent to let the young men be questioned as to their guilt, as is the custom of all colleges in such cases. He threatened if the question was put, to interfere & prevent their answering it." Atwater was afraid that Cooper's objections would undermine the authority of the faculty. "Tho' requested to speak in a lower tone," he complained of the professor, "he persisted in speaking so loudly as to be overheard by students without. Of course he has become much of a toast with those students who are disaffected."[76]

The increasing student disorders were probably the result of the political controversy surrounding the War of 1812. As a student wrote, "party spirit appears to rage with peculiar violence at present . . . Even here at College: the Students are infected with the Mania. And we squabble just as much as if we were the representatives of the Nation."[77] In May 1813 Dickinson suffered its worst vandalism to date—"wanton mischief and disgraceful filthiness, damaging the College building."[78] In July 1813 there was a rebellion over the study of Latin and Greek. The seriousness of the disorders was described by the nephew of President James Madison:

I have been rather unpleasantly situated for some time past. Their has been and is at present a great deal of commotion among the students and Faculty, and although I am not engaged in it in the remotest degree, still it is very disagreeable — their has been several expulsions and twenty one suspended for refusing to obey one of the laws of the institution. A very unfortunate affair took place about a fortnight ago. An amiable young man, (the only son of Mr. Champ Carter of Virginia) in a fray with another student received a blow on his head with a pair of snuffers which fractured his skull. The physicians were not able to remove the coagulated blood from the brain, and he expired on the eighth day.[79]

The breakdown of order intensified faculty strife, and by 1814 all the professors had turned against Atwater. Cooper in particular was unhappy and looking for another position. On July 12, 1815, the trustees voted that the professors must draw up weekly reports on "all delinquents or absentees." The implied charge that the faculty was not doing its duty was taken by the professors as a vote of no confidence. This led to the faculty's mass desertion (Atwater included) at the end of the year.[80]

A frantic search for a new staff kept the college going till December 1815 when there was a duel in which one young man was killed and three other students fled. To town and trustees alike, this was the last straw. College affairs ran downhill and the next fall the trustees voted "to suspend the business of this College for the present."[81] Thus the first college founded after the American Revolution closed, not to be reopened until the 1820s, and then as a denominational school. Perhaps harmony was too much to expect from the disparate elements of Carlisle, but there is little question that more moderate men than Atwater and Cooper might have kept the college alive. The seeds of faith sown by Jeremiah Atwater had fallen on hard ground. Coming to Dickinson to build another temple of prayer, he left it in ruins, a monument to the force and at times destructiveness of evangelical reform.

PRINCETON IN THE SPIDER'S WEB

On August 14, 1812, the Reverend Ashbel Green was elected president of Princeton. No one was more closely identified with evangelical education than this ambitious Philadelphia clergyman and Princeton trustee. Whether upbraiding the students after the Nassau Hall fire, sending spies into Smith's lectures to search out his heresies, or steeling the Board of Trustees against compromise during the great rebellion, Green had battled hard to save the college from anarchy and irreligion. Now, as president, he came to Princeton resolved "to reform it, or to fall under the attempt."[82] His administration saw a little of each. Although the reforms he made and the revival he engendered were highly significant, they were no more intriguing than the troubled man himself. It is usually an error to equate the history of an institution with the life of its executive, but to ignore Green's personal involvement with the college is to miss all the morbid gloom of his administration.

One of his first acts as president was to decree that all faculty meetings be opened with prayer. He was "greatly encouraged" when the serious admonitions of his first address to the students caused some of them to "shed tears." But finding that the majority of the students were not repentant—indeed, that "every kind of insubordination that they could devise was practiced"—he was forced to institute his reforms. First, he established the Princeton Bible Society in 1813. Second, he made Bible study mandatory and included it in year-end examinations. Third, he began sending periodic reports to parents on the moral conduct and literary standing of the students, later claiming credit for inventing report cards for American colleges. Finally, he forced the juniors and seniors to resume the study of Latin and Greek, reasoning that the difficulty of the classics was conducive to good discipline.[83] Throughout his administration he policed the campus with a pettiness bordering on the obsessive. Snowbound students were more than once forbidden to go sledding. In one instance students were reprimanded for throwing rocks at a tree on Sunday—an obvious violation of the Sabbath![84]

Although neither his reforms nor his personality endeared Green to most of the undergraduates, he professed great love for his students.[85] He was pleased in 1813 when a serious outbreak of illness allowed him to fulfill the promise he had made on coming to Princeton—to treat "every pupil as a child." He visited the sick "by day and by night" and even sent them food from his own table.[86] To some extent he was exploiting the suffering of the students, seeking to ingratiate himself with his pupils, but in a deeper sense Green tended to associate Princeton with sickness and death for personal reasons. In fact, one can only comprehend his fervent mission by discerning the strange manner in which his efforts to bring order and piety to the college were intertwined with his personal life.

Green traced the death of his first wife back to his acting presidency of the college after the fire, seeing her break in health not merely as a coincidence but as a consequence of his efforts. "On returning from visits to Princeton," he related, "I repeatedly found my wife much indisposed, probably from exposure or over-exertion in consequence of my absence." If he felt guilty about neglecting his wife, how could he better justify his actions than by redoubling his efforts to save the college? Or, if he subconsciously blamed the college for his loss, how better get revenge than by destroying the institution in the guise of reforming it? Whether this was his intent or not, it was almost the effect.[87] His wife finally passed away just before the 1807 rebellion, giving Green the opportunity he needed for losing himself in restoring discipline.

After the 1813 bout of illness among the students, he faced another crushing blow in the loss of his eldest son, a twenty-six-year-old attorney whom he had idolized. "He had a full belief in divine Revelation," Green later recalled. "He had examined and was complete master of the deistical controversy in all its parts and bearings, and could sooner and more fully put an infidel to silence than any other man I have ever known." Try as he would, however, he could never convince himself that his son had been saved. As a strict Calvinist he knew that justification did not depend on man's efforts but on the mysterious grace of God. Yet he felt guilty, fearing that he had placed too much stress on "scientific and intellectual distinctions" for himself and his children, making them unmindful of the world to come. "It certainly would now give me more comfort," he admitted, "if he had been unequivocally and eminently pious, than that he should have possessed all the brilliant talents by which he was undoubtedly distinguished." This was a turning point in Green's attitude toward intellect. He resolved "to be more earnest than I have ever yet been for the saving conversion of my children" and "to be more engaged for the conversion of young people in general, especially of my own dear pupils."[88]

Green's good intentions were momentarily frustrated, however, by renewed student disorders. He later described the days from November 9, 1813, to March 8, 1814, as "one of the most afflictive periods of my life." After a short, deceptive peace, "the roof of the privy was burned, and a kind of infernal machine was fired in the College edifice; many small crackers were also fired; theft was committed; the walls were scrawled on; there was clapping, hissing and screaming going on in the refectory." But the chaos on campus was overshadowed by personal crises. First Green's brother died. Then his second wife gave premature birth to a stillborn baby and subsequently died after great suffering. Very ill himself for over eight weeks, the president was distraught. "Show me, Oh God," he demanded, "why thou contendest with me."[89] Against this troubled backdrop loomed the Princeton revival of 1815.

When Princeton's long-sought awakening broke out in the second week of January 1815, the thankful president proclaimed that "the divine influence seemed to descend like the silent dew of heaven." In a letter to Jedidiah Morse he was equally modest, writing that the revival had "manifestly been wrought by the finger of God."[90] In ascribing the revival to Providence, Green was revealing the Old Side Presbyterian ambivalence toward religious revivals. Like other evangelicals they deplored religious declension and prayed for a quickening of the nation's faith. But they were strongly opposed to the physical exercises and emotional excesses of revivals or to the use of special "means" in their promotion. Of course all of Green's efforts since taking office had been directed toward an awakening. Once it arrived, however, he boasted that it began "without any special instructions, or other means" and assured his supporters that the whole event had been "remarkably free from extravagance and enthusiasm."[91] His analysis of the 1815 revival was almost a manual of how to promote a revival without really trying.

Green attributed the revival to four causes. First, the students' study of the Bible had made them "solemn and tender, beyond what they were themselves aware of at the time." Second, the town church had burned down two years earlier and since then the students had worshipped by themselves in the college prayer hall with the young men from the theological seminary. This allowed the professors to adapt their sermons to the youths. It also gave the students a direct participation in the worship service. Third, the president believed that his efforts to maintain discipline had "preserved the youth, generally from those practices, habits and vicious indulgences, which counteract, dissipate, and destroy all serious and religious impressions." His constant reproaches, that is, had made them aware of their total depravity. In fact, an act of discipline had actually sparked the revival, when a dismissed student was suddenly "seized with a remourse of conscience and anguish of mind that were very affecting." Finally, for more than a year before the revival, the twelve devout students in the college had been praying for an awakening, and as soon as it began they counseled their classmates "privately and tenderly, on the subject of religion."[92]

The immediate effect of the revival on the college was all that Green had hoped. He optimistically predicted to the trustees that a majority of the students would be converted. The rest, he was happy to report, were at least strict in religious observance. Although there were still a few infractions of the rules, "the public sentiment of the College, so far from being hostile to discipline, has called for it, has anticipated and gone before it, and has justified and sanctioned it whenever it has taken place."[93] It must have seemed that the president's reforms, so doubtful a year before, had finally transformed the college into a temple of prayer. Yet the reign of peace was of short duration. There is no need here to follow the remainder of Green's administration — the great riot of 1817 or his rupture with the trustees in 1822. After leaving Princeton he edited an influential Presbyterian periodical in which his demands for doctrinal purity contributed greatly to the Presbyterian schism of 1837.

It remains to be asked, however, why the effect of the revival was so transient, at least respecting discipline. Faced with this unpleasant fact, Green claimed that most of the converts had been seniors, and that the next year's entering students were of "a very different character, especially in point of morals and religion."[94] Historians of Princeton have too readily accepted his excuse. But a student letter written before the end of the school year by a junior gives a different account of the aftermath of the revival and a rather unflattering portrait of the president:

the short time which I have been here has disclosed such frequent and daily instances of hypocrisy and backsliding that all his fond hopes of this seminary being the fund from which our western frontiers are to be stocked with missionaries must soon vanish, and leave him the gloomy reflection that all his exertions . . . must at last avail nothing. Perhaps it was better that many of them were never converted, for there are many instances of those who have been the most seriously affected, who falling back into their old ways have become disgusted with their former professions again. Dr. Green does not appear to be sensible of this as he is a very reserved & haughty man and thinks himself condescending to speak to one of his pupils, without it be to chide him for some trivial offence, as for reading newspapers on Sunday, and many other such slight neglects, and he often reproaches them in the most insulting and opprobrious manner.[95]

By employing religion as a tool of discipline, the president vitiated the revival at Princeton. Rather than impart to the students a deepened sense of man's place in the world, he left them with a picayune set of rules about what one could or could not do on the Sabbath. Green's Princeton was regarded as intolerably strict by students of other colleges. "I do really pity the students of that institution," wrote a visitor from Harvard. "I think the government of it is too strict—it treats the students as mere children."[96] In this way Green the petty schoolmaster triumphed over Green the evangelist. On his very first trip to Philadelphia after the revival, Green became engaged to the woman who became his third wife. He had once again won the right to a normal life.

The Princeton revival was the crowning success of the early collegiate evangelical movement. Princeton had been "less the subject of revivals . . . than most colleges in New England." Its students came from "influential families in the southern and western States" and could now be expected to carry the Gospel into these former strongholds of deism.[97] It was truly a remarkable triumph. Never before in American history had there been so many campus revivals in so short a time. Student religious associations were growing into strong intercollegiate organizations capable of coordinating religious activities in the colleges. As the students of Andover informed their brethren at Dartmouth, "you have probably been informed of the concert of prayer held by pious students in Yale, Williams, Brown, Middlebury, & Harvard Colleges, & also by the students of this place. It is held on Sabbath mornings to pray particularly for revivals in Colleges & public schools."[98]

The climate of the colleges had changed greatly in the two decades since 1795. The Age of Reason was at an end. The year 1815 witnessed four major student revivals. To one devout undergraduate this signified Christ's second coming: "Nothing like this has ever been seen since the Apostolic age. Surely this, & [the] missionary spirit which prevails, indicate that Christ's Universal Empire is near at hand."[99] The Evangelical Age had truly come.

The Defensive Academe
and the Lost Generation

"THE INSUBORDINATION of our youth is now the greatest obstacle to their education," wrote Thomas Jefferson in 1823.[1] Student revolt had left a strong imprint on the American college. Its influence had been harmful not creative, ossifying rather than innovative. Falling attendance, faculty resignations, and loss of legislative or denominational financial support were some of the concrete effects. Less tangible but equally important was the fact that by disrupting the colleges revolt detracted from instruction. By focusing attention on misbehavior, it damaged the colleges in the public mind. And, by contributing to the general contraction of higher education at the turn of the nineteenth century, it played a large part in defining the old-time college.

With society seeming to come apart, academics tried to hold down their small part of the world by regulating student life, emphasizing the collegiate aspects of education. President Dwight told his students, "in this country we speak of our colleges both as colleges and universities, when they are neither. They are collegiate schools, such as Eton." Or, as the *Yale Report* of 1828 put it, "when removed from under the roof of their parents, and exposed to the untried scenes of temptation, it is necessary that some faithful and affectionate guardians take them by the hand, and guide their steps."[2] The old-time college was a paternalistic institution. It sought to instill steady habits, proper speech, good grooming, the rudiments of learning, at least a thin veneer of culture, and most of all what one of the famous old-time college presidents called "a good religious influence."[3] Christian doctrine was imparted in mandatory Sabbath services, in daily chapel prayers, and even in the classroom. In student religious societies, private counseling sessions, and campus revivals, the sparks of faith were fanned to flames. Earnest, pious professors served for students as models of the godly life. Religion and morality were primary not secondary considerations. As President Azel Backus declared in his inaugural address at Hamilton College in 1812, "mere science, without moral and religious habits, is a curse, and not a blessing to the community. Better for a youth, and for civil society, that he had lived in ignorance, than that he should issue from a college with irreligious and immoral principles."[4]

In matters of curriculum, student revolt fed a reaction away from experimental plans of study and back to Latin and Greek. The classics were associated not just with mental discipline but behavioral discipline as well. The dead languages were difficult to learn, requiring serious application, leaving little time for idle reading or temptation. The classics were also "safe," even antidotes to irreligion. There was a certain irony here — using pagan literature to shore up religious faith. Academics were aware that the classics might need to be bowdlerized. President Green cautioned that "classical reading itself, is not without a tendency to foster some notions and feeling which do not entirely accord with the spirit of the gospel."[5] But the ancient languages unlocked the wisdom of the past, and that for centuries had upheld the Christian faith. President Dwight explained, "the knowledge of the ancient languages opens to you access to writers who have formed standards of taste . . . Sound taste, sound sense, and *sound morals* go together; this is the law of the universe."[6] In addition, it was er-

roneously believed that God's word was originally "contained in
the Greek and Latin languages" and that knowledge of the ancient languages was therefore essential "in these times of doubt
and infidelity."[7] Having embraced a curriculum for the wrong
reasons—as a bulwark against dangerous ideas—academics were
never able to bring it to life. The deadly recitation method was actually not inappropriate for a subject designed merely to take up
space. The ancient languages remained not only safe, but safely
dead.[8]

The significance of these changes lay in their broader cultural
implications. The transformation of American higher education
after 1800 has been called "the great retrogression" and attributed
to "the pervasive national reaction from the Enlightenment," specifically "the epidemic of revivals, the rise of fundamentalism, and
the all but unchecked ragings of the denominational spirit."[9]
There is little doubt that American higher education did suffer a
decline around the turn of the nineteenth century. In 1814 the
trustees of Columbia described their institution as "a Spectacle
mortifying to its friends, humiliating to the City."[10] In 1816 Rut-
gers and Dickinson were closed, while Williams and William and
Mary contemplated relocating to keep from shutting down. When
he arrived at the University of Georgia in 1817, Reverend Robert
Finley, the president-elect, found it "in the lowest state that is possible; the contempt of the enemies of literature, the scorn of its
own particular enemies, and the pity of those who were once its
friends."[11]

These were not normal vicissitudes or chronic complaints.
Higher education was at its lowest ebb. But it is wrong to blame
the great retrogression on clerical-academic evangelicals. They
were the very ones who suffered most from the decline. The fact
was that American colleges had been relegated to an inferior status
in the new egalitarian American society. Samuel Miller's *A Brief
Retrospect of the Eighteenth Century* (1803) reported that most
colleges had "very inadequate funds." Want of fellowships and

scholarships discouraged the ablest men from academic life. With too few professors attempting to teach too many subjects, only a "very superficial knowledge" could be conveyed to the students. Hence the United States remained culturally subservient to Great Britain long after independence had been won.[12] At comparatively wealthy Yale, President Dwight had similar complaints. Demoralized professors had barely time enough to master their subjects, to say nothing of advancing the realm of knowledge. This was not the result of the nation's immaturity. In the colonial era Dwight's counterpart had received three or four times what Dwight received. "Our ancestors were liberal," he explained, "they gave a considerable sum to this college." But although "we talk a great deal about liberality," he went on, "I wish we acted more about it." "However painful it may be to make such a declaration, truth requires me to say that we are not liberal in support of our institutions, and that we do not properly appreciate the value of knowledge."[13] America would evolve with a defensive academe.

For the young, student revolt was part of a general breakdown of adolescent discipline. Many long-term changes contributed to this, such as the flux and mobility of American society after the Revolution, the erosion of the patriarchal family, the future-orientedness of national culture, and the adoption of egalitarian manners and styles.[14] Undergraduate resistance was not just a gradual development, however, not simply a response to new conditions, but a specific pattern of behavior developed during the Quasi-War with France and the subsequent political agitation. Once discovered it served as a *rite de passage* by which generations of upper-class youths could reenact the bold strokes of defiance which gave birth to the American nation, symbolically proving their manhood. Parents acquiesced in this. While they generally supported college governments during campus confrontations, they voiced no fear of freethinking or revolutionary intent. There was an absence of generational hatred. An outcry from parents halted those few attempts to call in civil authorities and courts to quell campus disorders.[15] By the end of this period parents seem to have accepted the fact that the days of youthful submissiveness were never coming back. Harrison Gray Otis wrote his wife regarding a disturbance at Harvard in 1818:

> I presume order is restored at Harvard. Old Mr. Adams mistakes the genius of the age, to tell of whipping and to practice scolding. *The principles of Government in States and Families are changed.* The understanding and the heart must be addressed by persuasion and reason, and the bayonet and rod reserved for the last emergency. A boy of 18 for all the purposes of Government, is as much a man as he will ever be.[16]

Whether lower-class adolescents were permitted their own forms of generational protest is still unknown.

Student revolt was indirectly political insofar as it reflected adolescent impatience to stand beside the Founders. Contemporary descriptions of the rising generation—which was perceived as a distinct postrevolutionary generation—captured this political flavor. The *Troy Gazette* of May 19, 1807, denounced the Princeton rebels as "young rights-of-boys politicians." In his *History of South Carolina* (1809), David Ramsay lamented that postrevolutionary youths were so "zealous for the rights of boys."[17] John Randolph complained that with a "smathering of Latin, drinking grog, and chewing tobacco, these striplings set up for legislators and statesmen."[18] Adolescent discontent was due in part to the revolutionary generation's reluctance to step aside. Not until Martin Van Buren's inauguration in 1837 did the United States have a President born after 1776. John Quincy Adams and Andrew Jackson, both born in 1767, had been actively involved in the War for Independence. For three score years after the Declaration of Independence, the United States would be led by men who remembered the Revolution.

Of all the young men, student evangelicals like Samuel Mills came the closest to finding an all-engrossing cause. The Sons-of-the-Founders psychological appeal was central to their movement. A clergyman recruiting ministerial candidates later wrote:

> I have met with unexpected success with the young men. They seem to understand that we are attacked by a more formidable enemy than our Fathers resisted in '76; and that the Education Society is just such a means as must be used to save our country, and transmit those blessings which we have received from the struggles of the *revolution*.[19]

Missionary enterprises were not the young men's cause alone, however, for the early founders of the Benevolent Empire—Morse, Dwight, Pearson, Green, Smith, and Boudinot—all were members of the revolutionary generation. Up to the 1830s student evangelicals were simply following their lead. Not until the Lane Rebels took up the banner of radical abolitionism in 1834, outraged their elders, and bolted Lane for Oberlin, would young evangelicals have a cause of their own.[20]

To a large extent the Sons of the Founders were a lost generation, born too late for the Revolution, too soon for the Civil War. Jefferson Davis was born in 1808, Lincoln in 1809. The Sons of the Founders had no rendezvous with destiny, though the accident of their birth was not entirely to blame. As twenty-eight-year-old Abraham Lincoln told the Springfield Young Men's Lyceum, every American generation faces the dilemma of being the descendents of the Founders. From birth they inherit the blessings of liberty. But it is not enough for them merely to support and maintain "an edifice that has been erected by others." His generation, he rightly predicted, would find itself by confronting the issues of slavery and abolitionism.[21] Each generation must make its place in history. The tragedy of the Sons of the Founders, and their revolt, was that they never found their cause.

NOTES

BIBLIOGRAPHY

INDEX

NOTES
---

1. *The Influence of the First Lapse*

1. Samuel Eliot Morison, *The Founding of Harvard College* (Cambridge, Mass., 1935), 259, 260; *Harvard College in the Seventeenth Century* (Cambridge, Mass., 1936), I, 76-78.

2. Morris Bishop, "The Lower Depths of Higher Education," *American Heritage,* 21 (Dec. 1969), 27-63; Lowell H. Harrison, "Rowdies, Riots, and Rebellions," *American History Illustrated* (July 1972), 18-29; David F. Allmendinger, Jr., "The Dangers of Ante-Bellum Student Life," *Journal of Social History,* 7 (Fall 1973), 75-85.

3. William C. Lane, "The Rebellion of 1766 in Harvard College," Colonial Society of Massachusetts *Transactions,* 10 (1905), 32-59.

4. Louis L. Tucker, *Puritan Protagonist: President Thomas Clap of Yale College* (Chapel Hill, 1962), chap. 10.

5. Sheldon S. Cohen, "Student Unrest in the Pre-Revolutionary Decade, 1765-1775," address to the American Historical Association, December 1971; *The Black Book, or the Book of Misdemeanors in King's College, New York, 1771-1775* (New York, Columbia University Press, 1931); Sheldon S. Cohen, "The Turkish Tyranny," *New England Quarterly,* 77 (Dec. 1974), 564-583.

6. Stephen Nissenbaum, ed., *The Great Awakening at Yale College* (Belmont, Calif., 1972), 59.

7. Nissenbaum, *Great Awakening at Yale College,* 221.

8. Richard L. Bushman, *From Puritan to Yankee: Character and the Social Order in Connecticut, 1690-1765* (New York, 1967), 241-251.

173

9. Bushman, *From Puritan to Yankee,* 256.

10. Benjamin Gale, *A Letter to a Member of the Lower House of the Assembly of the Colony of Connecticut* (New Haven, 1759), 19.

11. Pauline Maier, "Popular Uprisings and Civil Authority in Eighteenth-Century America," *William and Mary Quarterly,* 3d ser., 27 (Jan. 1970), 25.

12. John Graham, *A Letter to a Member of the Lower House of Representatives . . . in Vindication of Yale College* (New Haven, 1959), 16.

13. "There seems to be validity to Clap's repeated assertion that the Gale faction constantly urged the students to perpetrate acts of violence so as to discredit the administration and pave the way for his dismissal. The proof of this charge is admittedly hard to come by." Tucker, *Puritan Protagonist,* 231, n. 69.

14. Tucker, *Puritan Protagonist,* 252, n. 43.

15. Chauncey Whittelsey to Ezra Stiles, July 9, August 8, 1766, in Franklin Bowditch Dexter, ed., *Extracts from the Itineraries and Other Miscellanies of Ezra Stiles* (New Haven, 1916), 591.

16. Varnum Lansing Collins, *President Witherspoon, A Biography* (Princeton, 1925), I, 141.

17. Andrew Eliot to Thomas Hollis, December 25, 1769, in Massachusetts Historical Society *Collections,* 4th ser., 4 (1858), 447.

18. New York *Gazette,* July 30, 1770.

19. Seymour Martin Lipset, *Student Politics* (New York, 1971), iii.

20. "The Progress of Dulness" (1772, 1773), in Edwin T. Bowen, ed., *The Satirical Poems of John Trumbull* (Austin, Texas, 1962).

21. Lewis S. Feuer, *The Conflict of Generations: The Character and Significance of Student Movements* (New York, 1969), 319; Sheldon S. Cohen and Larry R. Gerlach, "Princeton in the Coming of the American Revolution," *New Jersey History,* 92 (Summer 1974), 92.

22. Lane, "The Rebellion of 1766 in Harvard College," 39, 40.

23. *The Connecticut Journal,* September 15, 1769.

24. Irving Brant, *James Madison: The Virginia Revolutionist* (New York, 1941), 91.

25. Hunter D. Farish, ed., *Journal and Letters of Philip Vickers Fithian, 1773-1774: A Plantation Tutor of the Old Dominion* (Williamsburg, 1945), 254.

26. Samuel Eliot Morison, *Three Centuries of Harvard* (Boston, 1936), 175, 176.

27. Henry Adams, "Harvard College, 1786-1787," *Historical Essays* (New York, 1891), 99.

28. *The Diary of William Bentley* (Salem, 1905), I, 252.

29. Tucker, *Puritan Protagonist,* 237, 238.

30. "An Essay on the Multiplicity of our Literary Institutions," (Boston) *The Monthly Anthology* (March 1807), 115.

31. Frederick Rudolph, ed., *Essays on Education in the Early Republic* (Cambridge, Mass., 1965); Meyer Reinhold, "Opponents of Classical Learning in America During the Revolutionary Period," American Philosophical Society *Publications,* 112 (1968), 221-234.

32. Thomas Jefferson Wertenbaker, *Princeton, 1746-1896* (Princeton, 1946), 123.

33. "On the State of Literature in New England," (Boston) *Panoplist* (April 1807), 522. This was a description of conditions in the 1790s.

34. "The Study of the Dead Languages," December 15, 1792, in Ray W. Irwin and Edna L. Jacobsen, eds., *A Columbia College Student in the Eighteenth Century: Essays by Daniel D. Tompkins* (Port Washington, N.Y., 1964), 6.

35. "Suitable Courses of Study," November 21, 1794, in *Columbia College Student in the Eighteenth Century,* 46.

36. Samuel Knox, "An Essay on the Best System of Liberal Education," in Rudolph, ed., *Essays on Education in the Early Republic,* 314.

37. Charles Nisbet to Joshua M. Wallace, June 8, 1793, in Richard Hofstadter and Wilson Smith, eds., *American Higher Education: A Documentary History* (Chicago, 1961), I, 254, 255.

38. (Boston) *The Monthly Anthology* (March 1807), 114.

39. Adams, "Harvard College, 1786-1787," 91.

40. Samuel Tyler, ed., *Memoir of Roger Brooke Taney* (Baltimore, 1876), 42.

41. Hugh Henry Brackenridge, *Modern Chivalry,* II (1793), ed. Lewis Leary (New Haven, 1965), 138-141.

42. Phyllis Vine Erenberg, "Change and Continuity: Values in American Higher Education, 1750-1800," Ph.D. diss., University of Michigan, 1974, pp. 228, 243, 263, 265. David L. Madsen estimates that "in 1810 the ratio of college student to the total population was about 1 in 1500; today, the figure is 1 in 30." *Early National Education, 1776-1830* (New York, 1974), 120.

43. Samuel Eliot Morison, "Precedence at Harvard College in the Seventeenth Century," American Antiquarian Society *Proceedings,* n.s.,

42 (1932), 371-431; Clifford K. Shipton, *New England Life in the Eighteenth Century* (Cambridge, Mass., 1963), xxvi; William L. Kingsley, ed., *Yale College, A Sketch of Its History* (New York, 1879), I, 95, 96.

44. Walter Bronson, *The History of Brown University, 1764-1914* (Providence, 1914), 116.

45. Bronson, *History of Brown University,* 518, 519.

46. Baxter Perry Smith, *The History of Dartmouth College* (Boston, 1878), 83.

47. Samuel Stanhope Smith to Charles Nisbet, February 4, 1785, in Michael Kraus, "Charles Nisbet and Samuel Stanhope Smith—Two Eighteenth Century Educators," *Princeton University Library Chronicle,* 6 (Nov. 1944), 26.

48. Samuel Miller, *Memoir of the Rev. Charles Nisbet* (New York, 1840), 228.

49. Samuel Stanhope Smith, *The Lectures, Corrected and Improved, Which Have Been Delivered for a Series of Years, in the College of New-Jersey, on the Subjects of Moral and Political Philosophy* (Trenton, 1812), II, 294-298, 309-312.

50. Leon Burr Richardson, *History of Dartmouth College* (Hanover, N.H., 1932), I, 200.

51. Adams, "Harvard College, 1786-1787," 102.

52. *Princeton University Library Chronicle,* 16 (1954), 17, 19.

53. Morison, *Three Centuries of Harvard,* 178.

54. Adams, "Harvard College, 1786-1787," 106.

55. R. D. W. Conner and others, eds., *A Documentary History of the University of North Carolina* (Chapel Hill, 1953), II, 147.

56. *Documentary History of the University of North Carolina,* I, 38.

57. *Letters of John Randolph to a Young Relative* (Philadelphia, 1834), 14, letter dated February 15, 1806.

2. *The Genius of Revolt*

1. Quantifying violence is methodologically problematic. As the military historian John Shy asked, "how much violence or destruction is consequential? how little, negligible?" in Stephen G. Kurtz and James H. Hutson, eds., *Essays on the American Revolution* (Chapel Hill, 1973), 126. The insurrections included here are William and Mary, 1800, 1802, 1808; Princeton, 1800, 1802, 1807; University of North Carolina, 1799,

1805; Williams, 1802, 1808; Brown, 1798, 1800; Harvard, 1800, 1807; as well as Dickinson 1798 and Dartmouth 1808.

2. Rudulphus H. Williams to William E. Green, April 8, 1798, in Robert Perkins Brown and others, eds., *Memories of Brown, Traditions and Recollections Gathered From Many Sources* (Providence, 1909), 29.

3. John Bassett Moore, ed., *The Works of James Buchanan* (Philadelphia, 1911), XII, 291-293.

4. "The Riotous Commencement of 1811," *Columbia University Quarterly,* 3 (June 1901), 229-238 and (Sept. 1901), 354-366.

5. William E. Green to Dr. John Green, June 25, 1798, in *Memories of Brown,* 29, 20.

6. Charles Coleman Sellers, *Dickinson College: A History* (Middletown, Conn., 1973), 119-124.

7. Charles Nisbet to John Witherspoon, December 3, 1793, in Miller, *Memoir of the Rev. Charles Nisbet,* 230.

8. Richard Hofstadter, *Academic Freedom in the Age of the College* (New York, 1955), 218.

9. Faculty Records, July 28, 30, 1800, in Arthur A. Richmond, III, "Jonathan Edwards, Jr., & Union College," *Union College Symposium,* 8 (Winter 1969/70), 27.

10. Report of the Committee on the Student Petition, Trustee Minutes, September 9, 1800, Union College Archives.

11. John London to Ebenezer Pettigrew, September 28, 1799, in Sarah McCulooh Lemmon, ed., *The Pettigrew Papers* (Raleigh, N.C., 1971), I, 244. See also Kemp P. Battle, *History of the University of North Carolina* (Raleigh, N.C., 1907), I, 155ff.

12. Willie Jones to the Trustees, November 23, 1799, in *Documentary History of the University of North Carolina,* II, 445.

13. "Extracts from the Diary of Timothy Fuller," Cambridge Historical Society *Publications,* 11 (Oct. 1916), 50, 51.

14. Moses Miller, Jr., to William Green, March 21, 1800, in *Memories of Brown,* 32.

15. Chapman Johnson to David Watson, May 18, 1800, in *The Virginia Magazine of History and Biography,* 29 (July 1921), 267-269.

16. Wertenbaker, *Princeton,* 137.

17. Samuel Stanhope Smith to Jedidiah Morse, March 10, 1802, Samuel Stanhope Smith Papers, Princeton University Library.

18. Niels Henry Sonne, *Liberal Kentucky, 1780-1828* (New York, 1939), 68-73.

19. Leverett Wilson Spring, *A History of Williams College* (Boston, 1917), 58.

20. Moses Stuart to Benjamin Silliman, December 21, 1802, and February 6, 1803, in George P. Fisher, *Life of Benjamin Silliman* (New York, 1866), 114-117.

21. *New-York Evening Post,* April 3, 1802.

22. *New-York Evening Post,* April 3, 1802.

23. *National Intelligencer,* May 10, 1802.

24. Wertenbaker, *Princeton,* 126-131.

25. Joseph McKeen, *The Inaugural Address, delivered in Brunswick, September 9, 1802* (Portland, 1807), 9, 10.

26. Eliphalet Nott to Samuel Nott, December, 1804, in C. Vann Santvoord, *Memoirs of Eliphalet Nott* (New York, 1876), 120, 121.

27. Henry Davis to Benjamin Silliman, December 22, 1806, Silliman Papers, Sterling Memorial Library, Yale University.

28. W. T. Hanson, Jr., *Early Life of John Howard Payne* (Boston, 1913), 58.

29. Student Petition, ca. August 13, 1805, Oversized Papers, University of North Carolina Archives.

30. Battle, *History of the University of North Carolina,* I, 200-215.

31. In *Three Centuries of Harvard* (Boston, 1936), 211, 212, Samuel Eliot Morison mentions an 1805 "Bread and Butter Rebellion" of which I can find no evidence. I have concluded that Morison confused this with the later 1807 rebellion which he omits. Yet he is correct in asserting that student complaints about the commons reached the trustees in 1805. See Thomas C. Amory, *Life of James Sullivan* (Boston, 1859), II, 214, 215.

32. Brooks Mather Kelley, *Yale: A History* (New Haven, 1974), 125.

33. James W. Alexander, *The Life of Archibald Alexander* (New York, 1855), 275, 276.

34. Spring, *History of Williams College,* 58, 59.

35. *William and Mary Quarterly,* 16 (1907), 120; 22 (1913-1914), 22.

36. Codman Hislop, *Eliphalet Nott* (Middletown, Conn., 1971), book 2, chap. 4.

37. (Boston) *New-England Palladium,* May 12, 1807.

38. (Richmond) *The Examiner,* April 10, 1802.

39. Minutes of the Meeting of the Board of Trustees, April 12, 1803, Princeton University Archives.

40. Governor Joseph Bloomfield, president of the Corporation of the College of New-Jersey to the president of Harvard University, April 11, 1807, Harvard University Archives. For responses to the Princeton letter see Timothy Dwight (Yale) May 16, 1807, Bishop James Madison (William and Mary) May 10, 1807, Eliphalet Nott (Union) May 9, 1807, Asa Messer (Brown) May 4, 1807, all found in the Maclean Collection, Princeton University Archives. Replies to the Harvard blacklist are John Wheelock (Dartmouth) to Samuel Webber, May 5, 1807, and Benjamin Moore (Columbia) to Samuel Webber, October 29, 1807, Harvard University Archives.

41. Trustee Minutes, December 10, 1807, typescript, III, 186-189, University of North Carolina Archives.

42. Daniel Clarke Sanders (University of Vermont) to John Wheelock, July 3, 1809, Gratz Collection, The Historical Society of Pennsylvania, Ebenezer Fitch (Williams) to John Wheelock, January 23, 1810, Dartmouth College Archives; Battle, *History of the University of North Carolina,* I, 237.

43. *Journal of the Proceedings of a Convention of Literary and Scientific Gentlemen* (New York, 1831), 145, 146. Rev. Dr. Jonathan Mayhew Wainwright, who made this comment, opposed the policy as too harsh.

44. In addition to the standard college histories see Samuel Eliot Morison, "The Great Rebellion in Harvard and the Resignation of President Kirkland," Colonial Society of Massachusetts *Transactions,* 27 (1928), 54-111; Robert Anthony Patrick McCaughey, "The Usable Past: A Study of the Harvard College Rebellion of 1834," *William and Mary Law Review,* 11 (Spring 1970); Barry A. Crouch, "Rusticated Rebel: Amos A. Lawrence and His Harvard Years," *Harvard Library Bulletin,* 20 (1972), 69-83.

45. Leonard L. Richards, *Gentlemen of Property and Standing: Anti-Abolition Mobs in Jacksonian America* (New York, 1970); David Grimsted, "Rioting in its Jacksonian Setting," *American Historical Review,* 77 (April 1972), 361-397.

46. Samuel F. Batchelder, *Bits of Harvard History* (Cambridge, Mass., 1924), 144, 145.

47. *The Diary of William Bentley* (Salem, 1911), III, 289.

48. The background to the rebellion is given in W. Phillips, "Anti-Don-Quixotism, or, A Vindication of the Students with respect to the late Occurrences in Harvard College," 1807, n.p., Harvard University Archives.

.

49. Quoted in James R. McGovern, "The Student Rebellion in Harvard College, 1807-1808," *Harvard Library Bulletin,* 19 (Oct. 1971), 342.

50. Records of the Faculty, March 25, 26, 1807, VIII, 28, Harvard University Archives.

51. Records of the Faculty, VIII, 30, 31, Harvard University Archives.

52. Joseph Tufts, *Don-Quixots at College; or, A History of the Gallant Adventures lately achieved by the combined students of Harvard University; interspersed with some Facetious reasoning, By a Senior* (Boston, 1807), 6.

53. *A Narrative of the Proceedings of the Corporation of Harvard College, relative to the Late Disorders in that Seminary* (Cambridge, 1807), 5.

54. "Journal of John Gallison," 1807, n.p., 5-7, Harvard University Archives.

55. *Narrative of the Proceedings of the Corporation,* 7, 15-17.

56. *Narrative of the Proceedings of the Corporation,* 13.

57. Levi Hedge to Daniel A. White, April 5, 1807, in McGovern, "The Student Rebellion in Harvard College," 345.

58. "The authors or instigators of the offence were not known. Those, who called the illegal meeting, or the offender who rang the bell, were not discovered. There was no evidence, who was the moderator or chairman; who harrangued the assembly, or who proposed the matter or form of the assembly," *Narrative of the Proceedings of the Corporation,* 9.

59. Levi Hedge to Daniel A. White, March 5, 1808, in McGovern, "The Student Rebellion in Harvard College," 347.

60. Levi Hedge to Daniel A. White, April 1807, in McGovern, "The Student Rebellion in Harvard College," 352, 353.

61. "Memoirs of the Life of Joseph Tufts," n.d., n.p., 64, 65, Harvard University Archives.

62. George Rudé, *The Crowd in History, A Study of Popular Disturbances in France and England 1730-1848* (New York, 1964), 10, 60, 253, 254.

63. Tufts, *Don-Quixots at College,* 20.

64. Phillips, "Anti-Don-Quixotism, or, A Vindication of the Students," Harvard University Archives.

65. *The Diary of William Bentley,* III, 289.

66. Petition of the Freshman Class, December 26, 1806, Corpora-

tion Papers, 1806-1807, Harvard University Archives; McGovern, "The Student Rebellion in Harvard College," 252.

67. Meeting of the President and Fellows of Harvard College, June 26, October 6, 1807, Corporation Papers, Harvard University Archives.

68. *Report of the Committee of the Overseers of Harvard College,* January 6, 1825, 52, Harvard University Archives.

69. L. M. Sargent, *The New-Milk Cheese, or the Comi-Heroic Thunderclap,* II, May 2, 1807, p. 45, Harvard University Archives.

70. "Memoirs of the Life of Joseph Tufts," 67, 69.

71. Asa Messer to Adoniram Judson, April 10, 1811, Messer Letterbook, Brown University Archives.

72. Ashbel Green, *To the Friends of the College of New Jersey* (Nassau Hall, February 20, 1817).

73. John Pierce to Reverend Reuben Smith, February 1816, Alumni File, Princeton University Archives.

74. William Stickney, ed., *Autobiography of Amos Kendall* (New York, 1872), 33-37.

75. Joseph R. Kett, "Adolescence and Youth in Nineteenth-Century America," 292.

76. E. J. Hobsbawm, *Primitive Rebels, Studies in Archaic Forms of Social Movement in the 19th and 20th Centuries* (New York, 1963), 150.

77. Timothy Dwight to Governor Joseph Bloomfield, May 16, 1807, Maclean Papers, Princeton University Archives.

78. Elias Boudinot to Ashbel Green, April 3, 1807, in George Adams Boyd, *Elias Boudinot, Patriot and Statesman, 1740-1821* (Princeton, 1952), 267.

79. Faculty Minutes, March 31, 1807, Princeton University Archives.

80. John Campbell to David Campbell, May 2, 1807, Campbell Papers, Duke University Library Manuscripts.

81. Thomas Telfair to Alexander Telfair, May 2, 1807, Telfair Papers, Duke University Library Manuscripts.

82. Joseph C. Breckenridge to Mrs. John Breckenridge, April 6, 1807, Breckenridge Papers, Manuscript Division, Library of Congress.

83. *Trenton True American,* May 11, 1807.

84. Ashbel Green to Samuel Stanhope Smith, May 5, 1807. Princeton University Archives.

85. "Statement of the Students of the College of New Jersey," April 15, 1807, Princeton University Archives.

86. Thomas Telfair to Alexander Telfair, May 2, 1807, Telfair

Papers, Duke University Library Manuscripts.

87. Joseph C. Breckenridge to Mrs. John Breckenridge, April 27, 1807, Breckenridge Papers, Manuscript Division, Library of Congress.

88. Statement of the Trustees of the College of New Jersey, April 10, 1807, Princeton University Archives.

89. David F. Allmendinger, Jr., "New England Students and the Revolution in Higher Education, 1800-1900," *History of Education Quarterly*, 11 (Winter 1971), 381-389.

90. See Lyman Beecher, *An Address of the Charitable Society for the Education of Indigent Pious Young Men, for the Ministry of the Gospel* (n.p., ca. 1814), 21-22; the only adequate treatment of the AES is John Rollefson, "The American Education Society, 1815-1837: Ministerial Education, and the United Front," seminar paper, University of California, Berkeley, 1974.

91. *Journal of the Proceedings of a Convention of Literary Gentlemen*, 35.

92. Henry Clay Cameron, *History of the American Whig Society* (Princeton, 1871); Charles Richard Williams, *The Cliosophic Society, Princeton University* (Princeton, 1916).

93. Alexander S. Johnson to James Iredell, January 28, 1807, Charles E. Johnson Collection, North Carolina State Archives.

94. James Iredell, Jr., to Robert Green, January 13, 1806, Charles E. Johnson Collection, North Carolina State Archives.

95. John Maclean, *History of the College of New Jersey* (Philadelphia, 1877), II, 79.

96. Maclean, *History of the College of New Jersey*, II, 76, 77.

97. Philanthropic Society Minutes, July 30, August 24, September 8, 1805, University of North Carolina Archives.

98. The Princeton Archives contains a list of the students expelled for the 1807 rebellion. The society leaders are identified in James Booth to James Iredell, March 4, 1807, Iredell Papers, Duke University Library Manuscripts.

99. Maclean, *History of the College of New Jersey*, II, 76. For the same observation at Harvard see W. Phillips, "Anti-Don-Quixotism, or, a Vindication of the Students," Harvard University Archives.

100. "History for 1807," Whig Society Annual Histories, 1802-1869, n.p., Princeton University Archives.

101. "History for 1805," Whig Society Annual Histories, 1802-1869, n.p., Princeton University Archives.

102. "History for 1807," Princeton University Archives.

103. Ralph Ketcham, "James Madison at Princeton," *Princeton University Library Chronicle,* 28 (Autumn 1966).

3. The Sons of the Founders

1. Thomas Jefferson to John Adams, July 5, 1814, in Lester J. Cappon, ed., *The Adams-Jefferson Letters* (Chapel Hill, 1959), II, 434.

2. Katherine Metcalf Roof, *Colonel William Smith and Lady* (Boston, 1929), 260, 230.

3. David Ramsay, *History of South Carolina, From Its First Settlement in 1670 to the Year 1808* (Charleston, 1809), II, 437.

4. Benjamin Rush, *A Plan for the Establishment of Public Schools and the Diffusion of Knowledge in Pennsylvania, to Which Are Added Thoughts upon the Mode of Education, Proper in a Republic* (Philadelphia, 1786), 24.

5. John Randolph to ward, January 8, 1807, *Letters of John Randolph to a Young Relative* (Philadelphia, 1834), 26.

6. Benjamin Waterhouse, *Cautions to Young Persons* (Cambridge, Mass., 1804), 27-29.

7. R. R. Palmer, *The Age of Democratic Revolution: The Struggle* (Princeton, 1964), chaps. 11, 12, 15.

8. James Morton Smith, *Freedom's Fetters: The Alien and Sedition Laws and American Civil Liberties* (Ithaca, 1956), 192.

9. Paul Leicester Ford, ed., *The Writings of Thomas Jefferson* (New York, 1905), VIII, 251, 252; Alexander De Conde, *The Quasi-War: The Politics and Diplomacy of the Undeclared War with France, 1797-1801* (New York, 1966), 83, 84.

10. John Bach McMaster, *A History of the People of the United States, From the Revolution to the Civil War* (New York, 1885), II, 381.

11. Abraham Bishop, *Proofs of a Conspiracy, against Christianity and the Government of the United States* (Hartford, 1802), 49.

12. Mercy Otis Warren, *History of the Rise, Progress and Termination of the American Revolution, Interspersed With Biographical, Political and Moral Observations* (Boston, 1805), III, 395.

13. Thomas Jefferson to William Greene Munford, June 18, 1799, in Julian P. Boyd, ed., *Thomas Jefferson on Science and Freedom* (Worcester, 1964), 60. This rare letter, never included in Jefferson's works, tells how he was taken advantage of by a brilliant, freethinking student of William and Mary.

14. Benjamin Austin, *Constitutional Republicanism, in Opposi-*

tion to Fallacious Federalism (Boston, 1803), 174, 175, 302-306. These essays were first printed in Boston's *Independent Chronicle,* October 15, 22, 1801.

15. Joseph F. Kett, "Adolescence and Youth in Nineteenth-Century America," *Journal of Interdisciplinary History,* 2 (Autumn 1971), 286.

16. The Union address is mentioned in George W. Bancker to Abraham B. Bancker, June 21, 1798, Bancker Papers, New-York Historical Society. For Yale's address see McMaster, *History of the People of the United States,* II, 381.

17. William Austin, ed., *A Selection of the Patriotic Addresses to the President . . . Together with the President's Answers* (Boston, 1798), 235-238, 103, 185.

18. Seymour Martin Lipset, *Student Politics* (New York, 1971), xxii; Peter Loewenberg, "Psychohistorical Origins of the Nazi Youth Cohort," *American Historical Review,* 76 (Dec. 1971), 1457-1502.

19. Thomas Jefferson to William Greene Munford, June 18, 1799, in Boyd, ed., *Jefferson on Science and Freedom,* 27, 56, 57; Thomas Jefferson to Joseph Priestley, March 21, 1801, in Ford, ed., *The Writings of Thomas Jefferson,* IX, 217. The publication of the latter letter nearly broke up the Adams-Jefferson friendship which mutual friends had worked so hard to restore. Lester J. Cappon, ed., *The Adams-Jefferson Letters,* II, 288.

20. Austin, *Selection of the Patriotic Addresses,* 27; Charles Francis Adams, ed., *The Works of John Adams* (Boston, 1854), IX, 212, 207.

21. Drilling at Union is mentioned in George W. Bancker to Abraham B. Bancker, July 15, 1798, Bancker Papers, New-York Historical Society; at Princeton in James Mercer Garnett, *Biographical Sketch of Hon. Charles Fenton Mercer* (Richmond, Va., 1911), 5; at Harvard in "Diary of Timothy Fuller," Cambridge Historical Society *Publications,* 11 (Oct. 1916), 35.

22. Henry Van Schaack to Theodore Sedgwick, January 21, 1798; Daniel Dewey to Sedgwick, June 16, 1798; Dewey to Sedgwick, June 22, 1798; Van Schaack to Sedgwick, July 4, 1798, Sedgwick Papers, Massachusetts Historical Society.

23. Richmond, *The Observatory: Or, A View of the Times,* June 14, 1798.

24. *Philadelphia Aurora,* June 18, 1798, in Noble E. Cunningham, Jr., *The Early Republic, 1789-1828* (New York, 1968), 60, 61.

25. Joseph C. Cabell to David Watson, July 8, 1798, Watson Pa-

pers, Manuscript Division, Library of Congress; Boyd, ed., *Jefferson on Science and Freedom,* 59.

26. "Extracts from the Diary of Timothy Fuller," 38; *The Diary of William Bentley,* II, 299, 300.

27. John H. Tudor, "Diary, 1800-1801," Harvard University Archives; "Extracts from the Diary of Timothy Fuller," 45.

28. Dr. John Warren to John Collins Warren, July 18, 1800, John C. Warren Papers, Massachusetts Historical Society.

29. Extract from the Proceedings of the Faculty, July 11, 1798, *William and Mary Quarterly,* 27 (April 1919), 232; McMaster, *History of the People of the United States,* II, 384; Cabell to Watson, July 8, 1798, Watson Papers, Manuscript Division, Library of Congress.

30. Alexander Slidell MacKenzie, *Life of Stephen Decatur, A Commodore in the Navy of the United States* (Boston, 1848), 15-24. One of the sons of the Founders wrote a biography of Decatur which well expressed his generation's thirst for glory. "How ignoble would Stephen and James Decatur have appeared, if, instead of devoting themselves to their country, and achieving deeds of glory as the foundation of *their own* fame, they had supinely reposed upon the high rank and reputation of their gallant father?" S. Putnam Waldo, *The Life and Character of Stephen Decatur* (Hartford, 1821), motto, 22, 23, 26, 42, 43.

31. Charles J. Ingersoll, *Recollections, Historical, Political, Biographical, and Social* (Philadelphia, 1861), I, 205, 206; William M. Meigs, *The Life of Charles Jared Ingersoll* (Philadelphia, 1897), 26-31.

32. Abigail Adams Smith to Abigail Adams, May 17, 1800, in Roof, *Colonel William Smith and Lady,* 255; see also John Henry Hobart to Charles Fenton Mercer, June 24, 1798, in *The Correspondence of John Henry Hobart* (New York, 1911), II, 90.

33. Petition of the Seniors at Harvard Against Certain Restrictions at the Commencement of 1798, Park Family Papers, Sterling Memorial Library, Yale University.

34. William Henry Channing, *Memoir of William Ellery Channing,* 2d ed. (Boston, 1848), I, 68-72.

35. James Walker Austin, ed., *Literary Papers of William Austin* (Boston, 1890), 391, emphasis added.

36. *Literary Papers of William Austin,* 124, emphasis added.

37. The authorship of *A Selection of the Patriotic Addresses* is admittedly uncertain. Most bibliographies assume that another, unknown, William Austin compiled the volume, probably because the known Austin was only twenty at the time. Yet Harvard's Houghton Li-

brary credits it to Austin the Harvard senior, and there is a good deal of indirect evidence to support this. *A Selection* bears exactly the same imprint as Austin's known work, *Strictures on Harvard University*—Boston, John W. Folsom printer, 1798—and the list of subscribers at the end of *A Selection* contains many of the Harvard Austin's relatives on both sides of the family, as though they were trying to subsidize their aspiring young kinsman's literary endeavors. There are stylistic similarities between the two works as well.

38. Sidney Willard, *Memories of Youth and Manhood* (Cambridge, Mass., 1855), II, 13-15.

39. [William Austin], *Strictures on Harvard University, By a Senior* (Boston, 1798), 25, 5, 8, 9, 29; Walter Austin, *William Austin, The Creator of Peter Rugg* (Boston, 1925), 58, 182.

40. Austin, *Strictures on Harvard University*, 8, 9.

41. H. W. L. Dana, "Allston at Harvard," and "Allston in Cambridgeport," Cambridge Historical Society, *Publications*, 29 (1948), 14-67.

42. Dana, "Allston at Harvard," 32.

43. Jared B. Flagg, *The Life and Letters of Washington Allston* (New York, 1892, 1969), 21-29.

44. John Campbell to David Campbell, September 7, 1806, Campbell Papers, Duke University Library Manuscripts.

45. Joseph C. Breckenridge to Alfred Grayson, January 9, 1807, in Lowell H. Harrison, "A Young Kentuckian at Princeton, 1807-1808: Joseph Cabell Breckenridge," *Filson Club History Quarterly*, 38 (Oct. 1964), 299.

46. James Booth to James Iredell, March 4, 1807, Iredell Papers, Duke University Library Manuscripts.

47. Joseph C. Breckenridge to Mrs. John Breckenridge, April 6, 1807, in Harrison, "A Young Kentuckian at Princeton," 303.

48. Mills Day to Thomas Day, December 24, 1802, Day Family Papers, Sterling Memorial Library, Yale University.

49. William Stickney, ed., *Autobiography of Amos Kendall* (New York, 1872), 50.

50. Ebenezer Fitch to John Eliot, May 19, 1802, Massachusetts Historical Society.

51. Robert E. Spiller, *Fenimore Cooper, Critic of His Times* (New York, 1931), 32.

52. Parke Godwin, *A Biography of William Cullen Bryant* (New

York, 1883), I, 70, 71; Tremaine McDowell, "Cullen Bryant at Williams College," *New England Quarterly*, 1 (Oct. 1928), 463.

53. *The Trial of Julian C. Verplanck, Hugh Maxwell, and Others, for a Riot, in Trinity Church, at the Commencement of 1811* (New York, 1821).

54. Richmond, "Jonathan Edwards, Jr., & Union College," 27.

55. *Autobiography of Amos Kendall*, 33-35.

56. Charles Sellers, *James K. Polk, Jacksonian, 1795-1843* (Princeton, 1957), 39-53.

57. Austin, *Constitutional Republicanism*, 171, 172; David Hackett Fischer, *The Revolution of American Conservatism: The Federalist Party in the Era of Jeffersonian Democracy* (New York, 1969), 30.

58. [Clement C. Moore], *Observations Upon Certain Passages in Mr. Jefferson's Notes on Virginia, Which Appear to Have a Tendency to Subvert Religion and Establish False Philosophy*, 3d ed. (New York, 1804), 30, 31.

59. Timothy Dwight, Baccalaureate Sermon, 1803 and 1813, in *Sermons* (New Haven, 1828), I, 417.

60. Samuel Stanhope Smith to William Hamilton, December 10, 1808, Hamilton Papers, Southern Historical Collection, University of North Carolina.

61. Faculty Minutes, April 22, 1805, Harvard University Archives; Minutes of the Board of Trustees, December 8, 1804, University of North Carolina Archives.

62. John M. Blum and others, *The National Experience, Part One*, 3d ed. (New York, 1973), 171; Samuel Eliot Morison, *The Oxford History of the American People* (New York, 1965), 380.

63. *History of the Adventures and Sufferings of Moses Smith* (Albany, 1814). Although Smith was "tricked" into participating, see Paul H. Musser, *James Nelson Barker, 1784-1858* (Philadelphia, 1929), 16, 17; Benjamin Rush to John Adams, June 10, 1806 ("Miranda has been the unfortunate cause of distress to more families than yours"), in L. H. Butterfield, ed., *Letters of Benjamin Rush* (Princeton, 1951), II, 920.

64. "Statement of the Students of the College of New Jersey," April 15, 1807, Princeton University Archives.

65. *Statement of Facts, Relative to the Late Proceedings at Harvard College, Published by the Students* (Boston, 1807), 8, 9, emphasis added.

66. J. L. Conner to G. A. L. Conner, September 22, 1805, North

Carolina *University Magazine* (April 1894), 332.

67. John Campbell to Maria Campbell, July 17, 1807, Campbell Papers, Duke University Library Manuscripts.

68. Moses Miller, Jr., to William Green, March 21, 1800, in *Memories of Brown*, 32.

69. Ramsay, *History of South Carolina*, II, 385, 386.

4. The Defenders of the Faith

1. Samuel Stanhope Smith to Charles Nisbet, November 26, 1784, in Kraus, "Charles Nisbet and Samuel Stanhope Smith," 20.

2. John Thornton Kirkland, *An Oration, at the request of the Society of Phi Beta Kappa, in the chapel of Harvard College, on the day of their anniversary, July 19, 1798* (Boston, 1798), 7, 8.

3. Winthrop Hudson, *American Protestantism* (Chicago, 1961), 50.

4. Joseph McKeen, *The Inaugural Address, delivered in Brunswick, September 9th, 1802* (Portland, Maine, 1802), 5.

5. S. G. Goodrich, *Recollections of a Lifetime* (New York, 1856), I, 196, 197.

6. *The Life of the Reverend Devereux Jarratt, Written by Himself* (Baltimore, 1806), 181.

7. Gary B. Nash, "The American Clergy and the French Revolution," *William and Mary Quarterly*, 3d ser., 13 (July 1965), 392-412; Henry F. May, "The Problem of the American Enlightenment," *New Literary History*, 1 (Winter 1970), 211.

8. Samuel McCorkle, *The Work of God for the French Revolution, and then her Reformation or Ruin; or, The novel and useful experiment of national deism, to us and all future ages* (Salisbury, N.C., 1798), 27.

9. David Brion Davis, ed., *The Fear of Conspiracy: Images of Un-American Subversion from the Revolution to the Present* (New York, 1971).

10. Harold S. Jantz, "Samuel Miller Papers at Princeton," *Princeton University Library Chronicle*, 4 (Feb. 1943), 74.

11. Timothy Dwight, *The Duty of Americans at the Present Crisis . . . Preached on the 4th of July, 1798* (New Haven, 1798), 31.

12. Jonathan Maxcy, *An Oration . . . on the Fourth of July, 1799* (Providence, 1799), 3.

13. Ebenezer Fitch, *Useful Knowledge and Religion, Recom-*

mended to the Pursuit and Improvement of the Young (Pittsfield, Mass., 1799), 25.

14. Vernon Stauffer, *New England and the Bavarian Illuminati* (New York, 1918).

15. John Robison, *Proofs of a Conspiracy* (Boston, The American Classics, 1967), 5. This is now in paperback because right-wing political groups trace the origin of communism to Illuminism.

16. Robison, *Proofs of a Conspiracy*, 121.

17. Robison, *Proofs of a Conspiracy*, 9.

18. Stauffer, *New England and the Bavarian Illuminati*, 227.

19. Jedidiah Morse, *A Sermon, Exhibiting the Present Dangers, and Consequent Duties of the Citizens of the United States of America* (Charlestown, Mass., 1799), 17.

20. Charles Nisbet to Samuel Miller, July 6, 1798, quoted in Miller, *Memoir of the Rev. Charles Nisbet*, 256.

21. David Tappan, *A Discourse Delivered in the Chapel of Harvard College* (Boston, 1798), 13, 14.

22. Samuel Stanhope Smith to Jedidiah Morse, February 23, 1799, Smith Papers, Princeton University Library Manuscripts.

23. Franklin Bowditch Dexter, *Biographical Sketches of the Graduates of Yale College* (New York, 1911), V, 153-155; Timothy Dwight to Jedidiah Morse, December 13, 1800, Morse Family Papers, Sterling Memorial Library, Yale University.

24. John Smith to Eliphalet Pearson, October 26, 1799, Park Family Papers, Sterling Memorial Library, Yale University.

25. Timothy Dwight to Jedidiah Morse, December 19, 1800, Morse Family Papers, Sterling Memorial Library, Yale University.

26. Benjamin Silliman, *An Oration, delivered at Hartford on the 6th of July, 1802, before the Society of the Cincinnati* (Hartford, 1802), 8n.

27. Eliphalet Pearson, "Exhibition Day Address," ca. 1808, Park Family Papers, Sterling Memorial Library, Yale University.

28. Sidney E. Mead, *The Lively Experiment: The Shaping of Christianity in America* (New York, 1963), 50.

29. Robison, *Proofs of a Conspiracy*, 58, 77, 81, 128, 263, 273.

30. Seth Payson, *Proofs of the Real Existence, and Dangerous Tendency of Illuminism* (Charlestown, Mass., 1802), 51, 90.

31. Timothy Dwight, *The Nature and Dangers of Infidel Philosophy*, Baccalaureate Sermon 1797, in *Sermons*, I, 347-355.

32. Joseph Lathrop, *A Sermon on the Dangers of the Times, From*

Infidelity and Immorality (Springfield, Mass., 1798), 22, 13.

33. *Minutes of the General Assembly* (Philadelphia, 1835), 181.

34. Stauffer, *New England and the Bavarian Illuminati,* 101.

35. Jedidiah Morse, *A Sermon . . . On the Existence, Progress, and Deleterious Effects of French Intrigue in the United States* (Boston, 1798), 22.

36. Payson, *Proofs of the Real Existence of Illuminism,* 189, 190, 191, 222n.

37. Leon Burr Richardson, *History of Dartmouth College,* I, 272.

38. Dexter, *Biographical Sketches of the Graduates of Yale,* V, 316; Willard, *Memories of Youth and Manhood,* II, 139.

39. Miller, *Memoir of the Rev. Charles Nisbet,* 269.

40. Samuel Phillips to Eliphalet Pearson, May 4, 1801, Park Family Papers, Sterling Memorial Library, Yale University.

41. Dr. Benjamin Waterhouse to Dr. James Tilton, March 24, 1815, Massachusetts Historical Society *Proceedings,* 54 (1920-21), 160.

42. William M. Meigs, *Life of Josiah Meigs* (Philadelphia, 1887), 35-51.

43. C. R. Hall, *A Scientist in the Early Republic, Samuel Latham Mitchill* (New York, 1934); N. G. Goodman, *Benjamin Rush, Physician and Citizen, 1746-1813* (Philadelphia, 1934).

44. Bishop, *Proofs of a Conspiracy,* 48, 163, 164.

45. James Cosens Ogden, *A View of the New-England Illuminati* (Philadelphia, 1799), 17; *Friendly Remarks to the People of Connecticut, Upon their College and Schools* (Litchfield, 1799).

46. "Literature of North Carolina," *Monthly Anthology and Boston Review* (July 1806), 356.

47. *Wilmington Gazette,* October 21, 1806.

48. Anonymous to Thomas Jefferson, June 29, 1802, Library of Congress Microfilm, vol. 124, 21410-21411; John Armstrong to Ephraim Kirby, November 2, 1801, Kirby Papers, Duke University Library Manuscripts.

49. George William Erving to unknown, July 5, 1804, Boston Public Library Manuscripts.

50. George W. Bancker to Abraham B. Bancker, June 21, 1798, Bancker Papers, New-York Historical Society.

51. William Garnett to Thomas Ruffin, September 24, 1804, in J. G. deR. Hamilton, ed., *The Papers of Thomas Ruffin* (Raleigh, Va., 1918), I, 56.

52. *New England Historical and Geneological Register,* 71 (Oct. 1927), 396.

53. James McDowell to Samuel McDowell Reid, February 23, 1814, *William and Mary Quarterly*, 8 (April 1900), 225, 226.

54. *President Dwight's Decisions of Questions Discussed by the Senior Class in Yale College, in 1813 and 1814*, from stenographic notes by Theodore Dwight, Jr. (New York, 1833), 102.

55. *Annual Report of the American Historical Association for the Year 1899*, vol. II: *Calhoun Correspondence* (Washington, 1900), 81.

56. Draft of a letter to the *Wilmington Gazette* which appeared in much abridged form on December 30, 1806, found in the University Papers, University of North Carolina Archives.

57. John S. Whitehead, *The Separation of College and State: Columbia, Dartmouth, Harvard, and Yale, 1776-1876* (New Haven, 1973).

58. Samuel Miller, *The Life of Samuel Miller* (Philadelphia, 1869), II, 11.

59. Eliphalet Pearson to Henry B. Pearson, February 22, 1813, Henry B. Pearson Papers, Beinecke Library, Yale University.

60. Timothy Dwight, "On Doing Good," Baccalaureate Sermon 1816, in *Sermons*, I, 540.

61. Charles I. Foster, *An Errand of Mercy: The Evangelical United Front, 1790-1837* (Chapel Hill, 1960).

62. The latest thrust which provides an excellent bibliography is Lois W. Banner, "Religious Benevolence as Social Control: A Critique of an Interpretation," *Journal of American History*, 60 (June 1973), 23-41.

63. *President Dwight's Decisions of Questions*, 331.

64. Samuel Dexter's legacy to Harvard, February 17, 1799, Dexter Papers, Massachusetts Historical Society.

65. Samuel Phillips Donation, June 22, 1802, Pearson Papers, Harvard University Archives.

66. Alexander Hamilton to James A. Bayard, April 1802, in Henry Cabot Lodge, ed., *The Works of Alexander Hamilton* (New York, 1904), X, 432-437. This was the letter in which he stated that "men are rather reasoning than reasonable animals, for the most part governed by the impulse of passion," to which he hoped fellow Federalists would increasingly appeal.

67. Sydney E. Ahlstrom, "The Scottish Philosophy and American Theology," *Church History*, 24 (Sept. 1955), 267.

68. Douglas Sloan, *The Scottish Enlightenment and the American College Ideal* (Columbia University, 1971).

69. Daniel Walker Howe, *The Unitarian Conscience: Harvard Moral Philosophy, 1805-1861* (Cambridge, Mass., 1970) and D. H. Meyer,

The Instructed Conscience: The Shaping of the American National Ethic (Philadelphia, 1972) are profound studies of the legacy of Common Sense in America.

5. The Progress of Vice and Irreligion

1. Daniel Clarke Sanders to John Wheelock, July 3, 1809, Gratz Collection, Historical Society of Pennsylvania. Professor Henry F. May of the University of California, Berkeley, brought this letter to my attention.

2. This account is heavily indebted to Niels Henry Sonne, *Liberal Kentucky, 1780-1828* (New York, 1939), 68-73. Testimony from the trial is from "Minutes of the Trial of the Students vs. James Welsh," Transylvania University Archives, Lexington, Ky.

3. *Kentucky Gazette,* March 26, 1802.

4. *Kentucky Gazette,* March 26, 1802.

5. Report of the Trustees of Transylvania University to the Kentucky House of Representatives, 1816, in Sonne, *Liberal Kentucky,* 148; see also 73-77.

6. Minutes of the Faculty, January 2, 1802, Princeton University Archives.

7. Minutes of the Faculty, January 2, 1802, Princeton University Archives.

8. Joseph Olden to Mary Middletown, March 7, 1802, *Princeton Press,* February 28, 1914, copy in Princeton University Archives.

9. "Memoirs of George Strawbridge," Princeton University Library.

10. Olden to Middletown, March 7, 1802, *Princeton Press.*

11. "Memoirs of George Strawbridge."

12. Samuel Stanhope Smith to Jedidiah Morse, March 10, 1802, Princeton University Library.

13. Charles Nisbet to Alexander Addison, March 16, 1802, Darlington Library, University of Pittsburgh.

14. Joseph Willard to Ashbel Green, November 26, 1802, Boston Public Library.

15. Caleb Upshur to the Trustees, May 4, 1802, Princeton University Archives.

16. "Memoirs of George Strawbridge."

17. [Ashbel Green], *An Address to the Students and Faculty of the College of New-Jersey* (Trenton, 1802), 4, 5, 10, 11, 15.

18. *Laws of the College of New-Jersey* (Philadelphia, 1802), 31, 32.

19. Records of the Proceedings of the Board of Trustees, May 3, 1803, 253, Transylvania University Archives.

20. Benjamin Rush to Ashbel Green, December 9, 1802, in L. H. Butterfield, ed., *Letters of Benjamin Rush* (Princeton, 1955), II, 853, 854.

21. *Address of the Trustees of the College of New-Jersey* (Philadelphia, 1802), 4.

22. Samuel E. McCorkle to Ernest Haywood, December 20, 1799, Ernest Haywood Papers, Southern Historical Collection, University of North Carolina.

23. William R. Davie to John Haywood, September 22, 1805, *James Sprunt Historical Monograph*, 7 (1907), 59, 60.

24. Bishop James Madison to James Monroe, December 23, 1803, Monroe Papers, Series I, Manuscript Division, Library of Congress.

25. Jedidiah Morse to Eliphalet Lyman, February 9, 1805, in James King Morse, *Jedidiah Morse, A Champion of New England Orthodoxy* (New York, 1939), 95.

26. (Boston) *The Repertory*, April 10, 1807.

27. *A Narrative of the Proceedings of the Corporation of Harvard College, Relative to the Late Disorders in that Seminary*, 10.

28. "Journal of John Gallison," [1807], Harvard University Archives, 3, 7, 8.

29. Timothy Dwight to Governor Joseph Bloomfield, May 16, 1807, Maclean Papers, Princeton University Archives.

30. James Madison to the College of New Jersey, May 10, 1807, Maclean Papers, Princeton University Archives.

31. Eliphalet Nott to Samuel Stanhope Smith, May 9, 1807, Maclean Papers, Princeton University Archives.

32. Boyd, *Elias Boudinot,* 253, 254.

33. Elias Boudinot, *The Age of Revelation* (Philadelphia, 1801), xii.

34. Elias Boudinot, "Address to the Students," 1807, Princeton University Archives.

35. *Troy Gazette,* May 19, 1807.

36. "To the Students," April 15, 1807, Princeton University Archives.

37. (Boston) *New England Palladium,* April 17, 1807.

38. *Boston Gazette,* August 4, 1806.

39. Charles Warren, *Jacobin and Junto, or Early American Politics as Viewed in the Diary of Dr. Nathaniel Ames, 1758-1822* (Cambridge, Mass., 1931), 183-214.

40. *Trial of Thomas O. Selfridge* (Boston, 1807), 128.

41. *Statement of Facts, Relative to the Late Proceedings at Harvard College,* published by the students (Boston, 1807), 8, 9.

42. Charles Beecher, ed., *Autobiography, Correspondence, Etc., of Lyman Beecher* (New York, 1864), I, 43.

43. As Henry F. May has warned, "to make use of Lyman Beecher's remark about Deism at Yale . . . is even worse than it would be to make Senator Joseph McCarthy the chief source for the spread of Communism at Harvard in the thirties." "The Problem of the American Enlightenment," *New Literary History,* 1 (Winter 1970), 212. Some have mistaken Edmund S. Morgan's defense of President Stiles to be a denial of student freethinking. Actually, Morgan states that "there can be no doubt that infidelity existed in Yale in the 1790s." "Ezra Stiles and Timothy Dwight," Massachusetts Historical Society *Proceedings,* 72 (1963), 109.

44. Francis Wayland, *A Memoir of the Life and Labors of the Rev. Adoniram Judson, D.D.* (Boston, 1853), I, 22-25.

45. John Pettigrew to Charles Pettigrew, April 12, 1796, *Documentary History of the University of North Carolina,* II, 11.

46. Joseph C. Cabell to David Watson, March 4, 1798, Watson Papers, Manuscript Division, Library of Congress.

47. Allen McLane, "Reminiscences of Princeton College," n.d., n.p., Princeton University Library.

48. Daniel Walker Hollis, *University of South Carolina* (Columbia, S.C., 1951), I, 53.

49. "Memoirs of the Life of Joseph Tufts," 42, 43.

50. "Letters from William and Mary College, 1798-1801," *Virginia Magazine of History and Biography,* 29 (April 1921), 145-147, 155-158.

51. Condorcet, *Outlines of an Historical View of the Progress of the Human Mind* (London, 1795), 4.

52. Philip S. Foner, ed., *The Complete Writings of Thomas Paine* (New York, 1945), I, 528, 464.

53. Increase N. Talbot, ed., *Diary of Thomas Robbins* (Boston, 1886), I, 12, 22.

54. *Memoir of William Ellery Channing,* I, 102.

55. Samuel Miller, *A Brief Retrospect of the Eighteenth Century* (New York, 1803), II, 29, 295, 297-298, 300.

56. McLane, "Reminiscences of Princeton College."
57. William Godwin, *Enquiry Concerning Political Justice* [1793], (Oxford, 1971), 102.
58. "Examination of Modern Ethics," *The Literary Miscellany,* 1 (Cambridge, Mass., 1805), 56.
59. Benjamin Rush to Ashbel Green, December 31, 1812, *Letters of Benjamin Rush,* II, 1173, 1174.
60. "Annual History for 1805," Whig Society Annual Histories, 1802-1869, Princeton University Archives.
61. James McLachlan, "The *Choice of Hercules:* American Student Societies in the Early 19th Century," in Lawrence Stone, ed., *The University in Society,* vol. II: *Europe, Scotland, and the United States from the 16th to the 20th Century* (Princeton, 1974), 476.
62. See Thomas Jefferson Hogg's engaging *Shelly at Oxford* (London, 1904), 219-226.

6. The Downfall of Republican Education

1. *The Age of Reason, Part I* [1794], in Foner, ed., *The Complete Writings of Thomas Paine,* I, 491.
2. Howard Mumford Jones, *America and French Culture, 1750-1848* (Chapel Hill, 1927), 201, 202; Spring, *History of Williams College,* 56.
3. Bishop Madison to Ezra Stiles, August 27, 1780, *William and Mary Quarterly,* 16 (1907-1908), 215.
4. Bishop Madison to Thomas Jefferson, February 1, 1800, *William and Mary Quarterly,* 2d ser., 5 (1925), 148.
5. St. George Tucker to Professor Ebeling, December 11, 1801, Tucker-Coleman Papers, William and Mary Library.
6. Herbert B. Adams, *Thomas Jefferson and the University of Virginia* (Washington, D.C., 1888), 43.
7. Joseph C. Cabell to David Watson, March 4, 1798, Watson Papers, Manuscript Division, Library of Congress.
8. Isaac Coles to Henry St. George Tucker, July 20, 1799, *William and Mary Quarterly,* 8 (1900), 159.
9. J. Shelton Watson to David Watson, December 24, 1799, *Virginia Magazine of History and Biography,* 29 (April 1921), 152.
10. Theodore Dwight, *An Oration, Delivered at New Haven, on the 7th of July, 1801* (Hartford, 1801), 42, 43.

11. Bishop Madison to James Madison, October 24, 1801, Madison Papers, William and Mary Library; *National Intelligencer*, November 20, 1801.

12. *Memoirs of Lieut.-Genl. Scott, LL.D., Written by Himself* (New York, 1864), I, 10.

13. Joseph C. Cabell to David Watson, April 6, 1801, *Virginia Magazine of History and Biography*, 29 (July 1921), 278.

14. Adams, *Thomas Jefferson and the University of Virginia*, 43.

15. Joseph C. Cabell to David Watson, March 4, 1798, Watson Papers, Manuscript Division, Library of Congress.

16. Jedidiah Morse, *The American Geography; or, A View of the Present Situation of the United States of America* (London, 1792), 383.

17. David Watson to Joseph C. Cabell, April 21, 1798, Cabell Papers, University of Virginia Library.

18. William T. Barry to Dr. John Barry, January 20, February 6, 1804, *William and Mary Quarterly*, 13 (1904-1905), 109-111.

19. Thomas L. Preston to Andrew Reid, Jr., January 7, 1802, *William and Mary Quarterly*, 8 (1900), 216.

20. *Williamsburg Courier*, November 22, 1814.

21. *William and Mary Quarterly*, 16 (1907-1908), 126; 8 (1900), 220; *The Virginia Argus*, March 24, 1809.

22. *President Dwight's Decisions of Questions*, 316.

23. Thomas Cruse to James Hamilton, February 25, 1810, Cruse Papers, University of Virginia Library. Cruse was helping the woman place her son in Dickinson College.

24. Thomas L. Preston to Andrew Reid, Jr., February 22, 1802, *William and Mary Quarterly*, 8 (1900), 216.

25. Henry St. George Tucker to Joseph C. Cabell, March 28, 1802, Cabell Collection, University of Virginia Library.

26. Coleman had studied under Eliphalet Pearson at Andover Academy. He thanked Pearson for preserving him "from being contaminated with the foul & pestilential doctrines of modern philosophism and infidelity." William Coleman to Eliphalet Pearson, December 25, 1802, Park Family Papers, Sterling Memorial Library, Yale University.

27. William Parker Cutler and Julia Perkins Cutler, eds., *Life, Journals and Correspondence of Rev. Manasseh Cutler, LL.D.* (Cincinnati, 1888), II, 172, journal entry of December 2, 1804.

28. (Boston) *Columbian Centinel, Massachusetts Federalist*, April 10, 1802; (Hartford) *The Connecticut Gazette*, April 12, 1802; *Boston Gazette*, April 15, 1802.

29. Bishop Madison to Thomas Jefferson, April 15, 1802, *William and Mary Quarterly,* 2d ser., 5 (1925), 151; *National Intelligencer,* May 10, 1802; *Philadelphia Aurora,* April 8, 1802.

30. (Richmond) *The Examiner,* May 8, 1802.

31. Henry St. George Tucker to Joseph C. Cabell, March 28, 1802, Cabell Collection, University of Virginia Library.

32. J. S. Watson to Peter Minor, November 19, 1803, Minor Papers, University of Virginia Library, quoted with the kind permission of Mr. Niles Stevens.

33. Colonial enrollment is taken from Richard Beale Davis, *Intellectual Life in Jefferson's Virginia, 1790-1830* (Chapel Hill, 1964), 50. For 1800 and 1801 see J. S. Watson to David Watson, October 26, 1800, and March 2, 1801, *Virginia Magazine of History and Biography,* 29 (April 1921), 155, 161. For 1802 see George Watson to James Minor, November 15, 1802, Minor Papers, University of Virginia Library. For 1805 see W. Radford to Andrew Reid, Jr., December 26, 1805, *William and Mary Quarterly,* 8 (1900), 219.

34. According to Davis, *Intellectual Life in Jefferson's Virginia,* 53, "in 1801-1803, it was markedly in decline."

35. (Richmond) *The Examiner,* April 10, 1802. For a student reaction to the rules see *The Virginia Argus,* November 17, 1802.

36. William T. Barry to Dr. John Barry, February 15, 1804, *William and Mary Quarterly,* 13 (1904-1905), 113.

37. St. George Tucker to the Board of Visitors, December 9, 1803, William and Mary Library.

38. Bishop Madison to James Monroe, December 23, 1803, Monroe Papers, Series I, Manuscript Division, Library of Congress.

39. Bishop Madison to Thomas Jefferson, October 7, 1807, Jefferson Papers, Manuscript Division, Library of Congress.

40. Thomas Jefferson to William Short, November 9, 1813, Jefferson Papers, William and Mary Library.

41. *Dictionary of American Biography,* XVII, 297, 298.

42. John Augustine Smith, *A Syllabus of the Lectures Delivered to the Senior Students in the College of William and Mary on Government* (Philadelphia, 1817), 5, 7.

43. J. P. K. Henshaw, *Memoir of the Life of the Rt. Rev. Richard Channing Moore* (Philadelphia, 1843), 166ff.

44. (Richmond) *The Enquirer,* November 12, 24, 1814.

45. John S. Whitehead, *The Separation of College and State: Columbia, Dartmouth, Harvard, and Yale, 1776-1876* (New Haven, 1973).

46. Battle, *History of the University of North Carolina*, I, 1, 2.

47. Luther L. Gobbel, *Church-State Relationships in Education in North Carolina since 1776* (Durham, N.C., 1938), 10.

48. Blackwell P. Robinson, *William R. Davie* (Chapel Hill, 1957); John F. Hurley and Julia Goode Eagan, *The Prophet of Zion-Parnassus: Samuel Eusebius McCorkle* (Richmond, 1934).

49. William R. Davie to James Hogg, August 9, 1797, *Documentary History of the University of North Carolina*, II, 196.

50. *Four Discourses on the General First Principles of Deism and Revelation Contrasted* (Salisbury, N.C., 1797).

51. McCorkle, *Work of God for the French Revolution*, 27.

52. This plan is in *Documentary History of the University of North Carolina*, I, 375-379. McCorkle's comments on corporal punishment are in *Work of God for the French Revolution*, 35, 36. No provision for such punishments appeared in the laws.

53. Charles W. Harris to Dr. Charles Harris, April 10, 1795, *Documentary History of the University of North Carolina*, I, 387.

54. William R. Davie to Joseph Caldwell, February 26, 1797, *James Sprunt Historical Monographs*, 7 (1907), 32. His plan is in Robinson, *William R. Davie*, Appendix C, 406-410.

55. Battle, *History of the University of North Carolina*, I, 100.

56. John H. Hobart to Joseph Caldwell, November 30, 1796, *Documentary History of the University of North Carolina*, II, 79.

57. *Documentary History of the University of North Carolina*, II, 383.

58. John H. Hobart to Joseph Caldwell, November 30, 1796, *Documentary History of the University of North Carolina*, II, 79.

59. Thomas G. Amis to Ebenezer Pettigrew, June 25, 1798, *Documentary History of the University of North Carolina*, II, 337.

60. Joseph Caldwell to John Haywood, November 4, 1799, *Documentary History of the University of North Carolina*, II, 442.

61. Willie Jones to the trustees, November 23, 1799, *Documentary History of the University of North Carolina*, II, 445.

62. Delbert Harold Gilpatrick, *Jeffersonian Democracy in North Carolina, 1789-1816* (New York, 1931), 127-130.

63. Battle, *History of the University of North Carolina*, I, 139.

64. J. Franklin Jameson, ed., "The Diary of Edward Hooker, 1805-1806," in American Historical Association *Annual Report for the Year 1896, Vol. I* (Washington, D.C., 1897), 48.

65. William R. Davie to John R. Eaton, December 27, 1801, *James Sprunt Historical Monographs*, 7 (1907), 48.

66. Guy Howard Miller, "A Contracting Community: American Presbyterians, Social Conflict, and Higher Education, 1730-1820," (Ph.D. diss., University of Michigan, 1970), 437.

67. Samuel E. McCorkle to Ernest Haywood, December 20, 1799, Ernest Haywood Papers, Southern Historical Collection, University of North Carolina.

68. Joseph Caldwell Papers, ca. 1800, Southern Historical Collection, University of North Carolina.

69. Draft of a letter to the *Wilmington Gazette,* which appeared in much abridged form on December 30, 1806, Joseph Caldwell Papers, Southern Historical Collection, University of North Carolina.

70. Joseph Caldwell, *A Discourse delivered at the University of North Carolina, at the Commencement in July, 1802* (Raleigh, N.C., 1802), 6, 32.

71. Minutes of the Board of Trustees, typescript, July 12, 1804, 87, 88, University of North Carolina Archives.

72. "Literature of North Carolina," *Monthly Anthology and Boston Review* (July 1806), 356.

73. George P. Schmidt, *The Liberal Arts College, A Chapter in American Cultural History* (New Brunswick, 1957), 15.

74. Whitehead, *Separation of College and State,* 47-50.

75. Alan Heimert and Perry Miller, eds., *The Great Awakening, Documents Illustrating the Crisis and Its Consequences* (New York, 1967), 340, 347.

76. Leonard J. Trinterud, *The Forming of an American Tradition: A Re-examination of Colonial Presbyterianism* (Philadelphia, 1949), chap. 9.

77. *The Works of the Rev. John Witherspoon,* 2d ed. (Philadelphia, 1925), II, 205.

78. Collins, *President Witherspoon,* II, 205, 222.

79. Willard Thorp, ed., *The Lives of Eighteen from Princeton* (Princeton, 1946), 100, 101.

80. John Campbell to David Campbell, May 6, 1806, Campbell Papers, Duke University Library.

81. Charles W. Harris to Dr. Charles Harris, April 10, 1795, *Documentary History of the University of North Carolina,* I, 389.

82. George P. Fisher, *Life of Benjamin Silliman* (New York, 1866), I, 110.

83. David F. Bowers, "The Smith-Blair Correspondence, 1786-1791," *Princeton University Library Chronicle,* 4 (June 1943), 123-134.

84. Thorp, *Lives of Eighteen from Princeton,* 99.

85. Samuel Stanhope Smith to Benjamin Rush, September 27, 1812, Princeton University Library.

86. Samuel Stanhope Smith, *An Essay on the Causes of the Variety of Complexion and Figure in the Human Species,* ed. Winthrop Jordon (Cambridge, Mass., 1965), xxiv.

87. James Iredell, Jr., to Ebenezer Pettigrew, January 11, 1805, Pettigrew Papers, North Carolina State Archives; Minutes of the Trustees of the College of New Jersey, April 17, 1809, Princeton University Archives.

88. Samuel Stanhope Smith to William Southerland Hamilton, December 10, 1808, Hamilton Papers, Southern Historical Collection, University of North Carolina.

89. William Garnett to Thomas Ruffin, September 24, October 22, December 31, 1804, in J. G. deR. Hamilton, ed., *The Papers of Thomas Ruffin* (Raleigh, 1918-1920), I, 56-61.

90. Sterling Ruffin to Thomas Ruffin, November 22, December 6, 1804, January 11, 1805, *Ruffin Papers,* I, 58-60, 63, 64.

91. Wertenbaker, *Princeton,* 144.

92. Maclean, *History of the College of New Jersey,* II, 73.

93. Samuel Miller, *The Life of Samuel Miller* (Philadelphia, 1869), I, 233.

94. James W. Alexander, *The Life of Archibald Alexander* (New York, 1855), 314, 315.

95. Benjamin Rush to Ashbel Green? May 22, 1807, *Letters of Benjamin Rush,* II, 946, 947.

96. Maclean, *History of the College of New Jersey,* II, 106.

97. Douglas Sloan, *The Scottish Enlightenment and the American College Ideal* (Columbia University, 1971), 169.

98. John Campbell to David Campbell, May 9, 1806, Campbell Papers, Duke University Library.

99. Wertenbaker, *Princeton,* 148, 149.

100. Alexander, *Life of Archibald Alexander,* 347, 348.

101. Thorp, *Lives of Eighteen from Princeton,* 99.

102. Sloan, *The Scottish Enlightenment,* 181.

103. *General Repository and Review,* 3 (April 1813), 255-265, in *American Higher Education: A Documentary History,* I, 83, 82.

104. Samuel Stanhope Smith to John Henry Hobart, January 17, 1817, in John McVickar, *The Professional Years of John Henry Hobart* (New York, 1836), 419.

105. *A History of Columbia University, 1754-1904* (New York, 1904), 87-92.

106. Frederick Rudolph, *The American College and University: A History* (New York, 1962), 113-115, 129.

107. Leonard Levy, *Jefferson and Civil Liberties: The Darker Side* (Cambridge, Mass., 1963), 151.

108. Levy, *Jefferson and Civil Liberties*, 148, 153, 152.

109. Jefferson to Thomas Cooper, November 2, 1822, in *American Higher Education: A Documentary History*, I, 396.

110. Jefferson to Joseph C. Cabell, January 24, 1816, in A. A. Liscomb and A. L. Burgh, eds., *The Writings of Thomas Jefferson* (Washington, 1903), XIV, 413.

111. Jefferson to George Ticknor, July 16, 1823, in *American Higher Education: A Documentary History*, I, 267.

112. Edmund Hubbard to Benjamin Walker, July 26, 1825, Walker to Hubbard, August 13, 1825, Hubbard to Robert Hubbard, November 8, 1825, Hubbard Family Papers, Southern Historical Collection, University of North Carolina.

113. Minutes of the Faculty, October 2, 6, 14, 1825, University of Virginia Archives.

114. Philip Alexander Bruce, *History of the University of Virginia, 1819-1919* (New York, 1920), II, 300.

115. Robley Dunglison, "Diary," microfilm, University of Virginia Archives, 287, 288.

116. George Pierson to Albert Pierson, November 2, 1825, Princeton University Library.

117. Minutes of the Board of Visitors, typescript, I, 102, 103, University of Virginia Archives.

7. Little Temples of Prayer

1. Clarence P. Shedd, *Two Centuries of Student Christian Movements* (New York, 1934), 33-60.

2. Walter P. Metzger, *Academic Freedom in the Age of the University* (New York, 1955), 36; Schmidt, *The Liberal Arts College*, 88.

3. Durfee, *History of Williams College*, 111.

4. Albert Hopkins, "Revivals of Religion in Williams College," *Journal of the American Education Society*, 13 (1841), 461.

5. *Autobiography of Lyman Beecher*, I, 43.

6. Edmund S. Morgan, "Ezra Stiles and Timothy Dwight," Massachusetts Historical Society *Proceedings*, 72 (1963), 101-117.

7. Timothy Dwight, *Travels; in New England and New York* (New Haven, 1821), I, 212, 213.

8. Brooks Mather Kelley, *Yale: A History* (New Haven, 1974), 125.

9. Dwight, *Travels,* I, 514.

10. Fisher, *Life of Benjamin Silliman,* I, 32.

11. Edward Lind Morse, ed., *Samuel F. B. Morse, His Letters and Journals* (New York, 1914), I, 10, 18.

12. Eliphalet Pearson to Henry B. Pearson, June 7, July 7, 1811, Henry B. Pearson Papers, Beinecke Library, Yale University.

13. Dwight, *Sermons,* I, 366, 367; "Diary of Jeremiah Evarts," November 8, 1801, Evarts Family Papers, Sterling Memorial Library, Yale University; *President Dwight's Decisions of Questons,* 81, 82; "Baccalaureate Sermon," 1809, in Dwight, *Sermons,* I, 457.

14. "Diary of Jeremiah Evarts," November 15, 1801.

15. Chauncey A. Goodrich, "A Narrative of Revivals of Religion in Yale College," *Journal of the American Education Society,* 10 (1838), 296.

16. Goodrich, "Narrative of Revivals in Yale College," 299, 300.

17. Mills Day to Jeremiah Day, June 20, 1802, Day Family Papers, Sterling Memorial Library, Yale University.

18. Benjamin Silliman to mother, June 11, 1802, in Fisher, *Life of Benjamin Silliman,* I, 83.

19. "A Brief Account of the Revival of Religion Now Prevailing at Yale College," *Connecticut Evangelical Magazine,* 3 (July 1802), 32.

20. Kelley, *Yale: A History,* 123.

21. "The Autobiography of Benjamin Silliman, Sr.," in Nathan Reingold, ed., *Science in Nineteenth-Century America,* (New York, 1964), 4.

22. Reingold, *Science in Nineteenth-Century America,* 1.

23. James Dow McCallum, *Eleazer Wheelock, Founder of Dartmouth College* (Hanover, 1939), 156, 157.

24. This is an old explanation revived in Donald B. Cole, *Jacksonian Democracy in New Hampshire, 1800-1851* (Cambridge, Mass., 1970), 33.

25. Leon Burr Richardson, *History of Dartmouth College* (Hanover, N.H., 1932), I, 315; Hofstadter, *Academic Freedom in the Age of the College,* 220; Richardson, *History of Dartmouth College,* I, 315.

26. *Life, Letters, and Journals of George Ticknor* (Boston, 1877), I, 5; *Autobiography of Amos Kendall,* 68; Frederick Hall to Nathaniel Shattuck, April 24, 1804, Dartmouth College Archives.

27. Richardson, *History of Dartmouth College,* I, 260.

28. Richardson, *History of Dartmouth College*, I, 291.

29. Francis N. Stites, *Private Interest and Public Gain: The Dartmouth College Case, 1819* (Amherst, 1972), 11.

30. John French to Nathaniel Shattuck, July 22, 1806, Dartmouth College Archives.

31. Benjamin Hale to Thomas Hale, May 20, 1815, Dartmouth College Archives.

32. Roswell Shurtleff to George C. Shattuck, Jr., January 6, 1806, Shattuck Papers, Massachusetts Historical Society. The following account of the revival and quotations are taken from this letter unless otherwise specified. There are a few allusions to this revival in the Dartmouth archives, but most historians have overlooked it: "A revival occurred in 1782, but no further movement of this kind is mentioned until 1815." Richardson, *History of Dartmouth College*, I, 275.

33. John French to Nathaniel Shattuck, July 22, 1806, Dartmouth College Archives.

34. A. Burnham to Roswell Shurtleff, January 18, 1806, Dartmouth College Archives.

35. John French to Nathaniel Shattuck, July 22, 1806, Dartmouth College Archives.

36. Roswell Shurtleff to George C. Shattuck, February 26, April 18, 1806, and March 24, 1808, Shattuck Papers, Massachusetts Historical Society.

37. *Autobiography of Amos Kendall*, 32-49.

38. *A Vindication of the Official Conduct of the Trustees of Dartmouth College* (Concord, N.H., 1815), 38, 39, 102, 50.

39. David M. Ludlum, *Social Ferment in Vermont, 1791-1850* (New York, 1939), 67.

40. Payson, *Proofs of the Real Existence, and Dangerous Tendency of Illuminism*, 252, 255.

41. Emily A. Smith, *The Life and Letters of Nathan Smith, M.B., M.D.* (New Haven, 1914). Details on the Medical School, unless otherwise cited, may be found in this source.

42. Richardson, *History of Dartmouth College*, I, 248, 259.

43. Joel Tyler Headley, *The Great Riots of New York, 1712 to 1873* (New York, 1873, 1971), 54-65; Linden F. Edwards, "Resurrection Riots During the Heroic Age of Anatomy in America," *Bulletin of the History of Medicine*, 25 (March-April 1951), 178-184.

44. *Autobiography of Amos Kendall*, 44-46.

45. *Life and Letters of Nathan Smith*, 51, 52.

46. *Life and Letters of Nathan Smith,* 84.

47. *Life and Letters of Nathan Smith,* 112.

48. Moses Pillsbury to Samuel Fletcher, May 6, 1811, Dartmouth College Archives.

49. Richardson, *History of Dartmouth College,* I, 300.

50. "I have found a school," he wrote in 1807, "which has required all the *logic* of a *strong arm* to *reason* them into subjection. The logic of the *head* availed but little. By the aid of the former we have almost produced order from a state of chaotic confusion. I have set out with a resolution to make myself a complete Bonaparte, & have nearly succeeded." Ebenezer Adams to George C. Shattuck, January 19, 1807, Shattuck Papers, Massachusetts Historical Society.

51. [John Wheelock], *Sketches of the History of Dartmouth College and Moor's Charity School* [n.p., 1815], 48, 49.

52. John King Lord, *A History of Dartmouth College, 1815-1909* (Concord, N.H., 1913), 106, gives the allegiances of the medical professors.

53. *Dictionary of American Biography,* XIII, 372-373, emphasis added.

54. In 1813 a writer described Dartmouth's sectarian status as "divided, but the Andoverian party [Shurtleff faction] expect to prevail." *General Repository and Review,* 3 (April 1813), 364, 365.

55. Samuel C. Allen to John Wheelock, July 1, 1815, Dartmouth College Archives.

56. Elijah Parish, *A Candid, Analytical Review of the Sketches of the History of Dartmouth College* (n.p., 1815), 27.

57. Wheelock, *Sketches of the History of Dartmouth College,* 96.

58. Charles Marsh to Reverend Francis Brown, 1815, in Richardson, *History of Dartmouth College,* I, 348.

59. Benoni Dewey, James Wheelock, Ben J. Gilbert, *A True and Concise Narrative of the Church Difficulties in the Vicinity of Dartmouth College* (Hanover, 1815), 59, 60.

60. Judge Jonathan Hubbard to John Wheelock, August 31, 1815, Dartmouth College Archives.

61. Benjamin Hale to Thomas Hale, July 6, 1815, Dartmouth College Archives.

62. *Vindication of the Trustees,* 26.

63. Benjamin Hale to Thomas Hale, July 6, 1815, Dartmouth College Archives.

64. Jonathan Freeman to Peyton Freeman, February 5, 1817, Dartmouth College Archives.

65. Jeremiah Atwater to Ashbel Green, July 21, 1811, in Charles Coleman Sellers, *Dickinson College: A History* (Middletown, Conn., 1973), 139.

66. Jeremiah Atwater to Benjamin Rush, March 11, 1811, in Sellers, *Dickinson College,* 141.

67. Jeremiah Atwater to Benjamin Rush, March 11, 1811, in Sellers, *Dickinson College,* 139. An interesting criticism of Dickinson's adoption of New England rules was made by Thomas Cruse, who was promoting the college among families in Virginia: "I cannot suppress one remark, that the College of Carlisle expects celebrity from adopting the rules & regulations of the New England Colleges, these seminaries of aristocracy that has been for ten years arrayed in hostility to our present government—I for myself feel ignoble that the first state in the Union had not talents to frame a code of laws & regulations for the government & prosperity of its own College." Thomas Cruse to Hon. James Hamilton, August 20, 1810, Cruse Collection, University of Virginia Library.

68. Jeremiah Atwater, *An Inaugural Address, delivered at the Public Commencement of Dickinson College* (Carlisle, 1809), 12, 3, 6, 16.

69. In his 1786 *Plan for the Establishment of Public Schools,* Rush said, "I cannot help bearing a testimony . . . against the custom of crowding boys together under one roof for the purpose of education. The practice is the gloomy remains of monkish ignorance and is as unfavorable to the improvement of the mind in useful learning as monasteries are to the spirit of religion. I grant this mode of secluding boys from the intercourse of private families has a tendency to make them scholars, but our business is to make them men, citizens, and Christians." Rudolph, *Essays on Education in the Early Republic,* 16, 17.

70. Jeremiah Atwater to Benjamin Rush, September 18, 1810, in Sellers, *Dickinson College,* 144.

71. *Laws of Dickinson College,* ca. 1810, Dickinson College Archives.

72. Jeremiah Atwater to Ashbel Green, July 20, 1811, Gratz Collection, Historical Society of Pennsylvania.

73. Jeremiah Atwater to Ashbel Green, July 20, 1811, in Sellers, *Dickinson College,* 145.

74. For Cooper's trial and imprisonment see Smith, *Freedom's Fet-*

ters, 307-333. Jefferson's quotation is from Sellers, *Dickinson College,* 151.

75. Jeremiah Atwater to Ashbel Green, February 23, 1812, Gratz Collection, Historical Society of Pennsylvania.

76. Jeremiah Atwater to Ashbel Green, February 23, 1812, in Sellers, *Dickinson College,* 154, 155.

77. James Somervell to Samuel Marsteller, February 1, 1813, Duke University Library.

78. Sellers, *Dickinson College,* 155.

79. Robert L. Madison to Dolley P. Madison, July 25, 1813, in Ralph L. Ketcham, "Uncle James Madison and Dickinson College," *Early Dickinsoniana: The Boyd Lee Spahr Lectures in Americana, 1957-1961* (Carlisle, 1961), 177.

80. Harry G. Good, *Benjamin Rush and His Services to American Education* (Berne, Indiana, 1918), 163.

81. Sellers, *Dickinson College,* 158.

82. J. H. Jones, ed., *The Life of Ashbel Green* (New York, 1849), 345. This work is made up of diary extracts and autobiographical recollections.

83. Minutes of the Faculty, November 10, 1812, Princeton University Archives; *Life of Ashbel Green,* 344, 346, 347. For compulsory Bible study see Green, *Report to the Trustees relative to a Revival of Religion* (New Haven, 1815), 5n.

84. James Mercer Garnett to parents, February 13, June 5, 1813, typescript, Princeton University Library.

85. A favorable account of the president by a student is Walter Kirkpatrick to Moria C. Cobb, January 20, 1813, September 21, 1814, alumni file, Princeton University Archives.

86. *Life of Ashbel Green,* 349.

87. *Life of Ashbel Green,* 297; Wertenbaker, *Princeton,* chap. 5.

88. *Life of Ashbel Green,* 353, 355, 356.

89. *Life of Ashbel Green,* 358, 359.

90. Green, *Report to the Trustees on A Revival of Religion,* 4; Ashbel Green to Jedidiah Morse, April 12, 1815, Green Papers, Princeton University Library.

91. Green, *Report to the Trustees on A Revival of Religion,* 3.

92. Green, *Report to the Trustees on A Revival of Religion,* 5-7.

93. *Life of Ashbel Green,* 379, 380.

94. *Life of Ashbel Green,* 385.

95. George K. Cabell to Joseph C. Cabell, June 15, 1815, Cabell Collection, University of Virginia Library.

96. John Haslett to William Moultrie Reid, September 10, 1818, Southern Historical Collection, University of North Carolina.

97. *Connecticut Evangelical Magazine,* 7 (June 1815), 235.

98. Andover to Dartmouth, August 12, 1815, in Shedd, *Two Centuries of Student Christian Movements,* 82.

99. Benjamin Hale to Thomas Hale, July 6, 1815, Dartmouth College Archives.

Afterword: The Defensive Academe and the Lost Generation

1. Thomas Jefferson to George Ticknor, July 16, 1823, in *American Higher Education: A Documentary History,* I, 267.

2. Dwight, *Decisions of Questions,* 205; *American Higher Education: A Documentary History,* I, 280.

3. Mark Hopkins, *An Inaugural Address, Delivered at Williams College* (Troy, 1836), 19, 20.

4. Walter Pilkington, *Hamilton College, 1812/1962* (Clinton, N.Y., 1962), 69, 70.

5. Ashbel Green, "The Word of God the Guide of Youth," *Discourses, Delivered in the College of New Jersey* (Philadelphia, 1822), 88.

6. Dwight, *Decisions of Questions,* 248.

7. "Remarks on Classical Learning," *The Monthly Miscellany,* 1 (Cambridge, Mass., 1805), 13, 19.

8. Richard Hofstadter rightly said that the failure of the old-time college was not that it taught the classics but that it trained no great classicists. *Academic Freedom in the Age of the College,* 228.

9. Hofstadter, *Academic Freedom in the Age of the College,* 209, 215.

10. *History of Columbia University,* 100.

11. E. Merton Coulter, *College Life in the Old South* (New York, 1928), 40.

12. Robert E. Spiller, ed., *The American Literary Revolution, 1783-1837* (New York, 1967), 53, 55.

13. Dwight, *Decisions of Questions,* 206, 207.

14. See John R. Gillis, "Essay Review: Youth in History: Progress and Prospects," *Journal of Social History,* 7 (Winter 1974), 204; Charles W. Janson, *Stranger in America* (London, 1807), 297; John Bristed, *Resources of the United States* (New York, 1818), 459, 460; William R. Davie to John Haywood, September 22, 1805, *James Sprunt Historical Monograph,* 7 (1907), 59, 60.

15. Edmund Quincy, *Life of Josiah Quincy* (Boston, 1868), 464ff;

Wertenbaker, *Princeton,* 168, 169.

16. Samuel Eliot Morison, *The Life and Letters of Harrison Gray Otis, Federalist, 1765-1848* (Boston, 1913), 254, 255, emphasis added.

17. Arthur W. Calhoun, *A Social History of the American Family, From Colonial Times to the Present* (Cleveland, 1918), II, 76.

18. *Letters of John Randolph to a Young Relative,* 26.

19. *The American Quarterly Register,* 3 (August 1830), 69.

20. Lois W. Banner, "Religion and Reform in the Early Republic: The Role of Youth," *American Quarterly,* 23 (December 1971), 688, 692.

21. "The Perpetuation of Our Political Institutions," Address Before the Springfield Young Men's Lyceum (1838), in Richard N. Current, ed., *The Political Thought of Abraham Lincoln* (Indianapolis, 1967), 12, 18, 20.

SELECTED BIBLIOGRAPHY

Unpublished Sources

In addition to the faculty records and trustee minutes of the colleges, the following manuscripts were most useful.

Jeremiah Atwater Papers, Gratz Collection, Historical Society of Pennsylvania.
George W. Bancker Papers, New-York Historical Society.
Joseph C. Breckinridge Papers, Library of Congress.
Joseph C. Cabell Papers, Library of Congress.
Joseph Caldwell Papers, Southern Historical Collection, University of North Carolina.
John Campbell Papers, Duke University Library.
Timothy Dwight Papers, Sterling Memorial Library, Yale University.
John Gallison Papers, Harvard University Archives.
James Mercer Garnett Papers, Princeton University Library.
Ashbel Green Papers, Princeton University Library, and Gratz Collection, Historical Society of Pennsylvania.
Bishop James Madison Papers, Library of Congress, and the College of William and Mary.
Charles Nisbet Papers, Dickinson College Archives.
Eliphalet Pearson Papers, Park Family Collection, Sterling Memorial Library, Yale University.

Roswell Shurtleff letters in George C. Shattuck Collection, Massachusetts
    Historical Society.
Samuel Stanhope Smith Papers, Princeton University Library.
Joseph Tufts Papers, Harvard University Archives.
David Watson Papers, Library of Congress.
John Wheelock Papers, Dartmouth College Archives.

Published Works

In addition to college histories, readily available and many already
mentioned in the notes above, the following were helpful.

Adams, Henry. "Harvard College, 1786-1787," *Historical Essays* (New
    York: Charles Scribners' Sons, 1891).
Alexander, James W. *The Life of Archibald Alexander* (New York:
    Charles Scribner, 1855).
Allmendinger, David F. Jr. "New England Students and the Revolution
    in Higher Education," *History of Education Quarterly,* 11 (Winter
    1971).
_____ "The Dangers of Ante-Bellum Student Life," *Journal of Social
    History,* 7 (Fall 1973).
Austin, William. *A Selection of the Patriotic Addresses to the President
    . . . Together with the President's Answers* (Boston: John W. Folsom,
    1798).
_____ *Strictures on Harvard University, By a Senior* (Boston: John W.
    Folsom, 1798).
Beecher, Charles, ed. *Autobiography, Correspondence, Etc. of Lyman
    Beecher,* 2 vols. (New York: Harper and Brothers, 1864).
Bell, Whitfield J. Jr. "Thomas Cooper as Professor of Chemistry at Dick-
    inson College, 1811-1815," *Journal of the History of Medicine,* 8
    (1953).
Boyd, Julian P., ed. *Thomas Jefferson On Science and Freedom: The
    Letter to the Student William Greene Munford, June 8, 1799, with a
    Foreword* (Worcester: A. J. St. Onge, 1964).
Caldwell, Joseph. *The Autobiography and Biography of Joseph Caldwell*
    (Chapel Hill: The University Magazine Pub., 1859).
Cameron, Henry Clay. *History of the American Whig Society* (Princeton,
    1871).
Collins, Varnum Lansing. *President Witherspoon: A Biography,* 2 vols.
    (Princeton: Princeton University Press, 1925).

A Columbia College Student in the Eighteenth Century, Essays by Daniel D. Tompkins, Class of 1795 (New York: Columbia University Press, 1940).

Crowe, Charles. "Bishop James Madison and the Republic of Virtue," *Journal of Southern History,* 30 (Feb. 1964).

Cunningham, Charles E. *Timothy Dwight, 1752-1817: A Biography* (New York: Macmillan, 1942).

Dana, H. W. L. "Allston at Harvard, 1796 to 1800," Cambridge Historical Society *Publications,* vol. 29, Proceedings of the Year 1943 (1948).

Dexter, Franklin B. "Student Life at Yale College, 1795-1817," American Antiquarian Society *Proceedings,* n.s., 27 (1917).

Dwight, Theodore Jr. *President Dwight's Decisions of Questions Discussed by the Senior Class in Yale College, in 1813 and 1814* (New York: Crocker & Brewster, 1833).

"Extracts from the Diary of Timothy Fuller, Jr., An Undergraduate in Harvard College, 1798-1801," Cambridge Historical Society *Proceedings,* 11 (Oct. 1916).

Fisher, George P. *Life of Benjamin Silliman,* 2 vols. (New York: Charles B. Scribner and Company, 1866).

Flagg, Jared B. *The Life and Letters of Washington Allston* (New York: Benjamin Blom, 1892, 1969).

"Glimpses of Old College Life," *William and Mary Quarterly,* 8 (Jan., April 1900).

Govan, Thomas P. "Nicholas Biddle at Princeton, 1799-1801," *Princeton University Library Chronicle,* 9 (Feb. 1948).

Green, Ashbel. *An Address to the Students and Faculty of the College of New Jersey* (Trenton, 1802).

_____ *Report to the Trustees . . . relative to a Revival of Religion* (New Haven, 1815).

Harrison, Lowell H. "A Young Kentuckian at Princeton, 1806-1810: Joseph Cabell Breckenridge," *The Filson Club History Quarterly,* 38 (Oct. 1964).

Hislop, Codman. *Eliphalet Nott* (Middletown: Wesleyan University Press, 1973).

Hofstadter, Richard. *Academic Freedom in the Age of the College* (Chicago: University of Chicago Press, 1955).

_____ and Smith, Wilson. *American Higher Education: A Documentary History,* 2 vols. (Chicago: University of Chicago Press, 1961).

Howe, Daniel Walker. *The Unitarian Conscience: Harvard Moral Philos-*

212   BIBLIOGRAPHY

ophy, 1805-1861 (Cambridge: Harvard University Press, 1970).
Hurley, James F., and Goode, Julia Eagan. *The Prophet of Zion Parnassus: Samuel Eusebius McCorkle* (Richmond, Va.: Presbyterian Committee of Publication, 1934).
Ingersoll, Charles J. *Recollections, Historical, Political, Biographical, and Social,* 2 vols. (Philadelphia: J. B. Lippincott & Co., 1861).
Jones, J. H., ed. *The Life of Ashbel Green* (New York: R. Carter and Brothers, 1849).
Kraus, Michael. "Charles Nisbet and Samuel Stanhope Smith," *Princeton University Library Chronicle,* 6 (Nov. 1944).
Lane, William Coolidge. "Dr. Benjamin Waterhouse and Harvard University," Cambridge Historical Society *Publications,* 4 (1909).
"Letters of William T. Barry," *William and Mary Quarterly,* 13 (1904-1905).
"Letters to David Watson," *Virginia Magazine of History and Biography,* 29 (April, July 1921).
"Letters from William and Mary College, 1798-1801," *Virginia Magazine of History and Biography,* 29 (April 1921).
McDowell, Tremaine. "Cullen Bryant at Williams College," *New England Quarterly,* 1 (Oct. 1928).
McGovern, James R. "The Student Rebellion in Harvard College, 1807-1808," *Harvard Library Bulletin,* 19 (Oct. 1971).
Meigs, William M. *Life of Josiah Meigs* (Philadelphia: J. P. Murphey, 1887).
Meyer, D. H. *The Instructed Conscience: The Shaping of the American National Ethic* (Philadelphia: University of Pennsylvania Press, 1972).
Miller, Samuel. *Memoir of the Rev. Charles Nisbet, D.D.* (New York: Robert Carter, 1840).
Miller, Samuel Jr. *The Life of Samuel Miller,* 2 vols. (Philadelphia: Claxton, Remsen, and Haffelfinger, 1869).
Morgan, Edmund S. "Ezra Stiles and Timothy Dwight," Massachusetts Historical Society *Proceedings,* 72 (1963).
———— *The Gentle Puritan: A Life of Ezra Stiles* (New Haven: Yale University Press, 1962).
Richmond, Arthur A. "Jonathan Edwards, Jr., & Union College," *Union College Symposium,* 8 (Winter 1969/70).
Robinson, Blackwell P. *William R. Davie* (Chapel Hill: University of North Carolina Press, 1957).

Rudolph, Frederick. *The American College and University: A History* (New York: Random House, 1962).

———— *Essays on Education in the Early Republic* (Cambridge: Harvard University Press, 1965).

Sloan, Douglas. *The Scottish Enlightenment and the American College Ideal* (New York: Columbia University Press, 1971).

Smith, Emily A. *The Life and Letters of Nathan Smith, M.B., M.D.* (New Haven: Yale University Press, 1914).

A Statement of Facts, relative to the late proceedings in Harvard College, Cambridge, Published by the Students (Boston, 1807).

Stickney, William, ed. *Autobiography of Amos Kendall* (Baltimore: John Murphey & Co., 1876).

Ticknor, George. *Life, Letters, and Journals of George Ticknor*, 2 vols. (Boston: James R. Osgood and Company, 1877).

Tufts, Joseph. *Don Quixots at College; or, a History of the Gallant Adventures lately achieved by the combined students of Harvard University; interspersed with some facetious reasoning. By a Senior* (Boston: Etheridge & Bliss, 1807).

Tyler, Samuel. *Memoir of Roger Brooke Taney, LL.D.* (Baltimore, John Murphey & Co., 1876).

Van Santvoord, C. *Memoirs of Eliphalet Nott* (New York: Sheldon and Company, 1870).

A Vindication of the Official Conduct of the Trustees of Dartmouth College (Concord, N.H., 1815).

Waterhouse, Benjamin. *Cautions to Young Persons, concerning health . . . shewing the Evil Tendency of the Use of Tobacco upon Young Persons; more especially the Pernicious Effects of Smoking Cigarrs; with observations on the Use of Ardent and Vinous Spirits in general* (Cambridge, 1804).

Wheelock, John. *Sketches of the History of Dartmouth College and Moor's Charity School* [n.p., 1815].

Whitehead, John S. *The Separation of College and State: Columbia, Dartmouth, Harvard, and Yale, 1776-1876* (New Haven: Yale University Press, 1973).

Willard, Sidney. *Memories of Youth and Manhood*, 2 vols. (Cambridge: John Bartlett, 1855).

Williams, Charles Richard. *The Cliosophic Society, Princeton* (Princeton: Princeton University Press, 1916).

INDEX

215